Towards
a Truly Catholic Church
An Ecclesiology for the Third Millennium

Thomas P. Rausch, S.J.

A Michael Glazier Book

LITURGICAL PRESS
Collegeville, Minnesota

www.litpress.org

A Michael Glazier Book published by the Liturgical Press

Cover design by Ann Blattner. Cover art: *Loaves and Fishes*, © 2003 by John August Swanson, serigraph, 24" x 36", www.JohnAugustSwanson.com. Used with permission.

1	2	3	4	5	6	7	8

Library of Congress Cataloging-in-Publication Data

Rausch, Thomas P.
    Towards a truly Catholic Church : an ecclesiology for the third millennium / Thomas P. Rausch.
      p. cm.
    "A Michael Glazier book."
    Summary: "Ecclesiology which takes into account the Second Vatican Council, ecumenism, and globalization"—Provided by publisher.
    Includes bibliographical references and index.
    ISBN-13: 978-0-8146-5187-2 (pbk. : alk. paper)
    ISBN-10: 0-8146-5187-9 (pbk. : alk. paper)
    1. Catholic Church—History—1965– 2. Catholic Church—History—21st century. I. Title.
BX1390.R365 2005
262'.02—dc22
                                                          2005004752

For Sister Heidi
of the Community of Grandchamp

In Memoriam

Contents

Abbreviations

Documents of Vatican II

CD   *Christus Dominus*: Decree on the Pastoral Office of Bishops in the Church

DH   *Dignitatis humanae*: Declaration on Religious Freedom

DV   *Dei verbum*: Dogmatic Constitution on Divine Revelation

GS   *Gaudium et spes*: Pastoral Constitution on the Church in the Modern World

LG   *Lumen gentium*: Dogmatic Constitution on the Church

NA   *Nostra aetate*: Declaration on the Relationship of the Church to Non-Christian Religions

OE   *Orientalium ecclesarium*: Decree on the Eastern Catholic Churches

SC   *Sacrosanctum concilium*: Constitution on the Sacred Liturgy

UR   *Unitatis redintegratio*: Decree on Ecumenism

Other

ARCIC   Anglican-Roman Catholic International Commission

AAS   *Acta Apostolicae Sedis*

BEM   World Council of Churches, *Baptism, Eucharist and Ministry* (WCC: Geneva, 1982).

CDF   Congregation for the Doctrine of the Faith

COCU   Consultation on Church Union

DS   Denzinger-Schönmetzer, *Enchiridion Symbolorum* 33rd ed. (Freiburg: Herder, 1965)

ELCA   Evangelical Lutheran Church in America

PCPCU   Pontifical Council for Promoting Christian Unity

USCCB   United States Conference of Catholic Bishops

WCC   World Council of Churches

Acknowledgements

This is a book on ecclesiology, the theology of the Church. How do we understand the Church theologically, what are its New Testament roots, how have its structures emerged historically, what are its possibilities today? Though I write from the perspective of the Roman Catholic tradition, I've tried to draw on the works of Orthodox, Protestant, and Evangelical scholars as well. While I will refer to some of them in the Introduction, I'd like to acknowledge a number of theologians whose works have been particularly helpful to me in preparing this book.

Hans Küng's book *The Church*, first published in 1967, has been perhaps the best work on ecclesiology since the Second Vatican Council.[1] Since then, however, much has happened in the area of ecclesiology. The present volume hopes to take into account the considerable work in historical, theological, and feminist scholarship as well as the progress made through some forty years of ecumenical dialogue.

The first volume of Roger Haight's new work on the Church, *Historical Ecclesiology*, was very helpful, particularly his efforts to develop an ecclesiology from below and to show the emergence of diverse ecclesiologies throughout the Church's history.[2] As always, Haight raises important methodological questions. Also very helpful was John Burkhard's new work, *Apostolicity Then and Now*.[3] Apostolicity has long been considered the neuralgic ecumenical question; Burkhard's careful research helps to place it in a new context.

[1] Hans Küng, *The Church*, trans. Ray and Rosaleen Ockenden (New York: Sheed and Ward, 1967).

[2] Roger Haight, *Christian Community in History*, Vol I: *Historical Ecclesiology* (New York: Continuum, 2004). Vol. II, *Comparative Ecclesiology* (New York: Continuum, 2005) appeared too late for inclusion in this work.

[3] John J. Burkhard, *Apostolicity Then and Now: An Ecumenical Church in a Postmodern World* (Collegeville, MN: The Liturgical Press, 2004).

The works of Miroslav Volf and Veli-Matti Kärkkäinen have brought the Free Church and Pentecostal traditions into the conversation on ecclesiology.[4] Robert Schreiter has insisted that this conversation should take place in the context of a multicultural Church and the process known as "globalization."[5] The work of Cardinal Avery Dulles over the years establishes him as the dean of Roman Catholic ecclesiologists. While I have drawn with appreciation on the work of these and other scholars, the interpretation remains my own.

Many others helped in developing this volume, among them John A. Coleman, S.J., Jeffrey Gros, F.S.C., Richard Gaillardetz, Frank Oveis, Cecil M. Robeck, Jr., and Mark Twomey. The basic idea for the book came from my colleague Jeffrey Siker. Catherine Clifford of St. Paul's College, Ottawa, read the manuscript and offered many valuable suggestions. My graduate assistant, Ryan Ignatius Pratt, helped with the research and Barbara Murphy assisted with proofing the text and compiling the index. To all these I am very grateful.

A final note. Pope John Paul II died shortly before this manuscript went to the printers. Throughout his ministry this remarkable Pope showed in numerous ways the potential of the papacy for ecclesial leadership on a global level and Catholics and non-Catholics alike mourned his passing. He was succeeded on the Chair of Peter by Cardinal Joseph Ratzinger, who took the name of Benedict XVI. In his years as a university professor Ratzinger distinguished himself for his work in ecclesiology and his expertise in ecumenical theology. Thus he brings special gifts to gather the churches together as he embarks on his ministry as Bishop of Rome. May God grant him the fullness of the Spirit.

Thomas P. Rausch, S.J.

[4] Miroslav Volf, *After Our Likeness: The Church as the Image of the Trinity* (Grand Rapids, MI: William B. Eerdmans, 1998); Veli-Matti Kärkkäinen, *An Introduction to Ecclesiology: Ecumenical, Historical and Global Perspectives* (Downers Grove, IL: InterVarsity, 2002).

[5] Robert J. Schreiter, *The New Catholicity: Theology Between the Global and the Local* (Maryknoll, NY: Orbis, 1997).

Introduction

What do we mean by "Church"? Is it one or many, visible or invisible, local or universal, hierarchical or congregational in its structure, sacramental or kerygmatic in its expression? Most Christians—whether Roman Catholic, Orthodox, mainline Protestant, or Evangelical—tend to view Christian history through the lenses of their own particular traditions. Because of these lenses, their vision of what has been and what should be takes on a particular theological color. They presume that the Church has always been one, or always been many, or they privilege the particular or the universal expression of the Church.

Those in the Catholic tradition, understood broadly—Anglican, Orthodox, and Roman Catholic, generally look back to an originally undivided Church. While the Reformers saw the Reformation as a reform movement within the universal Church, some Protestants today, particularly those in the great confessional traditions, start from the fact of a divided Christianity, and so tend to understand the Church as a plurality of separate confessions. From this perspective, they envision the Church of tomorrow as an ecumenical community of churches that maintain their own confessional identities and structures while re-establishing communion in preaching, eucharistic sharing, ministry, and service. Many of those in the Free Church tradition, with their roots in the Radical Reformation, have adopted a restorationist ecclesiology; they see their churches as "restoring" the apostolic Church of the New Testament that had fallen or been lost as a result of Constantine's establishment of Christianity.

The Church: One or Many?

What does the New Testament say about the Church? Does the New Testament canon ground the unity of the Church or the diversity of the churches? The distinguished Tübingen New Testament scholar Ernst Käsemann first

1

posed this question in 1951 at an ecumenical symposium sponsored by the theological faculty at Göttingen in Germany.[1] He argued that the variability of the New Testament *kerygma*, the extraordinary variety of theological positions in primitive Christianity, and the incompatibility of some of these positions all lead to the conclusion that "the New Testament canon does not, as such, constitute the foundation of the unity of the Church. On the contrary, as such (that is, in its accessibility to the historian) it provides the basis for the multiplicity of the confessions."[2]

Käsemann gave classic expression to his thesis in an address to the World Council of Churches' Fourth World Conference on Faith and Order at Montreal in July 1963, an assembly that took place between the second and third sessions of the Second Vatican Council. He argued that the New Testament presents not a uniform ecclesiology but a series of ecclesiologies, Jewish Christian, Hellenistic, Pauline, "enthusiastic," Johannine, and "early Catholic." His conclusion: "The unity of the Church has been, is and remains primarily an eschatological datum, which is only achieved in so far as it is received as a gift."[3]

Following Käsemann, Catholic biblical scholar Raymond Brown gave a second address, the first time a Roman Catholic had spoken to a WCC world conference. Brown acknowledged that strong differences of outlook could be found among the various New Testament writers as well as the impossibility of reducing New Testament ecclesiologies to a theological uniformity. At the same time, in his response to Käsemann Brown argued that there is "a *unity in belief* that is present in all stages of NT thought about the Church."[4] He pointed to three elements common to all New Testament ecclesiologies: a consciousness of a continuity with Israel; apostolicity, in the sense that the Church from the beginning possessed some kind of organization based on the Twelve and the apostles in general; and finally, that from its inception the Christian community practiced baptism and shared in the Eucharist.

[1] Ernst Käsemann, "Begrundet der neutestamentliche Kanon die Einheit der Kirche?" *Evangelische Theologie* 11 (1951–52) 13–21; ET "The Canon of the New Testament and the Unity of the Church," in Käsemann, *Essays on New Testament Themes* (London: SCM Press, 1964) 95–107.

[2] Käsemann, "The Canon of the New Testament and the Unity of the Church," 103.

[3] Ernst Käsemann, "Unity and Diversity in New Testament Ecclesiology," *Novum Testamentum* 6 (1963) 295.

[4] Raymond E. Brown, "Unity and Diversity in New Testament Ecclesiology," *Novum Testamentum* 6 (1963) 302, emphasis in original; his article is reprinted in his *New Testament Essays* (New York: Paulist Press, 1965) 36–47.

More recently, James D. G. Dunn has advanced an argument similar to Käsemann's. Dunn locates the center of the New Testament in the unity between the historical Jesus and the exalted Christ, the one in whom Christians encountered God's saving power.[5] Beyond this "canon within the canon," Dunn sees no single normative form of Christianity in the first century, no unity rooted in the New Testament; what the canon gives us is the irreducible diversity of Christianity. Some scholars today go even further, beyond the canon, to include other, usually considered heterodox forms of early Christianity.[6]

Käsemann and Dunn are correct about the diversity of early Christianity—Jewish, Hellenistic, Apocalyptic, and early Catholic, in large part the product of the various missionary movements and the different communities that resulted. In a later work, Brown outlines a spectrum of Christian movements, from ultraconservative Jewish Christians and their Gentile converts at one extreme who insisted on full observance of the Mosaic Law, to the radical Hellenists at the other, Jewish Christians and their Gentile converts who were unable to see any continuing significance in the Jewish cults and feasts.[7]

Roger Haight's position is more nuanced; in his study of historical ecclesiology he points to a tension in the early Church between pluralism and unity. While the pluralism is obvious, "the value of unity suffused the community wherever it existed and according to all of its historical witnesses. The metaphors for the unity of the Church abound."[8] The Church was neither a single organization nor a plurality of isolated churches. He describes the Christian movement as one characterized by the principle of subsidiarity, which by allowing local decisions to be made on local levels "preserves an integral whole church as a union of churches."[9]

Thus it would be inaccurate to portray the New Testament period as analogous to that of today's divided Christianity, or to reduce the New Testament itself to discrete theologies, without any center or development. The New Testament Christians shared a common biblical tradition and the

[5] James D. G. Dunn, *Unity and Diversity in the New Testament: An Inquiry into the Character of Earliest Christianity: Second Edition* (London: SCM Press, 1990) 369; first published 1977.

[6] Bart D. Ehrman, *Lost Christianities: The Battles for Scripture and the Faiths We Never Knew* (Oxford/New York: Oxford University Press, 2003).

[7] Raymond E. Brown in Raymond E. Brown and John P. Meier, *Antioch and Rome: New Testament Cradles of Catholic Christianity* (New York: Paulist Press, 1983) 2–9.

[8] Roger Haight, *Christian Community in History*, Vol I: *Historical Ecclesiology* (New York: Continuum, 2004) 132–33.

[9] Ibid., 133.

rituals of baptism and Eucharist. They recognized or came to accept a pastoral office already linked to the apostles within the New Testament period. Christians from the different churches were able to live with considerable diversity in both theology and ecclesiology; nevertheless they did not repudiate or reject one another. They maintained communion (*koinōnia*) with each other. The later New Testament books speak of Church in an absolute or universal sense. In Colossians and Ephesians, Christ is the head of the Church, his body (Col 1:18; Eph 4:15). Overcoming all divisions, the Church is the People of God (1 Pet 2:10). In John's Gospel Jesus prays that there be one flock and one shepherd (John 10:16). Perhaps as early as 110, Ignatius of Antioch referred to the whole, universal or "catholic" (*katholikē*) Church (Smyrn 8:2).[10]

So how do we understand the Church? And how do we speak meaningfully of the Church in the third millennium? To say the word "Church" is to invoke a number of different theologies[11] or models[12] of what Church is and how Church should be understood. Therefore it is important to address at least briefly the question of method in ecclesiology.

Methodological Observations

To speak of Church is to speak of a reality at once christological, pneumatological, historical, and eschatological; it is rooted in biblical symbol and story, history and tradition, theology and doctrine. The life of the Church is enriched by diverse theologies and different ecclesiological visions. While some traditions, for example, the Roman Catholic, place considerable emphasis on the Church's christological foundations, others like the Orthodox and the Pentecostal stress the pneumatological. Catholic and Orthodox Christians believe that the Church is a visible, historical community with hierarchical elements. Many Protestants see the real Church as the invisible community of the elect. Different ways of structuring the Church have emerged over the centuries: papal, episcopal, presbyteral, or congregational. An ecclesiology for the third millennium should respect this diversity; at the same time, it should try to incorporate the following principles.

[10] Some scholars argue for a later date, closer to 140 for Ignatius. See John J. Burkhard, *Apostolicity Then and Now: An Ecumenical Church in a Postmodern World* (Collegeville, MN: Liturgical Press, 2004) 213–14, note 27.

[11] See for example, Veli-Matti Kärkkäinen, *An Introduction to Ecclesiology: Ecumenical, Historical, and Global Perspectives* (Downers Grove, IL: InterVarsity) 200.

[12] Avery Dulles, *Models of the Church* (Garden City, NY: Doubleday, 1974); see also his *Models of the Church, Expanded Edition* (Garden City, NY: Doubleday, 1987).

First, the Church today must remain rooted in the teaching and actions of Jesus; therefore it has to have a christological foundation. The earliest Christians are united by their experience of God's saving presence in Christ. But the question is complicated. Much of what is attributed to Jesus in the Gospels represents the emerging tradition of the primitive Church rather than the words and deeds of the Jesus of history. While Jesus did not provide a constitution for the Church, Catholic and Orthodox Christians see certain ecclesiological implications that flow from his life and ministry. These include his preaching on the reign of God, the Jesus movement called to proclaim and embody it, the constitution of the Twelve as a college or fixed group at its center, and the Lord's Supper (which the later Church would call the Eucharist). Haight's argument that the Church is self-constituting, arising out of practice,[13] while true in a general sense, does not seem to pay sufficient attention to those elements in the Church's life that have a christological foundation. A viable ecclesiology needs to take account of what can be traced to the historical Jesus, and therefore is of dominical institution.

Second, the Church has also a pneumatological foundation—so important in Orthodox ecclesiology—that is the source of its life, vitality, and diversity. The guiding principle of the early Christian communities was the Spirit of the risen Jesus that brought the Church into existence. Like the wind, the Spirit blows where it will (cf. John 3:8). A viable ecclesiology must take care not to extinguish the Spirit if it is to respect human freedom, renew the Church's structures, and remain open to the new and the unexpected.

There is mutuality between Christology and Pneumatology. The Spirit works through Jesus in his historical ministry while the risen Jesus pours out the Spirit on his own, animating the community of disciples as Church. "The christological aspect creates the objective and unchangeable features of the Church, while the pneumatological aspect brings into being the subjective side of the Church. In other words, the christological aspects guarantee stability, while in its pneumatological aspects the Church has a dynamic character."[14] The challenge for ecclesiology is maintaining the proper balance. An over-emphasis on the christological can result in a sterile, top down institutionalism while Pneumatology separated from Christology easily leads to enthusiasms, sectarianism, and ecclesiological individualism.[15]

[13] Haight, *Historical Ecclesiology*, 131.

[14] Veli-Matti Kärkkäinen, "Spirit, Church and Christ: An Ecumenical Inquiry into a Pneumatological Ecclesiology" *One in Christ* 4 (2000) 341.

[15] See for example, Ronald Knox, *Enthusiasm: A Chapter in the History of Religion, with Special Reference to the XVII and XVIII Centuries* (New York: Oxford University Press, 1950).

Third, while the New Testament provides an important foundation for understanding the Church, its origins cannot be understood in pre-critical terms. The New Testament describes the Church much more often in the mythopoetic language of the Scriptures than in the theological or doctrinal language of the later tradition. A pre-critical approach to the text traps an interpreter or a tradition in a literalism or fundamentalism that fails to distinguish between the text and the subject matter it mediates, what Paul Ricoeur has called a "first naiveté."[16] For example, it is as problematic to build an entire ecclesiology on a text such as "where two or three are gathered together in my name, there am I in the midst of them" (Matt 18:20) as it would be to construct a Christology on a single text such as "He is the image of the invisible God, the firstborn of all creation" (Col 1:15). Just as the New Testament offers a diversity of Christologies that reflect the Church's developing understanding of the mystery of Jesus, so too a similar development is evident in relation to ecclesiology.

Similarly, both Roman Catholics and Pentecostals tend towards an overly idealized understanding of the apostolic Church, while failing to recognize the truth of each other's positions. For example, some Catholics move rapidly from "you are Peter and upon this rock I will build my church" (Matt 16:18) to the entire papal structure of the Church. On the other hand, some Pentecostals have difficulty in recognizing the ecclesial reality of a community that doesn't look like the Church of 1 Corinthians in all its charismatic richness. The Final Report of the international dialogue between representatives of the World Alliance of Reformed Churches and some classical Pentecostal churches and leaders notes that "a careful reading of Paul's letters leads Reformed Christians to the conviction that it would be wrong to concentrate attention on the so-called supernatural gifts, such as *glossolalia* and healing," since in the Pauline lists of spiritual gifts, "the more common gifts, such as leading, organizing, and teaching, are mentioned in juxtaposition with the more spectacular gifts."[17]

The New Testament abounds in miracle stories, extraordinary manifestations of the Spirit, symbols, and metaphors. Those stories, symbols, and metaphors need to be taken seriously but not always literally; when unpacked and understood against the tradition out of which they developed, they continue to prove a rich source of meaning for ecclesiology.

[16] See Sandra M. Schneiders, *The Revelatory Text: Interpreting the New Testament as Sacred Scripture*, Second Edition (Collegeville, MN: Liturgical Press, 1999) 169–72.

[17] *The Final Report of the International Dialogue between Representatives of the World Alliance of Reformed Churches and Some Classical Pentecostal Churches and Leaders 1996–2000*, (no. 32); see Cyberjournal for Pentecostal-Charismatic Research.

Finally, Church history is also an important source for ecclesiology. Throughout its long history the Church's self-understanding has grown and structures have emerged which have supported and sustained its life. While not every practice or usage has stood the test of time, many have been recognized as Spirit-inspired developments in the Church's life. It is difficult to dismiss a suggested reform or development as "against the tradition" when there is clear evidence of an earlier practice. At the same time, while the activity of the Spirit is important, if the Church is an historical, visible, even developing community, it cannot be created anew in every age. Thus knowledge of Church history is essential.

If we look at the Church historically, the first millennium can be seen as the era of the united Church. There were some exceptions. Some ancient churches lost communion with the universal Church in the fifth century because of differences over Christology: the Nestorian or East Syrian Churches after the Council of Ephesus (431), the Copts in Egypt and Armenians after Chalcedon (451). But for the most part the *ecclesia catholica* or Church catholic lived as a communion of churches, united with each other and with the bishop of Rome. With the loss of communion between the Greek East and the Latin West in 1054 and then with the Reformation in the sixteenth century, the second millennium became the millennium of the divided Church. And unfortunately, once the charism of unity was lost, the churches continued to divide.

Today many hope that the third millennium, witness to the rapid growth of the Church in Asia and the global south, will see the divided churches rediscover a new unity in Christ and enter into full communion with each other. Thus our discussion of the Church needs to be framed by three contexts: the Second Vatican Council, the modern ecumenical movement, and the phenomenon known as globalization.

Three Contexts

The Second Vatican Council

For Roman Catholics, a contemporary ecclesiology has to take account of the Second Vatican Council (1962-65). John O'Malley has compared the council to two other great reforming movements in the history of the Church, the Gregorian Reform in the eleventh century and the Lutheran Reformation in the sixteenth.[18] In a real sense, at Vatican II the Roman

---

[18] John W. O'Malley, *Tradition and Transition: Historical Perspectives on Vatican II* (Wilmington, DE: Michael Glazier, 1988) 17.

Vat II
threads

Catholic Church finally came to terms with modernity, a challenge that remains for some other churches. After Rome's decades of long struggle
against "modernism," the council's documents reflected to a considerable
degree modernity's historical-critical ways of thinking. The council accepted the principle of religious liberty (DH 2), already presumed in Western Europe and North America.[19] Its Pastoral Constitution on the Church in
the Modern World represented a clear turn towards the world, placing the
Church at its service. Reversing its earlier position, the council committed
the Catholic Church officially to the ecumenical movement and encouraged
dialogue with other religions (NA 2). Finally, its renewal or *aggiornamento*
provided a new self-understanding for contemporary Catholicism.

But the ecclesiological vision of the council emerged only after a long,
difficult, and often bitter struggle between opposing points of view, a progressive majority and a more traditional minority. This historical context
needs to be understood. Most members of the Roman Curia were against
the very idea of a council, but when Pope John XXIII's resolve to hold it
became clear, they sought to at least "manage" it. Richard Gaillardetz
summarizes the problems faced by the bishops as the council opened:
"Commissions ill-disposed to reform, rules intended to marginalize all but
curial officials, poor draft documents, the lack of a council plan—all these
factors contributed to the low expectations for any substantive reform as
the opening of the council approached."[20]

The minority was operating largely out of a traditional, heavily scholastic Roman theology. Based on the Roman manuals and the official teachings of the magisterium, particularly of the most recent popes, this
abstract, deductive, top down approach to theology has been described as
"classicist," in contrast to one based on historical consciousness.[21] The
more progressive bishops at the council were much more open to currents
of renewal such as the modern biblical movement and the liturgical movement, both of which were rich in promise for the renewal of the Church's
life, worship, and theology. They also had the advantage of having theological advisors or "experts" (*periti*) who had been influenced by what was

[19] See José Casanova, "Globalizing Catholicism and the Return to a 'Universal'
Church," in *Transnational Religion and Fading States*, ed. Susanne Hoeber Rudolph and
James Piscatori (Bolder, CO: Westview Press, 1997) 130–32.

[20] Richard R. Gaillardetz, "What Can We Learn From Vatican II," in *The Catholic
Church in the 21ˢᵗ Century: Finding Hope for Its Future in the Wisdom of the Past*, ed.
Michael J. Himes (Liguori, MO: Liguori, 2004) 86.

[21] See Bernard J. F. Lonergan, "The Transition from a Classicist World View to Historical Mindedness," *A Second Collection*, ed. William F. J. Ryan and Bernard J. Tyrrell (London: Darton, Longman and Todd, 1974) 1–9.

known as the "new theology" (*nouvelle théologie*), a movement in France beginning in the 1940s that sought to renew Catholic theology by a return (*ressourcement*) to the biblical, patristic, and liturgical sources that had so enriched the Church of the first millennium.[22]

The important shift in ecclesial self-understanding that the council affected moved official Catholic ecclesiology from the sixteenth century to the twentieth and helped it to view other churches in a different light.

An Ecumenical Approach

Thus an ecclesiology for the third millennium needs to be self-consciously ecumenical. Unity belongs to the essential nature of the Church; a divided Church is a deficient sign; its disunity negatively impacts its mission. Ecumenism calls all the churches to repentance. In the words of the Second Vatican Council's Decree on Ecumenism, "There can be no ecumenism worthy of the name without interior conversion" (UR 7).[23] Furthermore, as Roger Haight observes, the object of ecclesiology must always be the whole Christian movement as "no single church exhausts the church, even though the church in principle subsists in every church."[24]

My own position is that of a Roman Catholic theologian long involved in ecumenical dialogue who strives to be faithful to his own tradition and still critical. For Roman Catholics, some developments have been officially affirmed by the Church's magisterium, and so have taken on doctrinal or even dogmatic status. Other official teachings have been modified in the light of their reception by scholars and the faithful, and even dogmatic teachings can be reinterpreted, for example, as the Second Vatican Council reinterpreted the teachings of Vatican I on papal infallibility by placing it in the context of its teachings on episcopal collegiality.

Therefore difficult ecclesiological questions are not always resolved simply by citing statements of some Roman congregation or even of the magisterium. At the same time, this doctrinal tradition also needs to be acknowledged and respected in developing an ecclesiology.

It is not possible in a book like this to do justice to the rich ecclesiological variety of the Protestant traditions. While I have made an effort to draw on diverse Protestant sources, I would like to use two statements of

[22] See Paul Lakeland, "The Road to Vatican II," in his *The Liberation of the Laity: In Search of an Accountable Church* (New York: Continuum, 2003) 17–48.

[23] For the text of the council's documents I will use Austin Flannery's (general editor), *Vatican Council II: The Basic Sixteen Documents: Constitutions, Decrees, Declarations* (New York: Costello/Dublin, Ireland, Dominican Publications, 1996).

[24] Haight, *Historical Ecclesiology*, 263.

the World Council of Churches to represent contemporary mainstream Protestantism, the 1982 statement *Baptism, Eucharist and Ministry*,[25] and a second document, still in preparation and presently titled *The Nature and Mission of the Church: A Stage on the Way to a Common Statement*.[26]

Baptism, Eucharist and Ministry (*BEM*), developed by the WCC's Faith and Order Commission with the assistance of Protestant, Orthodox, and Roman Catholic scholars and approved at its meeting at Lima, Peru in 1982, is probably the most significant ecumenical statement since the Second Vatican Council's Decree on Ecumenism. *BEM* represents a consensus statement of theologians; it is not yet an agreement of churches. Nevertheless, as a theological consensus on these foundational sacraments from representatives of such widely different traditions, it is "unprecedented in the modern ecumenical movement."[27] The second document on ecclesiology, the WCC's study on *The Nature and Mission of the Church*, was commissioned by the Fifth World Assembly of the WCC at Santiago de Compostela, Spain in 1993.

While ecclesiology has long occupied a central place in Roman Catholic theology,[28] it has not played a strong role in Evangelical theology, as a number of Evangelical commentators have recently acknowledged.[29] For example, Donald Bloesch speaks of the "appalling neglect of ecclesiology" in Evangelicalism,[30] and Southern Baptist theologian Timothy George has acknowledged that Evangelicalism "is called upon to set forth a clear, compelling ecclesiology in the light of new conversations and developing relations with their Roman Catholic brothers and sisters."[31]

Recently two fine Evangelical contributions to ecclesiology have appeared. Miroslav Volf's *After Our Likeness* is an impressive effort to develop a Free Church ecclesiology that has been enriched by dialogue with

---

[25] *Baptism, Eucharist and Ministry* (Geneva: WCC, 1982); see also *Baptism, Eucharist and Ministry 1982-1990: Report on the Process and Responses* (Geneva: WCC, 1990).

[26] *The Nature and Mission of the Church: A Stage on the Way to a Common Statement* (Faith and Order Paper No. 181) (January 2005).

[27] *BEM*, ix.

[28] See Avery Dulles, "A Half Century of Ecclesiology," *Theological Studies* 50/3 (1989) 419–42.

[29] See George Vandervelde, "Ecclesiology in the Breach: Evangelical Soundings," *Evangelical Review of Theology* 23/1 (1999) 30–31.

[30] Donald Bloesch, *The Future of Evangelical Christianity* (Garden City, NY: Doubleday, 1983) 127.

[31] Timothy George, "Toward an Evangelical Ecclesiology," in Thomas P. Rausch (ed.), *Catholics and Evangelicals: Do They Share A Common Future* (New York: Paulist Press, 2000) 123.

Catholic and Orthodox voices.[32] So is Finnish Pentecostal Veli-Matti Kärkkäinen's comparative study, *An Introduction to Ecclesiology*.[33] This new interest in ecclesiology by Evangelical theologians in the Free Church tradition is a welcome development. I will draw on their works.

A Global Context

With people linked today by email, an electronic nervous system that has made communications on a planetary level virtually instantaneous, globalization becomes the context for any serious and genuinely "catholic" consideration of the Church. The Church is now in its third millennium. The life of the Church, however, is not static. Though it seems from a number of perspectives to be declining in Western Europe and North America, Philip Jenkins' book *The Next Christendom* charts its incredible growth in the global south, a phenomenon virtually unnoticed by most secular commentators. Jenkins points out that the churches that have grown most dramatically have been the Roman Catholic, Evangelical, and Pentecostal communities.[34]

The demographic figures are startling. At the beginning of the twentieth century, eighty percent of the world's Christians were of Caucasian origin, living mostly in the northern hemisphere. But by early in the twenty-first century, they will count for only twenty percent of world Christianity. The most rapidly growing churches are in Africa, South Korea, and the People's Republic of China. There are more Christians today in Africa than in North America. Pentecostal Christians grew from 74 million in 1970 to an estimated 497 million by 1997, an increase of 670 percent.[35] The expansion of Pentecostal communities across the southern hemisphere amounts to a "new reformation," paralleled by the rapid growth of non-traditional churches, often identified as African Indigenous

---

[32] Miroslav Volf, *After Our Likeness: The Church as the Image of the Trinity* (Grand Rapids, MI: William B. Eerdmans, 1998); Volf defines "Free Churches" as involving primarily those churches with a congregationalist constitution, and secondarily, those affirming a consistent separation of Church and state; 9, nt 2.

[33] Veli-Matti Kärkkäinen, *An Introduction to Ecclesiology: Ecumenical, Historical and Global Perspectives* (Downers Grove, IL: InterVaristy Press, 2002).

[34] Philip Jenkins, *The Next Christendom: The Coming of Global Christianity* (Oxford: Oxford University Press, 2002) 7.

[35] See Robert J. Schreiter, "The World Church and Its Mission: A Theological Perspective," *Proceedings of the Canon Law Society of America* 59 (1997), 49–50; also *World Christian Encyclopedia: A Comparative Survey of Churches and Religions in the Modern World*, ed. David B. Barrett, George T. Kurian, Todd M. Johnson (Oxford/New York: Oxford University Press, 2001).

or African Independent churches.[36] If many of these churches in the southern hemisphere are more conservative, commentators like Peter Phan point out that this does not describe Asian Christianity, particularly Asian Catholicism.[37]

This enormous shift of the Christian majority from the northern hemisphere to Asia and the global south means that these churches will play an increasing influential role in setting the agenda for the world Church. There are already signs of this happening. The growth of more participative churches in the non-Western world seems to imply for Miroslav Volf that the Protestant Christendom of the future will reflect the Free Church tradition, while episcopal churches will have to integrate elements from this tradition into their own ecclesial lives, both theologically and practically.[38] Liberation theology has spread far beyond its origins in Latin America. *Dominus Iesus*, the controversial declaration of the Congregation for the Doctrine of the Faith promulgated in 2000, was the result of tensions between Rome and the Asian churches over how best to proclaim Christ in an Asian context.[39] The threat to the integrity of the Anglican Communion occasioned by the ordination of a non-celibate gay bishop by the Episcopal Diocese of New Hampshire in 2004 was driven by the protests of the Anglican bishops of Africa. And many Roman Catholics expect to see a pope from Africa, Asia, or Latin America in the near future.

Conclusion

At the end of this introduction I need to make a note on terminology. In calling this book *Towards a Truly Catholic Church*, I recognize that neither "catholicity" nor the word "catholic" is an exclusive characteristic of the Roman Catholic Church. That Church refers to itself in its official documents simply as the Catholic Church, though some Protestant and Evangelical Christians who claim catholicity for their churches as well as the Orthodox object to Rome's appropriation of the word "catholic" for itself. On the other hand, Eastern rite Catholics (some twenty-two Eastern churches in communion with Rome) protest that the Catholic Church is larger than the Western, Latin-rite Roman Catholic Church. They do not

---

[36] Jenkins, *The New Christendom*, 7.
[37] Peter C. Phan, "The Next Christianity," *America* 188/3 (2003) 9–11.
[38] Volf, *After Our Likeness*, 11–13.
[39] CDF, "*Dominus Iesus*," *Origins* 30/14 (2000) 209-19; see Thomas C. Fox, *Pentecost in Asia: A New Way of Being Church* (Marknoll, NY: Orbis, 2002) 192.

consider themselves Roman Catholics but see themselves as part of the communion of the Catholic Church.

With this in mind, I have used both names here, referring more formally to the Roman Catholic Church, but also using Catholic Church in both its official and more comprehensive sense. The Second Vatican Council recognizes that the divisions among Christians prevent the Catholic Church from realizing the fullness of catholicity proper to her (UR 4). Thus I will use the terms "truly catholic Church" and "*ecclesia catholica*" in a more inclusive sense of a communion of churches and communions which includes but goes beyond the Roman Catholic Church.

Because the Second Vatican Council is foundational to an understanding of the contemporary Roman Catholic Church we will begin with the council's two ecclesiological documents, the Dogmatic Constitution on the Church (*Lumen gentium*) and the Pastoral Constitution on the Church in the Modern World (*Gaudium et spes*). In subsequent chapters we will consider various biblical metaphors and theological models that have described the Church, as well as its apostolic ministry, its ways of safeguarding its apostolic tradition, and its marks. Finally, we will look at the Church in the context of globalization. How might the different churches move towards a becoming a truly "catholic" Church, and what challenges would such a goal present to other Christians as well as to Roman Catholics?

CHAPTER 1

Lumen Gentium

The Second Vatican Council changed the way Roman Catholics understand their Church. Prior to Vatican II, most Catholics ascribed to the Church and its official ministers an authority that today they would give only to God. There was no distinction between God's will and Church pronouncement, particularly in the area of moral theology. To ignore a Church prohibition was to sin against God. Avery Dulles terms this understanding of the Church, stressing its structures of governance and its authority to impose doctrine and discipline with spiritual sanctions, an "institutional" model of Church.[1] While a Church will always have an institutional dimension, the almost exclusively institutional, or perhaps more accurately, juridical understanding of the Catholic Church was to change considerably with the council.

The schema on the Church that the council fathers received on November 23, 1962 reflected such an institutional ecclesiology. Prepared by the council's Theological Commission under Cardinal Ottaviani, the titles of its chapters are indicative of its approach.

1. The nature of the Church militant.
2. The members of the Church and the necessity of the Church for salvation.
3. The episcopate as the highest grade of the sacrament of orders; the priesthood.
4. Residential bishops.
5. The state of evangelical perfection.
6. The laity.
7. The teaching office (magisterium) of the Church.

[1] Avery Dulles, *Models of the Church* (Garden City, NY: Doubleday & Company, 1974) 35.

8. Authority and obedience in the Church.
9. Relationships between Church and State and religious tolerance.
10. The necessity of proclaiming the gospel to all peoples and in the whole world.
11. Ecumenism.
Appendix: Virgin Mary, Mother of God and Mother of Men.[2]

The first two chapters stressed the institutional structure and authority of the Church and the criteria for membership. The following two take up the episcopal office, though with a strong emphasis on papal authority. A chapter on the religious life is followed by two more on authority and obedience, then by a chapter on the relationship of Church and state that demands special favor for the Catholic Church. The final chapter was on evangelization.[3] The order of the titles indicates a lack of a clear focus for the schema beyond its emphasis on structure and authority.

Though many fathers spoke against the schema at the first session of the council, it was Cardinal Suenens of Malines-Brussels who suggested a radical new direction. Calling attention to Pope John XXIII's suggestions in his opening address, he proposed that the council's treatment of the Church should take place in two stages. First, it should look at the Church in its inner life (*ecclesia ad intra*). This would allow a treatment of the Church as the mystery of Christ living in his mystical body, as well as of its missionary, sacramental, and worship life. The second stage should address the Church in its relations with the outside world (*ecclesia ad extra*), addressing the dignity of the human person, social justice, the evangelization of the poor, and the question of war and peace. Thus the Church could be involved in a triple dialogue: with the faithful, with other Christians, then referred to as "our separated brethren," and with the world.[4]

Suenens' suggestions were ultimately to bear fruit in the Second Vatican Council's two great documents on the Church, the Dogmatic Constitution

---

[2] See Gérard Philips, "History of the Constitution," in *Commentary on the Documents of Vatican II*, Vol. I, ed. Herbert Vorgrimler (New York: Herder and Herder, 1967) 106.

[3] See Joseph A. Komonchak, "The Significance of Vatican Council II for Ecclesiology," in Peter C. Phan (ed.), *The Gift of the Church: A Textbook on Ecclesiology in Honor of Patrick Granfield, O.S.B.* (Collegeville, MN: The Liturgical Press, 2000) 72–73.

[4] See Giuseppe Ruggieri, "Beyond an Ecclesiology of Polemics: The Debate on the Church," 116–17 in Giuseppe Alberigo and Joseph A. Komonchak, (ed.), *History of Vatican II*, Vol. II: *The Formation of the Council's Identity, First Period and Intersession, October 1962–September 1963* (Maryknoll, NY: Orbis, 1997) 343–44; also Xavier Rynne, *Vatican Council II: An Authoritative One-Volume Version of the Four Historical Books* (New York: Farrar, Straus and Giroux, 1968) 109–123.

on the Church, known from its first two words as *Lumen gentium*, and the Pastoral Constitution on the Church in the Modern World, *Gaudium et spes*. In this chapter we will consider the debate on *Lumen gentium* and then, more carefully, what the Constitution actually said. After a hard-fought battle, the Constitution developed an ecclesial self-understanding for the Roman Catholic Church that would carry it into the third millennium. In the following chapter we will consider *Gaudium et spes*.

The Debate on *De Ecclesia*

With the title *De Ecclesia*, the schema on the Church sounded like a chapter in a Roman seminary manual. And it reflected the traditional manualist theology. Characteristic themes included the primacy of the Church as a visible organization, and thus the image of the Church as a "body," an exclusive identification of the Roman Catholic Church with the mystical body of Christ, a concept of membership that was dependent on acknowledgment of the authority of the pope, thus a juridical definition rather than one based on the spiritual power of baptism, the papacy as the source of all jurisdiction in the Church, a maximum extension of the range of the infallible magisterium, a constant concern to safeguard authority, and an ecumenical minimalism.[5]

The First Session

Cardinal Ottaviani's introduction to the discussion reflected the profound divisions that had surfaced in the November 1962 debate on the schema on divine revelation, so much criticized by the majority of the bishops that Pope John had ordered that it be withdrawn. Ottaviani observed ironically that "he expected the usual litany: the schema was not ecumenical, it was scholastic, it was not pastoral, it was negative, and so on."[6] He was not wrong. The actual debate on the schema lasted from December 1 to December 7. As the fathers took to the floor to voice their reactions, it quickly became evident that the schema was not to the liking of the majority. From their interventions came many of the images and themes that would find their way into what became the council's Dogmatic Constitution on the Church. Here I can only summarize briefly.[7]

---

[5] Ruggieri, "Beyond an Ecclesiology of Polemics," 285–86.
[6] Ibid., 329.
[7] Rynne, *Vatican* Council II, 109-123; also Ruggeri, "Beyond an Ecclesiology," 332–40.

The first speaker, Cardinal Liénart (Lille) thanked the Commission for its work. But he observed that the schema failed to emphasize one of the implications of its stress on the Church as the mystical body of Christ, namely, that it was therefore a mystery. He also objected to article 7 which seemed to identify the mystical body with the "Roman Church." Some defended the schema, or asked that it be strengthened. A Polish bishop suggested changing the Creed to read, "I believe in the Holy, Catholic, and *Petrine* Church." Others called attention to its overemphasis on the rights of the Church, its failure to mention the Church as sacrament and as people of God, the importance of freedom of conscience, and recent developments in ecclesiology; they challenged its superficial use of Scripture, its inadequate treatment of episcopal collegiality, limiting it to residential bishops and its exercise to extraordinary circumstances, and its reduction of the laity to the status of subjects.

In a much cited intervention, Bishop Emile de Smedt of Bruges summarized his criticisms under three points. First of all, the document should avoid all forms of "triumphalism," that pompous and self-righteous style of speaking so characteristic of *L'Osservatore Romano* and Roman documents. The "Church militant" language seemed to describe the members of the Church as though arrayed for battle, very different from the sheepfold imagery of Jesus. Second, the "clericalism" of the schema was offensive to many. The Church should be understood as the people of God, not a pyramid of pope, bishops, priests, and people. Members of the hierarchy exercise a ministry or service, like Jesus who came "not to be served but to serve" (cf. Mark 10:45). Finally, the schema was too "juridical," reflecting a legalistic spirit rather than the maternal nature of the Church.

Perhaps most significant was the speech of Cardinal Suenens. He called for a redrafting of the schema. Vatican I had been the council of the primacy. Vatican II, he argued, should be the council of the Church, the "light of the nations," preaching the gospel to all the nations and entering into a dialogue with the world. His address was received with sustained applause. The next day, December 5, Cardinal Montini (Milan) seconded Cardinal Suenens' approach. He emphasized that it was up to the council fathers to address the collegiality of the episcopate and give a truly ecumenical outlook to the Church. To do so, it was necessary to return the schema to the Theological Commission, to be completely revised.

One of the last interventions was that of Cardinal Lecaro (Bologna) on December 6. Speaking on behalf of many who had come to Rome from Latin America and the Francophone world, he urged that the council speak of the Church as "the Church of the poor," a theme Pope John had mentioned in his radio address to the assembling bishops on September 11, 1962. Following this address, a paper from the Pope was read, detailing the work to be done during the intersession. The Pope called for a revision of the schemas discussed during the first session, to bring them into line with the goals of the council. Thus the need for a vote on the schema on the Church was obviated, and after a final closing address by the Pope, the first session came to a close. It was to be his last appearance at the council. That summer, on June 3, 1963, Pope John XXIII died.

The Election of Paul VI

In the conclave that followed Pope John's death, Giovanni Montini, the Cardinal Archbishop of Milan who had urged the complete revision of the schema on the Church, was elected to the chair of Peter. Taking the name Paul VI, he soon began to put his own stamp on the council. On September 15 he announced the creation of a steering committee composed of four cardinals; three of its members, Döpfner, Lecaro, and Suenens were known for their progressive views. Nor could the fourth, Cardinal Agagianian, representing the Eastern churches, be called a strict traditionalist. On September 21 the Pope gave an address to members of the Roman Curia. While he sought to reassure them of his esteem for their work, he made it clear that they should accept the council and that he expected that there would be "a conformity of minds with what the pope commands or desires."[8]

The Second Session

When the debate on the schema on the Church resumed on September 30, 1963, the fathers had a second draft to consider. It consisted of only four chapters:

1. The mystery of the Church.
2. The hierarchical constitution of the Church and the episcopate in particular.
3. The people of God and the laity in particular.
4. The call to holiness in the Church.

As the session began, the bishops appeared more confident; they were finding their voice. Frings (Cologne) called for an explicit emphasis on the

---

[8] Alberto Melloni, "The Beginning of the Second Period: The Great Debate on the Church," in Giuseppe Alberigo and Joseph A. Komonchak, (ed.), *History of Vatican II:* Vol. III, *Second Period and Intersession, September 1963–September 1964* (Maryknoll, NY: Orbis, 2000) 14.

Church as sacrament. Silva (Conceptión, Chile) asked for the inclusion of the concept of *koinōnia* or communion and the integration of the Trinity into the image of the Church. After considerable discussion, the chapter on the people of God and the laity was divided in two, and the former became Chapter II. Alfrink (Utrecht) suggested that the phrase "Peter and the apostles" would be better expressed as "Peter and the other apostles," putting Peter back within the apostolic college. Cardinal Lecaro (Bologna) insisted that all the baptized belonged to the Church and therefore the proper language for membership was of complete or incomplete incorporation. Debate continued on a number of issues. Should the permanent diaconate be restored? Was there a need for a separate document on Mary, the "Mother of the Church," or should the schema on Mary be included in the document on the Church, a question that generated considerable passion. The vote on October 29 was very close, 1,114 voting to include the schema within the document on the Church, and 1,074 for two separate documents.

The most extensive debate was on collegiality and how it should be understood. Did the episcopate constitute a "body" or a "college," what was its proper relation to the pope, and should there be something like a council of bishops to come together periodically from all countries to advise the pope? An important vote on October 30 showed a strong majority (between 74 and 98 percent) in favor of recognizing the episcopacy as the highest level of the sacrament of orders, the inclusion of a bishop into the college by consecration, the succession of the college of bishops to that of the apostles, their exercise of full and supreme power by divine right, and the restoration of the permanent diaconate.[9]

The vote was decisive; as Melloni writes, "After October 30 collegiality and Vatican II were synonymous."[10] Subcommissions would work to revise the chapters of the schema. Yet on the floor of the council, the debate went on. After representatives of the Holy Office argued that the October 30 vote was only a straw ballot, a particularly sharp exchange took place on November 8. Cardinal Frings took the floor to argue that the vote clearly indicated the mind of the fathers. He argued that conciliar commissions were instruments of the council and its fathers, not the reverse. That included the Holy Office, "whose procedure in many respects is no longer suited to our age, harms the Church, and is scandalous to many."[11]

[9] Mellonni, "The Beginning of the Second Period," *History of Vatican II*, Vol. III, 105; cf. Rynne, *Vatican Council II*, 214.

[10] Ibid., 108.

[11] Joseph Famerée, "Bishops and Dioceses and the Communications Media (November 5–25, 1963)," in *History of Vatican II*, Vol. III, 127.

His remarks several times drew applause, though such displays were forbidden by the rules. After several other interventions, Cardinal Ottaviani responded to defend the Holy Office in a voice choked and angry. He protested the words spoken against the Holy Office; to attack it was to attack the pope, its president. He reaffirmed his position that collegiality had not yet been defined, that the ballot was "only a straw vote," and that he did not see how collegiality could be derived from Scripture.[12]

Finally Pope Paul was forced to intervene. On November 15 he called together those who guided the council—the council presidents, the members of the Coordinating Commission, and the moderators who, led by Cardinal Lecaro, reassured him about the good progress of the council and the unity of the council's majority with the Pope. On November 21, the Pope announced the expansion of the conciliar commissions, to make them more representative. In his address on December 4 bringing the session to a close, the Pope acknowledged the "arduous and intricate" nature of the discussions and his own concern to allow the fathers perfect "freedom of expression" for the council's work.[13]

The Third Session

Opening the third session of the council on September 14, 1964, Pope Paul recalled that Vatican I had addressed the primacy and infallibility of the papal office, but was unable to complete its work by developing a theology of the episcopacy. This in his view constituted "the weightiest and most delicate" task of Vatican II, and so its work was very much in continuity with Vatican I.[14] Awaiting the bishops was a third draft of *De Ecclesia*, now known in English as the Dogmatic Constitution on the Church, or by its Latin title, *Lumen gentium*. It was a very different document.

1. The Mystery of the Church.
2. The People of God.
3. The Hierarchical Structure of the Church, with Special Reference to the Episcopate.
4. The Laity.
5. The Call of the Whole Church to Holiness.
6. Religious.

---

[12] Ibid., 129; see also Rynne, *Vatican Council II*, 223.

[13] Rynne, *Vatican Council II*, 264.

[14] Richard P. McBrien, "The Church (*Lumen Gentium*)," in Adrian Hastings (ed.), *Modern Catholicism: Vatican II and After* (New York: Oxford University Press, 1991) 86.

7. The Eschatological Nature of the Pilgrim Church and her union with the Heavenly Church.
8. The Role of the Blessed Virgin Mary, Mother of God, in the Mystery of Christ and the Church.
Addenda: Prefatory Note of Explanation.

Among the interventions during the third session was a protest by Cardinal Suenens against the Church's canonization process; he objected to the fact that those officially declared saints were mostly Europeans and members of religious orders (85 percent), and that the process was complicated, expensive, and discriminatory against the laity. There was continuing opposition from the minority on collegiality. A group of fourteen Italian bishops, including some curial cardinals, petitioned the Pope to remove the schema on the Church from the council's agenda, arguing that it was tainted by heresy. Some Spanish bishops were handing out pamphlets urging the fathers to vote against collegiality. But by now there was a strong majority in favor of the proposed teaching. In a surprising turn of events, Italian Archbishop Pietro Parente, assessor of the Holy Office who had distinguished himself for his conservative views at the first two sessions, spoke in favor of the amended text.

A critical moment was reached when on November 14 the fathers received a "fat booklet" containing additions to Chapters III and IV of *De Ecclesia*.[15] Included in it was an Explanatory Note (*Nota Explicative Praevia*). The background of the Note is complex. Attributed to "superior authority," it was known to the fathers that it came from the Theological Commission, though it had been "requested, willed, revised, reviewed and approved" by Pope Paul VI apparently in an effort to bring the minority around to an acceptance of the schema.[16] The Note, which sees itself as *the* norm for the interpretation of Chapter III, insisted on four points: first, the word "college" in the schema was not to be taken in a juridical sense as to imply a body of equals who delegated their powers to a president; second, the bishop's powers came from consecration or episcopal ordination, but the exercise of these powers had to be in "hierarchical communion with the head and members of the Church"; third, the college could not exist without its head, the pope, even though the pope could exercise his role personally rather than collegially; and fourth, the college continues to exist, but only exercises its powers at intervals, and never without its head.

[15] Rynne, *Vatican Council II*, 406.
[16] Rynne, quoting G. Caprile's comments in *L'Ossevatore Romano* (Feb. 29, 1965) and *La Civiltà Cattolica* (March 1, 1965), *Vatican Council II*, 410.

Many members of the majority did not appreciate this last minute intervention. Nevertheless, the long struggle to produce the Dogmatic Constitution on the Church was at an end, and the majority had carried the day. On November 21, the constitution was accepted by 2,151 fathers, with only 5 opposed. The vote was virtually unanimous.

The Text

Lumen gentium represents an official articulation of the Roman Catholic Church's self-understanding at the end of the second millennium. One of the council's two "dogmatic constitutions," it is official teaching. Even if the constitution does not define new dogmas, it reinterprets the teachings of Vatican I considerably by placing papal primacy and infallibility in the new context of its teaching on collegiality.

Rather than describing the Church in the scholastic categories long dominant in the tradition, the constitution is much more biblical and historical in its approach. Biblical images of the Church abound; it is the People of God (Chapter II), the Body of Christ (LG 7), and temple of the Spirit (LG 4). Thus the constitution moves beyond an exclusively christological approach to the Church to include the pneumatological; its framework is Trinitarian, seeing the Church as a communion in the life of the Trinity (LG 2-4). Other images include the Church as sheepfold, cultivated field, building, household and dwelling of God, the Jerusalem that is above, spotless spouse of the spotless lamb, and mother (LG 6).

The constitution is more sensitive to historical development than previous magisterial documents. For example, it states that "the divinely established ecclesiastical ministry is exercised in different degrees by those who even from antiquity have been called bishops, priests and deacons" (LG 28),[17] unlike Trent, which speaks of the traditional threefold ministry as a "hierarchy established by divine ordinance" (DS 1776).

Most significantly, its approach is more pastoral than juridical, and thus very different from the clerical and monarchical ecclesiology of the two preceding centuries. While the first draft of *De Ecclesia* had stressed the visible, institutional aspects of the Church, the opening chapter of *Lumen gentium* speaks of the Church as a mystery in which God calls humans to share in the life of the Trinity. One is incorporated into the Church by baptism, not by submission to papal authority, though full incorporation means those who

[17] Text from Austin Flannery, (ed.), *Vatican Council II: the Basic Sixteen Documents: Constitutions, Decrees, Declarations*, a completely revised translation in inclusive language (Northport, NY: Costello Publishing, 1996).

"accept its entire structure and all the means of salvation established within it and who in its visible structure are united with Christ, who rules it though the Supreme Pontiff and the bishops, by the bonds of profession of faith, the sacraments, ecclesiastical government, and communion" (LG 14).

Principal Themes

To better understand the ecclesiology of *Lumen gentium*, we will approach it in terms of five important themes: its image of the Church, teaching on the episcopate, theology of the laity, relation to other Christian churches, and view of non-Christians.

Image of the Church

It can be argued that Vatican II's ruling image of Church is that of the people of God. After introducing the Church as a mysterious share in the divine life in Chapter I, Chapter II treats the Church as the people of God. Placing this chapter before Chapter III on the hierarchical structure of the Church moves away from the institutional image of the Church as a pyramid of pope, bishops, priests, and people; still less can "the Church" be reduced to the hierarchy, as is so often the case in popular language even today. The Church is the whole people of God, chosen and prefigured in Israel, made a new people in Christ, and ordered towards the salvation of the entire human race (LG 9-10). It is a pilgrim Church, a Church on the way, marked by a world that will pass away and looking forward to a perfection and fulfillment that will be realized only in the eschatological future (LG 48).

Also important for the council's ecclesiology are the images of the Church as sacrament (LG 1; cf. 11, 48), as Body of Christ (LG 7), and as mystery (LG Chapter I). The opening paragraph of *Lumen gentium* speaks of the Church as "a kind of sacrament [*velut sacramentum*] of intimate union with God, and of the unity of all [human]kind."[18] Gone is the "Church militant" imagery suggested by the first chapter of the initial draft of the schema *De Ecclesia*, while speaking of the Church as mystery places more emphasis on its inner life of grace than on its external structure.

The concept of the Church as sacrament is ecumenically helpful, for it broadens the traditional understanding of sacramentality and recenters the seven sacraments within the life of the Church, underlining the fundamental, evangelical nature of the Church as "the seed and the beginning"

---

[18] Translation from Walter M. Abbott (ed.), trans. ed. Joseph Gallagher *The Documents of Vatican II* (New York: Guild Press, 1966).

of the kingdom of God (LG 5). It also implies that the Church must be visible and embody in its life the justice it symbolizes. In the words of the 1971 Synod of Bishops statement, *Justice in the World*, "While the Church is bound to give witness to justice, she recognizes that anyone who ventures to speak to people about justice must first be just in their eyes. Hence we must undertake an examination of the modes of acting and of the possessions and life style found within the Church itself" (no. 3).

The images of the Church as people of God, sacrament, Body of Christ, mystery, and pilgrim Church are very different from the institutional, "perfect society" (*societas perfecta*) model that appeared in the first draft of the Constitution on the Church, prepared but never actually promulgated by Vatican I.[19] To speak of the Church as a perfect society is to affirm its difference from and superiority to other societies and institutions, with the implication that it has nothing to learn from them, particularly in terms of the representative structures and constitutional checks and balances which moderate the exercise of authority.

Finally, in shifting from a universalistic ecclesiology to an ecclesiology of communion, an ecclesiology that sees the whole Church as a communion of churches, Vatican II effected what has been called a "Copernican revolution" in ecclesiology.[20]

Teaching on the Episcopate

The long debates over collegiality that marked the first three sessions of the council resulted finally in its most "important doctrinal achievements," its teaching on the hierarchical office in Chapter III.[21] The issue of hierarchy for many has negative connotations; it needs to be addressed specifically. For many, hierarchy means a structure of subordination and dominance, as opposed to more egalitarian structures. And it's true that it has often been understood that way in the tradition. For example, the work of pseudo-Dionysius, an early sixth century Greek author, was extremely influential in the twelfth and thirteenth centuries. For Dionysius, without being applied specifically to the Church, hierarchy was a sacred order of

[19] See "The First Draft of the Constitution on the Church of Christ," Chapter III, in *The Teaching of the Catholic Church*, Josef Neuner and Heinrich Roos (Staten Island, NY: Alba House, 1967) 213–214.

[20] Joseph A. Komonchak, "The Local Church and the Church Catholic: The Contemporary Theological Problematic," *The Jurist* 52 (1952) 432.

[21] The language is that of Avery Dulles, from his introduction to the Dogmatic Constitution on the Church in *The Documents of Vatican II*, ed. Walter M. Abbott (New York, Guild Press, 1966) 12.

levels of reality, roles, and activities that imitates and mediates the saving activity of the triune God.[22] But hierarchy does not necessarily mean the dominance of some social units by others. Using a scientific or ontological model of hierarchy that he finds in the works of thinkers such as Michael Polanyi, Ian Barbour, and Arthur Peacocke, Terance Nichols speaks of "participatory" hierarchies, an ontological/social structure in which "higher" wholes, rather than dominating "lower" ones, allow them to function according to their own laws, while integrating them into larger systems.[23] Such structures characterize many societies and nature itself. In ecclesiological terms, hierarchy really means a principle of order, that the Church has an office. It is a positive gift to the Church, not a negative development.

In formal language, chapter III states the council's intention "to profess before all and to declare the teaching on bishops." Bishops are successors of the apostles who together with the pope govern the house of the living God (LG 18); they do this by divine institution (LG 20). Episcopal consecration confers the fullness of the sacrament of orders, and with it the office of sanctifying, teaching, and governing, though these offices can only be exercised in hierarchical communion with the head and members of the college (LG 21).

Just as "St. Peter and the other apostles constitute one apostolic college," so the bishops are joined together in a college or body. The order of bishops together "with its head, the Supreme Pontiff, and never apart from him . . . is the subject of supreme and full authority over the universal church" (LG 22) and exercises with him the "infallibility promised to the church" (LG 25). Significantly, section 25 adds that to the resulting definitions of pope and bishops the assent of the Church can never be wanting, on account of the activity of the Holy Spirit, thereby emphasizing that the Spirit works in the whole Church to maintain its unity (*sensus fidelium*), and not just in the hierarchy.[24] Bishops are to be understood, not as vicars of the pope, but as heads of local or "particular" churches; as vicars and legates of Christ they govern "the particular churches assigned to them" (LG 27). It is "in and from these that the one and unique Catholic Church exists" (LG 23).

---

[22] See Roger Haight, *Christian Community in History*, Vol. I: *Historical Ecclesiology* (New York: Continuum, 2004) 301–05.

[23] See Terence L. Nichols, *That All May Be One: Hierarchy and Participation in the Church*, (Collegeville, MN: The Liturgical Press, 1997) 14–17. Nichols bases his work on Arthur Koestler's "holon" theory; see his "Beyond Atomism and Holism—the Concept of the Holon," in Koestler and J. R. Smythies, (ed.), *Beyond Reductionism* (Boston: Beacon Press, 1971) 192–216.

[24] See Richard R. Gaillardetz, *By What Authority? A Primer on Scripture, the Magisterium, and the Sense of the Faithful* (Collegeville, MN: The Liturgical Press, 2003) 107–20.

The council's teaching on the collegial nature of the episcopal office, spelled out here and in its Decree on the Pastoral Office of Bishops in the Church (*Christus Dominus*), represented in many ways a retrieval of the way the Church was understood in the first millennium. First, the description of the bishops as the pastors or heads of local churches is evidence that the Church itself is not a single, monolithic institution, but a communion of churches. Various references to bonds of union and love (LG 22, 23, 25) or "hierarchical communion" (LG 21, 22, 25) or simply "communion" (LG 25), linking bishops to each other and to the bishop of Rome, provided a foundation for the ecclesiology of communion (*koinonia*) which would prove so fruitful in the post-conciliar period.[25]

Secondly, as members of the episcopal college united with its head, the bishop of Rome, bishops exercise supreme and full power over the universal Church, particularly when gathered for an ecumenical council. They assist him at Synods of Bishops (CD 5), a collegial structure announced by Paul VI on September 15, 1965. Therefore the Church cannot be understood as a papal monarchy; its government is collegial, even though the pope can exercise his power personally, as the *Nota Praevia* emphasized.

collegial

Third, by including the bishops in the exercise of the Church's infallibility and by making reference to the assent of the Church, the council provided a new context for the interpretation of the teaching of the First Vatican Council (1870) on papal infallibility.

Theology of the Laity

Another very significant accomplishment was the council's articulation of a theology of the laity. In the centuries since the Council of Trent, the clericalizing and centralizing of the Church's authority reduced the laity for all intensive purposes to passive members. This view came to expression in a 1906 encyclical of Pope Pius X:

Mistake!

> It follows that the Church is essentially an unequal society, that is, a society comprising two categories of persons, the Pastors and the flock. . . . So distinct are these categories that with the pastoral body only rest the necessary right and authority for promoting the end of the society and directing all its members towards that end; the one duty of the multitude is to allow themselves to be led, and, like a docile flock, to follow the Pastors.[26]

[25] The *Nota Praevia*, no. 2 provides an explanation of hierarchical communion.
[26] Pope Pius X, *Vehementor nos*, no. 8; ET, *The Papal Encyclicals*, vol. 3., ed. Claudia Carlen (New York: McGrath, 1981) 47–48.

A movement in the decades prior to Vatican II described the "lay aposto-late" as "the collaboration of the laity in the apostolic tasks proper to the hierarchy,"[27] language which suggested that the mission or apostolate of the Church really belonged to the hierarchy. Missing was any sense of the dignity and vocation of the lay person.

The more conservative bishops were very much against the new theol-ogy of the laity that was beginning to make an impact on the council fa-thers. The Dominican Yves Congar had been disciplined, in part because of curial unhappiness over his book, *Lay People in the Church.*[28] The Curia's Cardinal Ruffini attacked this theology directly. He argued that the constitution should not speak of a "mission of the laity" when in fact their mission came to them only through the hierarchy. And he objected to the idea that the charisms or spiritual gifts, so important to St. Paul (1 Cor 12-14), were still widespread in the Church, arguing that today they were very rare. Others had problems with speaking of the "universal priesthood" or "priesthood of the faithful," fearful that this would blur the distinction be-tween the ordained priesthood and that of the rest of the Church.[29]

Nevertheless, *Lumen gentium* took a number of significant steps to de-velop a theology of the laity. First, it used the biblical image of the people of God to describe the Church (LG Chapter II) as we have seen. Second, it emphasized that the whole Church, not just priests and religious, are called to holiness (LG Chapter V). This means that the old language, de-scribing the religious life as a "state of perfection" or "higher way" no longer seems appropriate (cf. Chapter VI). Third, it taught that both the baptized and the ordained share in the one priesthood of Christ, though in different ways, for the two priesthoods differ in essence and not only in degree (LG 10). Fourth, in spite of Cardinal Ruffini's intervention, the council reclaimed the charismata or spiritual gifts, both "hierarchic and charismatic" (LG 4, cf. 12, 30), thus stressing the laity's share in the charismatic or pneumatological structure of the Church. Finally, it began using ministry language, though somewhat hesitantly, in regard to the laity. In an important study, Elissa Rinere shows that the terms "minister" and "ministry" appear over two hundred times in the documents; nineteen times they are used in reference to the activity of lay people.[30]

---

[27] Pius XII, "Allocution to Italian Catholic Action," *Acta apostolica sedis* 32 (1940) 362.

[28] Yves Congar, *Lay People in the Church; a Study for a Theology of the Laity* (West-minster, MD: Newman Press, 1957).

[29] See Rynne, *Vatican Council II*, 192.

[30] Elissa Rinere, "Conciliar and Canonical Applications of 'Ministry' to the Laity," *The Jurist* 47 (1987) 205.

Chapter IV teaches that lay men and women share in their own way in Christ's priestly, prophetic, and kingly functions; their vocation is to "seek the kingdom of God by engaging in temporal affairs" (LG 31). Through the sacraments of baptism and confirmation, they share in the mission of the Church, "appointed to this apostolate by the Lord himself." Thus lay people have their own apostolate; they are not merely cooperators with the hierarchy. They can also be called to more direct cooperation in the apostolate of the hierarchy, exercising certain church functions (LG 33) and "providing some sacred functions to the best of their ability" when ordained ministers are lacking (LG 35). This still rather hesitant language opened up what would become in the post Vatican II Church the "ministry explosion" as well as a new appreciation of the vocation of the laity, based on their baptismal dignity.

It would also lead to further reflection on their share in the mission of the Church, and thus, to some participation in its decision-making processes. According to canon law, the lay faithful can only "cooperate in the exercise" of the power of governance or "jurisdiction" which belongs to those in sacred orders (can. 129); if called to a council or synod their vote is only consultative (can. 443, nos. 4, 5). But as Hugh Lawrence argues, if all members of the Church share a common priesthood, that involves rethinking of the ways that all participate in the mission of Christ. "In general, the co-responsibility of lay Christians for the mission of the Church necessarily involves their participation in its governance."[31] Finally, the Church has only begun to ponder what fully recognizing the gifts of women in the Church might mean.

Relation to Other Christian Churches

Although the Catholic Church had continued to recognize the Orthodox churches as churches after the division between East and West in 1054, in the twentieth century its ecclesial language had become increasingly exclusive. Pope Pius XI stated that no one could be in the one Church of Christ without submission to the pope[32] and Pius XII identified the Mystical Body of Christ with the Roman Catholic Church in his 1943 encyclical *Mystici corporis* (no. 13), implying that only Catholics are members of

---

[31] Hugh Lawrence, "Ordination and Governance" in *Authority in the Roman Catholic Church: Theory and Practice*, ed. Bernard Hoose (Burlington, VT: Ashgate, 2002) 81; see also Edward Schillebeeckx, *Church: The Human Story of God*, trans. John Bowden (New York: Crossroad, 1990) 209.

[32] *AAS* 20 (1928) 15

the Body of Christ.[33] In his 1950 encyclical *Humani generis* he stated again that Catholics must hold that the mystical body of Christ and the Roman Catholic Church are one and the same thing.[34] This same exclusive language appeared in the first draft of the schema, *De Ecclesia*: "The Roman Catholic Church is the Mystical Body of Christ . . . and only the one that is Roman Catholic has the right to be called church."[35]

During the debates at Vatican II's first session, a number of fathers criticized this language. The document ultimately approved by the fathers in 1964 took a number of steps to reformulate the Catholic understanding of the relation of the Catholic Church to other Christian communities. First, the original schema's exclusive identification of the Mystical Body of Christ with the Catholic Church was qualified in the 1963 text; while it still asserted that the church of Christ is the Roman Catholic Church, it added that "many elements of sanctification can be found outside its total structure" and that such are "things properly belonging to the church of Christ." Thus there was an emerging recognition of elements of sanctification, implying some ecclesial reality beyond the boundaries of the Roman Catholic Church.

Secondly, in speaking of the relation between the Church of Christ and the Catholic Church, the 1964 text that became *Lumen gentium* changed *is* to *subsists in*, so that it now states that the "unique church of Christ . . . . constituted and organized as a society in the present world, subsists in the Catholic Church" (LG 8). This small change was extremely significant, as it signified that the Roman Catholic Church was no longer claiming an exclusive identity or strict equation between the Church of Christ and itself.

Finally, the text adopted the language of "churches and ecclesial communities" to refer to other Christian churches. This, together with the change from *is* to *subsists in*, suggests that the Church of Christ, if truly present in the Catholic Church, is also present in various ways in other churches and ecclesial communities. The council had no problem in using the word "church" in referring to the Orthodox churches (UR, chapter III), and post-conciliar discussion made clear that the word "church" was included in the phrase "churches and ecclesial communities" to include the Old Catholics who, like the Orthodox, were considered to have valid orders and a valid Eucharist.[36] Because the council understands the Catholic Church

[33] The same teaching appears in the Pius XII's 1950 encyclical, *Humani generis* (no. 27).

[34] See Francis A. Sullivan, *The Church We Believe In: One, Holy, Catholic and Apostolic* (New York: Paulist, 1988) 16; text in *AAS* 42 (1950) 571.

[35] *Acta Synodalia Concilii Vaticani II* (Vatican City, 1970 ff), I/4, 15; cited by Sullivan, *The Church We Believe In*, 23.

[36] Jerome Hamer, "La terminologie ecclésiologique de Vatican II et les ministères protestants," *Documentation catholique* 68 (1971) 628.

as having "all the means of salvation," it speaks of Catholics as being "fully incorporated" into the Church (LG 14). At the same time, those baptized in other churches or ecclesial communities are linked to the Catholic Church by baptism, faith, and the Holy Spirit (LG 15). They have been brought through baptism into a real but "imperfect" communion with the Catholic Church (UR 3). Going a step further, the 1993 Roman Catholic Ecumenical Directory acknowledges a partial or certain communion" between the Catholic Church and other "churches and ecclesial communities."[37]

View of Non-Christians

After considering other Christians, *Lumen gentium* addresses the relationship of those "who have not yet accepted the Gospel" but are related to the people of God in various ways. First, it speaks of the Jewish people, "beloved for the sake of their fathers, for God never regrets his gifts or his call," and then of Muslims: "they profess to hold the faith of Abraham, and together with us they adore the one, merciful God." Finally, it addresses those who belong to other world religions, or no religion at all:

> Those who, through no fault of their own, do not know the Gospel of Christ or his church, but who nevertheless seek God with a sincere heart, and, moved by grace, try in their actions to do his will as they know it through the dictates of their conscience—these too may attain eternal salvation. Nor will divine providence deny the assistance necessary for salvation to those who, without any fault of theirs, have not yet arrived at an explicit knowledge of God, and who, not without grace, strive to lead a good life (LG 16).

Here the council clearly recognizes the possibility of salvation for those who have neither been baptized nor evangelized. It does not, as is sometimes alleged, move to a doctrine of universal salvation, for it acknowledges the power of sin, or what it refers to as the deceptions of the "Evil One." Nevertheless, in its teaching on God's universal salvific will and the presence of grace in those who have not been evangelized the council is moving Catholic teaching significantly forward. Sullivan speaks of this as "a decisive change in Catholic thinking about the salvation of those 'outside.'"[38]

---

[37] Pontifical Council for Promoting Christian Unity, *Directory for the Application of Principles and Norms on Ecumenism,*" no. 18; text in *Origins* 23 (July 29, 1993) 133.
[38] Francis A. Sullivan, *Salvation Outside the Church? Tracing the History of the Catholic Response* (New York: Paulist, 1992) 160.

Catholic theologians differ today as regards the implications of this change for Catholic doctrine. Building on the council's understanding of the Church as a "sign and instrument" of God's salvation for all peoples, a theme he sees reflected in the third and fourth eucharistic prayers, Sullivan sees Vatican II as presenting in a positive way the traditional axiom, "no salvation outside the Church."[39] Others, for example Karl Rahner, argue that salvific grace, which is always embodied, can be made available for non-Christians through the practice of their religions and so those religions must be seen as capable of having a positive significance.[40] Jacques Dupuis asks, does God become present to other people of non-Christian religious traditions in the very practice of their religions? "The answer has to be 'yes.' Their religious practice is indeed what gives expression to their experience of God and of the mystery of Christ. It is the visible element, the sign, the sacrament of that experience."[41]

Though Pope John Paul II has done more to advance interreligious dialogue than any pope in history, he insists that all salvation is through Christ. The magisterium has not yet spoken authoritatively on the possibility of other religions mediating salvation. But the Catholic Church's ability to recognize that non-Christians are not excluded from God's salvific grace makes it far more able to enter into dialogue with the great world religions, and thus, with all the world's peoples.

Conclusion

Lumen gentium has remained one of the most significant documents of the council because of its teaching in a number of key areas. Its greatest achievement was its doctrine of collegiality, even if its implications have not always been honored in the post-conciliar Church. Its teaching that the college of bishops, together with its head, is "the subject of full and supreme authority over the universal church" (LG 22) and its reinterpretation of the teaching of Vatican I on how the Church's infallibility comes to expression, will continue to challenge and hopefully to shape the way authority is exercised in the Church of the future.

---

[39] Ibid., 160–61.

[40] Karl Rahner, "Christianity and the Non-Christian Religions," *Theological Investigations* 5, trans. Karl-H. Kruger (Baltimore: Helicon, 1966) 125; see James Fredericks, "The Catholic Church and Other Religious Paths," *Theological Studies* 64 (2003) 217–54.

[41] Jacques Dupuis, *Christianity and the Religions: From Confrontation to Dialogue*, trans. Phillip Berryman (Maryknoll, NY: Orbis, 2002) 188.

In moving beyond Pius XII's identification of the Catholic Church with the mystical body of Christ, and by laying the foundation for an ecclesiology of communion, *Lumen gentium* made possible a new relationship between the Roman Catholic Church and other Christian churches. Because of the Dogmatic Constitution on the Church, together with the Decree on Ecumenism, the Roman Catholic Church is now firmly committed to the ecumenical movement.

Lumen Gentium's chapter on the laity makes clear that lay men and women can no longer be considered as adjuncts to the ordained. Equipped with gifts of the Spirit, appointed to their apostolate by baptism and confirmation, and sharing in the priestly, prophetic, and kingly office of Christ, the laity shares in the Church's mission to the world.

The chapter on the laity in some ways seems less developed than other chapters in the Constitution. It is still somewhat hesitant in articulating how lay men and women share in the threefold office of Christ and leaves unresolved questions such as their ability to exercise ministries, preach, or share in church decision-making and government. While it affirms that there is no inequality in Christ or the Church "arising from race or nationality, social condition or sex" (LG 32), it does not address the closing of certain roles to women, an issue that would surface in the post-conciliar Church. The term "laity" is defined negatively, meaning all those who are not in holy orders or a religious state (LG 31).

The entire document betrays a schizophrenia that reflects the attempts at the council to reconcile majority and minority positions; for example, the language repeatedly juxtaposes the conciliar nature of the episcopal office with the primacy of the bishop of Rome and the lack of clarity on the relations between the two is never resolved. Walter Kasper contends that the term *communio hierarchia* (LG 21) represents a "typical compromise formulation, which points to a juxtaposition of sacramental *communio* ecclesiology and juristic unity ecclesiology."[42]

The fact, however, that not all issues were successfully negotiated or resolved takes nothing away from its accomplishments. In a real sense, in changing the way the Roman Catholic Church understood itself, it also pointed the way to the Church's further development.

---

[42] Walter Kasper, *Theology and Church*, trans. Margaret Kohl (New York; Crossroad, 1989) 158.

CHAPTER 2

Gaudium et Spes

In his intervention on the schema on the Church (*De Ecclesia*) at the first session of the Second Vatican Council, Cardinal Suenens had suggested that the council should also address the Church in its relations with the outside world. He called particular attention to the dignity of the human person, social justice, the evangelization of the poor, and the question of war and peace.

But the ultimate credit for what became the Pastoral Constitution on the Church in the Modern World (*Gaudium et spes*) belongs to Pope John XXIII. In a radio address on September 11, 1962, he had spoken of the Church's concern for peace between peoples and for social justice. A "Message to Humanity," sent to the council fathers by the Pope nine days after the council opened and issued in their name, expressed the intention of the council fathers to "emphasize whatever concerns the dignity of man, whatever contributes to a genuine community of peoples."[1] Finally, Pope John's two encyclicals, *Mater et Magistra* (1960) and *Pacem in Terris* (1963) were influential in the development of the pastoral constitution.

The Debate on *Gaudium et Spes*

The schema was introduced on October 20, 1964, at the third session. Referred to as Schema 13 (originally as Schema 17), it had been drafted by a subcommission under Bishop Guano (Livorno, Italy) with the able assistance of Bernard Häring. It was Guano who had suggested in May of

---

[1] John XXIII, Text in Walter M. Abbott, *Documents of Vatican II* (New York: Guild Press, 1966) 5.

1963 that the schema be identified as a "pastoral constitution."[2] The text went through many versions. One father commented that the schema was the council's Noah's Ark into which were placed all those themes for which no other home could be found.

In introducing the schema to the council fathers Bishop Guano noted its difference in tone. It was not a definitive statement but intended to begin a dialogue on some of the problems facing the world and the Church: "The Church cannot remain closed up within herself as in a fortress, intent only on defending her own interests and members. The Church recognizes that she is living in the world, sharing the life of men [and women] in order to give them the life of God."[3] The schema was very different from others brought before the fathers. Addressed to all humankind, it was drafted largely in French and circulated in other modern languages (though Latin remained the official text). The initial reaction to the schema was surprisingly positive; though some in the minority were against it, the vote on October 23 to continue discussion was 1,579 to 296.

The most extensive discussion of Schema 13 took place at the fourth session, September 1965.[4] While most were positive about the extensive revisions made in the 1964 text, the wide-ranging discussion criticized its still excessively optimistic tone, questioned whether or not it should be identified as a pastoral constitution, and noted the need to focus not on "the world today" but "the Church in the world today." Some called for a more explicit incorporation of the Church's social doctrine and there was discussion about how to deal with atheism, including the recognition that many atheists were true humanists striving to build a better world and saw religion as an obstacle. The chapter on marriage raised questions about how to speak meaningfully about the purpose of marriage and recognize explicitly the value of human love.

The discussion on Chapter V, on "The Community of Nations and the Building Up of Peace," coincided with Pope Paul VI's dramatic visit to the United Nations' General Assembly in New York on October 4. The slight figure of the Pope speaking before that body was widely understood as symbolic of a reforming Church's desire to put itself at the service of the world it had so long described only in negative tones. After the Pope's return, the discussion touched on conscientious objection, whether the use of modern

---

[2] Charles Moeller, "History of the Constitution," in *Commentary on the Documents of Vatican II*, Vol. V, *Pastoral Constitution on the Church in the Modern World*, ed. Herbert Vorgrimler (New York: Herder and Herder, 1969) 56.

[3] Rynne, *Vatican Council II*, 344.

[4] Ibid., 466–511, 546–67.

weapons could ever be moral, support for the establishment of public authority at the world level, and assistance to developing nations. A surprise to many of the fathers was Cardinal Ottaviani's eloquent anti-war address, in which he broadened the concept of war to include guerrilla warfare, sabotage, and terrorism, all of which he condemned. He also defended the right of a people to rebel against a government planning an aggressive war and called for greater support of international bodies such as the International Court of Justice at the Hague and the United Nations as a way of addressing international conflicts. The efforts of some of the U.S. bishops led by Archbishop Philip Hannan of New Orleans, a former paratroop chaplain, to amend the chapter on the grounds that it was disparaging to the United States led to a softening of the text, though it was still too strong for Hannan.

The Text

The longest document to come out of the council, *Gaudium et spes* has a Preface, an Introduction, and two parts: "The Church and the Human Vocation" (Part I) and "Some More Urgent Problems" (Part II). From its eloquent opening sentences, it is obvious that this is a very different kind of ecclesiastical document: "The joys and hopes, the grief and anguish of the people of our time, especially of those who are poor or afflicted, are the joys and hopes, the grief and anguish of the followers of Christ as well" (GS 1). Gone is the image of the Church militant, the fortress Church arrayed against the world for battle. Here is the pilgrim Church (LG Chapter VII) in solidarity with the world and its history.

Thus the tone of *Gaudium et spes* is pastoral. Its basic approach has been described as evangelical, stressing the biblical goodness of creation. The text avoids technical theological language and the natural law analysis typical of the early social encyclicals. Nor does it issue condemnations, except for one against indiscriminate warfare targeting whole cities, which it condemns as a crime against God and humanity.[5] Its concern is not condemnation, but dialogue, recognizing that the Spirit is present in the world as well as the Church.

But *Gaudium et spes* has also a sound theological foundation. John Markey sees a strong correlation between the ecclesiological principles of *Lumen gentium* and their elaboration and application in *Gaudium et spes*. These principles are rooted in the theology of the Mystical Body of Christ so important prior to the council and provide the foundation for the ecclesiology

[5] Enda McDonagh, "The Church in the Modern World (*Gaudium et Spes*), in Adrian Hastings (ed.), *Modern Catholicism: Vatican II and After* (New York: Oxford University Press, 1991) 97–99.

of communion that characterizes the post-Vatican II Catholic Church. Specifically, Markey points to three ecclesiological principles evident in both constitutions: a theological foundation in a renewed *pneumatology, community* as the dominant image, and *sacramentality* as an organizing concept.[6]

Introduction

The Introduction describes the Church as "reading the signs of the times," a favorite expression of Pope John XXIII. As it does this, it is becoming aware of the great contrasts between the growing wealth and well-being of some and the hunger and extreme need of so many, the ideological divisions (GS 4), the accelerated pace of history (GS 5), and the profound changes in the social order brought on by industrialization, urbanization, socialization, and personalization (GS 6). These changes challenge institutions, laws, and ways of thinking, including the attitude of many towards religion (GS 7) and have led to growing tensions between peoples, races, and social classes (GS 8). "Hungry nations cry out to their affluent neighbors; women claim parity with men in fact as well as of right" (GS 9). Because of these changes in the world and the aspirations and questions of so many men and women, the Church, relying on the inspiration of Christ, wants to speak to all people (GS 10). The Church wants to enter into a dialogue with the world.

Part I: The Church and the Human Vocation

Chapter I: The Dignity of the Human Person

Part I begins by reflecting on the dignity of human persons, created in "the image of God" and able to know and love their creator (GS 12). Here is the foundational principle of Catholic social teaching, including its profound respect for human life, from the unborn to the elderly as well as the poor, the homeless, or the prisoner on death row. The following sections develop a theological anthropology, reflecting on the reality of sin, the dignity of the human intellect and the moral conscience, freedom, and the mystery of death (GS 13-19). Joseph Ratzinger calls the section on freedom (GS 17) "one of the least satisfactory in the whole document," as it excludes the New Testament doctrine of freedom, is not rooted in Christology, and cannot stand up to either theological or philosophical criticism.[7]

[6] John J. Markey, *Creating Communion: The Theology of the Constitutions of the Church* (Hyde Park, NY: New City Press, 2003) 94–97.
[7] Joseph Ratzinger, "The Dignity of the Human Person," in Vorgrimler, *Commentary on the Documents of Vatican II*, Vol. V, 136–40 at 136–37.

The constitution devotes two sections to modern atheism and the attitude of the Church towards those who do not have faith, deploring the discrimination between believers and unbelievers practiced by some public authorities that ends up denying the rights of persons. It calls for a dialogue so that both might work towards "right order" where all might live together (GS 21). In keeping with its pastoral approach, the council refrained from naming Marxism or communism specifically, but its call for a respectful dialogue with unbelievers marked an important step forward. At the end of this chapter on the dignity of the person, the constitution returns to Christology; in the Word made flesh, human destiny is revealed and the mystery of the human enlightened (GS 22).

Chapter II: The Human Community

The second chapter, noting the growing interdependence of all people, recalls the Church's teaching on human society (GS 23). Just as Scripture teaches the inseparability of love of God and one's neighbor (GS 24), so human beings are social by nature. Because the betterment of the person and the improvement of society are mutually interdependent (GS 25) attention to the common good, "the sum total of social conditions which allow people, either as groups or individuals, to reach their fulfillment," becomes more important (GS 26). Here in its reference to the common good the council lifts up another controlling value of Catholic social thought. The essential equality of all—including women, whose personal rights and dignity are singled out by the council fathers—must be respected. In speaking of personal human rights, equality, and human dignity, the council calls all to work for social justice and international peace (GS 29), to move beyond an individualistic morality that does not take into account social obligations, and to insure that all may participate in "communal enterprises" (GS 31), for humans have been created and called to salvation, not as individuals, but to be a people (GS 32).

Chapter III: Humanity's Activity in the Universe

The third chapter celebrates what it sees as the human family gradually coming to recognize itself as a single worldwide community. It acknowledges that the Church "does not always have a ready answer to every question," but "is eager to associate the light of revelation with the experience of humanity in trying to clarify the course upon which it has recently entered" (GS 33). Its approach here, correlating revelation with human experience, is very different from a more traditional, deductive way of teaching.[8] Human activity is recognized as a value that corresponds to the plan of God (GS 34). But it must always be harmonized with the authentic interests of human beings; therefore technical progress is of less value than progress towards justice, peace, and a more humane social environment (GS 35). The rightful autonomy of earthly affairs, an important affirmation for the council, does not mean that the revelation of God (GS 36) or the reality of sin can be ignored (GS 37).

Chapter IV: Role of the Church in the Modern World

Treating of the mutual relationship of the Church and the world, chapter IV speaks of the Church as traveling the same journey as all of humanity, acknowledging the contributions of other churches and ecclesial communities in making history more human (GS 40). In teaching men and women to follow Christ the Church helps them become more human themselves and contributes to the humanization of history. The Gospel entrusted to the Church safeguards personal dignity and human freedom; the Church proclaims human rights to safeguard these values and shows how they are rooted in divine law (GS 41). Though the Church does not have a mission in the political, social, or economic order, and because its mission and nature is universal, it is able to call all peoples to put aside conflicts and work together for the good of all (GS 42).

Lay Christians especially are called to witness to Christ at the very heart of the human community (GS 43). Just as the Church has much to contribute to the world, so also it has profited from the development of humankind and from the evolution of social life, that it might understand its "visible social structure" or constitution more deeply (GS 44). Here is an important acknowledgement that the Church has something to learn from the world for its own social structure and life.

Part II: Some More Urgent Problems

The second part of the constitution turns from a general consideration of the dignity of human persons and their role in creation to a more specific focus on some urgent contemporary problems.

---

[8] Richard Gaillardetz, "The Ecclesiological Foundations of Modern Catholic Social Teaching," in forthcoming *Commentary on Catholic Social Teaching*, ed. Kenneth Himes (Washington, DC: Georgetown University Press).

Chapter I: The Dignity of Marriage and the Family

Noting the threats to marriage and family life (GS 47), Chapter I speaks of marriage as divinely instituted, a sacramental participation in the divine love, and it states explicitly that "the institution of marriage and married love are ordered to the procreation and education of the offspring" (GS 48; cf. 50), moving beyond the traditional language of the "primary and secondary" ends of marriage. Married love, modeled on Christ's love for the Church, is uniquely expressed "by the exercise of the acts proper to marriage," a delicate way of speaking of their sexual union (GS 49). Thus the value of conjugal love is central to the constitution's treatment of marriage, while the idea of responsible parenthood is suggested by speaking of married couples "cooperating with the love of God the Creator" and being "in a certain sense, its interpreters" (GS 50). The constitution did not discuss birth control, beyond saying that the faithful were not to use methods disapproved by the Church's teaching authority, and noting in a footnote that the issue was being considered by a special commission set up by Pope Paul VI (GS 51).

Chapter II: Proper Development of Culture

The constitution sees culture as referring "to all those things which go to the refining and developing of humanity's diverse mental and physical endowments" (GS 53). Noting that the great changes brought on by developments in technology, science, and communication have resulted in the creation of new "mass-cultures" (GS 54), the council anticipates the phenomenon of "globalization." While human beings are the architects of culture and are giving birth to a new humanism (GS 55), the challenge remains to ensure that all are able to share in the benefits of culture and that the autonomy claimed by culture does not result in an earthbound humanism, hostile to religion (GS 56). Despite these dangers, culture can liberate the human spirit and draw it to the worship of the creator; therefore Christians should see culture as a positive value (GS 57) and work to bring the good news of Christ to the renewal of culture (GS 58). Humans, including women, have a right to develop themselves culturally; those capable of higher education should have access to it (GS 60).

Article 62 gives special attention to theology. Acknowledging the tensions that have arisen between culture and Christian thought, the text calls for more efficient ways of "communicating doctrine," citing John XXIII's famous distinction between the truths of faith and the manner of expressing them, and calling for the incorporation of the findings of secular sciences, especially psychology, into the Church's pastoral care. Those teaching theology in seminaries and universities should cooperate with scholars in other disciplines and more members of the laity should receive an adequate theological formation. To contribute to the advancement of theological studies, "the faithful, both clerical and lay, should be accorded a lawful freedom of inquiry, of thought, and of expression, tempered by humility and courage in whatever branch of study they have specialized" (GS 62).

For theologians, this stress on freedom of inquiry was particularly welcome in a Church in which scholars such as Karl Rahner, Yves Congar, Henri De Lubac, Marie-Dominique Chenu, Teilhard de Chardin, and John Courtney Murray had only recently been disciplined, silenced, or forbidden to write on certain topics. It was to contribute to the tremendous development in theology in the period after the council that would see a new cooperation between theology and culture and the opening of graduate programs in theology to lay men and women.

Chapter III: Economic and Social Life

The chapter on economic life begins by calling attention to the growing problems of poverty, social inequalities, living and working conditions unworthy of human dignity, and the threats to peace from the divisions between economically advanced and underdeveloped countries. While encouraging economic progress, the constitution teaches that the "ultimate and basic purpose of economic production does not consist merely in producing more goods, nor in profit or prestige; economic production is meant to be at the service of humanity in its totality, taking into account people's material needs" (GS 64). In other words, profit cannot be the ultimate motive; the economy must serve people. This fundamental principle was to reappear in the U.S. Catholic Bishops' 1986 pastoral letter, *Economic Justice for All*.[9] That the economy might benefit as many people as possible, the constitution states that economic development must remain under the control of the many, not just the few (GS 65), and that principles of justice and equity should govern production, agriculture, working conditions, and developing economies (GS 67). Other principles include the right to work, just wages, respect for human needs, and making available opportunities for professional development (GS 67), as well as the rights of workers to participate in decision-making and to form unions (GS 68).

While the constitution recognizes in a nuanced way the right to private property, it places more emphasis on the social nature of the earth's goods;

[9] *Economic Justice for All: Pastoral Letter on Catholic Social Teaching and the U.S. Economy* (Washington, DC: USCCB, 1986).

they are to be shared by all and those "in extreme necessity are entitled to take what they need from the riches of others." It reminds individuals and governments to remember the saying of the Church fathers: "Feed the people dying of hunger, because if you do not feed them you are killing them" (GS 69). The remaining sections stress the social nature of investment, property, and large estates and the obligation of the state to provide for the common good (GS 70-71). Finally, it states that Christians who seek first the kingdom of God and are engaged in the struggle for justice have much to contribute to the prosperity of humanity and to world peace (GS 72). This section and the following draw heavily on the Church's social teaching, particularly John XXIII's encyclical, *Mater et Magistra*.

Chapter IV: The Political Community

Acknowledging profound changes in political life around the world, *Gaudium et spes* reaffirms the right to freedom of assembly, expression, and religion and the rights of minority groups within countries (GS 73); it acknowledges the reality of political pluralism and affirms that citizens have the right to defend their rights against abuses by public authority (GS 74); and it repeats again that all citizens have a right to participate in civic life (GS 75). Implicit here is an endorsement of democratic structures that had emerged in the last two centuries, something the Church had been reluctant to do. The Catholic Church had come a long way from Pope Pius IX's *Syllabus of Errors* (1864), a document listing eighty errors of the modern world, concluding with a condemnation of the idea that "The Roman Pontiff can and ought to reconcile and harmonize himself with progress, with liberalism, and with modern civilization" (no. 80). The final section emphasizes that the Church is not tied to any political system, that the state and the Church are autonomous and independent of each other, and that both should be at the service of the personal and social good of individuals (GS 76).

Chapter V: Fostering of Peace and Establishment of a Community of Nations

The context for the long chapter on the fostering of peace was the Cold War between the United States and the Soviet Union, with its threat of nuclear annihilation. It begins by speaking of a "moment of supreme crisis" in the human race's advance towards maturity (GS 77). It makes clear that peace is more than the maintenance of a balance of power between opposing forces. It is the fruit of a right ordering of things, brought about by the perfect reign of justice (GS 78). Behind the council's language here is

Augustine's concept of peace as the "tranquility of order," an inner harmony in social relationships based on justice and love.[10]

The council affirms the right to conscientious objection. After condemning genocide and stating that governments have a right to lawful self-defense "once all peaceful efforts have failed" (GS 79), it argues that the proliferation of modern weapons and their devastating potential call for a completely fresh appraisal of war. Echoing recent popes, the council declares: "Every act of war directed to the indiscriminate destruction of whole cities or vast areas with their inhabitants is a crime against God and humanity" (GS 80). Though it did not specifically condemn the possession of nuclear weapons as a deterrent, it raised objections against the status quo, speaking of the arms race as "one of the greatest curses on the human race," not least because of its impact on the poor (GS 81). It called also for a complete outlawing of war by international agreement and the establishment of an international authority with effective power to ensure security for all (GS 2). The establishment of peace demands the elimination of injustice (GS 83), a commitment to the universal common good, particularly through the support of international organizations (GS 84), and international cooperation on economic matters to address the inequalities between peoples (GS 85). Clearly the council recommends a multilateral approach to justice and peace. Christians, their churches, and international Catholic organizations should work for the establishment of a just and equitable international order (GS 88-90).

The brief conclusion, echoing the opening of *Lumen gentium*, describes the Church's mission as to "gather together in one spirit all women and men of every nation, race and culture" and calls for a joint effort with other Christians to serve the human family. It expresses the eagerness of the Church to enter into a dialogue that excludes no one (GS 92) and to strive to recognize Christ in the person of all men and women (GS 93).

Conclusion

Gaudium et spes represents one of the Second Vatican Council's greatest achievements. Like *Lumen gentium*, it marked a significant change in the Church's self-understanding. Catholics and non-Catholics alike greeted its promulgation with great enthusiasm. In its concern for equal opportunity for women, its positive appreciation of culture, its sense for what is now called globalization, its pointing to social and economic

---

[10] *De Civitate Dei* XIX, 13, 1.

inequities as threats to peace and calling for a multilateral approach to justice issues, it was clearly prophetic. Yet it has not sustained the same kind of interest that has continued to be shown for *Lumen gentium* in the years since the council and many today are unfamiliar with its text.

The pastoral constitution is not without certain weaknesses. It is not always as explicit as the social encyclicals have been. Had more emphasis been placed on Jesus' symbol of the kingdom rather than on the mediating function of the Church, it might have been able to develop a clearer vision.[11]

But *Gaudium et spes* has had no less momentous an impact than *Lumen gentium*. In many ways it was revolutionary. Abandoning the defensive posture that had characterized the Roman Catholic Church since the Reformation, the pastoral constitution sought to embrace all that was good in the modern world and put the Church at its service. It represented the turn towards the poor that Pope John XXIII had called for at the beginning of the council. And to a remarkable extent, it succeeded in making issues of social justice and the plight of the poor central to the concerns of the Church.

The post-conciliar Church was to address these issues with new energy. New papal encyclicals, national episcopal conferences, and the liberation and feminist theologies that developed in the post-conciliar period were quick to take up the challenge. Few could have predicted how rapidly the Church's social posture would change. Today the Church's social role is taken for granted.

---

[11] See McDonagh, "The Church in the Modern World," 111.

CHAPTER 3

Metaphors and Models of Church

I n his seminal study, *Models of the Church*,[1] Avery Dulles reminded his readers of a remark of Gustave Weigel in the last article published before his death. Weigel had observed that in its two thousand year history, the Church had been described, "not so much by verbal definitions as in the light of images."[2] While the council's Dogmatic Constitution on the Church (*Lumen gentium*) is profoundly theological, the constitution itself, like the New Testament, uses a rich variety of metaphors. They include the Church as the people of God, the Body of Christ, the temple or household of God, the new Jerusalem, a pilgrim Church, the initial budding forth of the Kingdom, and the sacrament of the unity of the human race (cf. LG 6). Many of these ecclesial metaphors come from the New Testament.

There are a number of ways to approach the Church from the perspective of the New Testament. In his book, *The Church*, Hans Küng analyzes the Church in terms of three New Testament metaphors: people of God, creation of the Spirit, and Body of Christ.[3] Ernst Käsemann argued that the New Testament presents a series of ecclesiologies, Jewish Christian, Hellenistic, Pauline, "enthusiastic," Johannine, and "early Catholic" as we saw in the Introduction.[4] Similarly, Raymond Brown studies "the churches the apostles left behind" as they are reflected in the different New Testament

---

[1] Avery Dulles, *Models of the Church* (Garden City, NY: Doubleday, 1974), 17; I will use here Dulles' *Models of the Church, Expanded Edition* (Garden City, NY: Doubleday, 1987).

[2] Gustave Weigel, "How is the Council Going?" *America* 109 (1963) 730.

[3] Hans Küng, *The Church*, trans. Ray and Rosaleen Ockenden (New York: Sheed and Ward, 1967).

[4] Ernst Käsemann, "Unity and Diversity in New Testament Ecclesiology," *Novum Testamentum* 6 (1963) 290–97.

literary traditions, Pauline, Petrine, Johannine, and Matthian.[5] Daniel Harrington combines the two previous approaches, analyzing topics such as the Jesus movement, worship, and people of God as well as New Testament literary traditions, Pauline, Synoptic, and Johannine.[6] Finally, the WCC Faith and Order Commission paper, *The Nature and Mission of the Church*, presents the Church in relation to the Trinity, using the metaphors of people of God, Body of Christ, and Temple of the Holy Spirit, as well as the biblical notion of *koinōnia*/communion.[7]

In this chapter we will turn to those New Testament documents that reflect both the history of the primitive Christian community and the theologies that tell us how the first Christians understood their life in Christ. The New Testament gives us first, the word for Church, *ekklēsia*, as well as three root metaphors which spell out what *ekklēsia* is—people of God, Body of Christ, and Temple of the Spirit. These three root metaphors express the fundamentally Trinitarian nature of the Church. The Church is a people gathered by God, united in Christ as his Body, a community of believers animated by his Spirit; to live in Christ is to share in God's life as a Trinity of persons. The mission of the Church is that of Christ, to reveal God's love through Word and sacrament and to be itself a sacrament or instrument of the communion of all people with God and with one another (LG 1).

As we review these metaphors, we will follow a cross-traditions approach in order to illustrate Brown's point that there is a "unity in belief" about the Church in the various stages of the New Testament.[8] The idea of the Church as the people of God, implicit in the idea of the *ekklēsia*, is presupposed throughout the New Testament, but it is developed particularly in Paul's letters, 1 Peter, and the letter to the Hebrews. While Body of Christ is exclusively Pauline, the idea of the Church as a community in the Spirit can be seen in Paul, Luke/Acts, and the Johannine tradition. In the final section we will consider briefly Avery Dulles' six theological models of Church.

---

[5] Raymond E. Brown, *The Churches the Apostles Left Behind* (New York: Paulist Press, 1984).

[6] Daniel J. Harrington, *The Church According to the New Testament: What the Wisdom and Witness of Early Christianity Teach Us Today* (Franklin, WI: Sheed & Ward, 2001).

[7] WCC, Faith and Order Commission, *The Nature and Mission of the Church: A Stage on the Way to a Common Statement* (Faith and Order Paper No. 181) nos. 17–57.

[8] Raymond E. Brown, "Unity and Diversity in New Testament Ecclesiology," *Novum Testamentum* 6 (1963) 302; see Introduction, p. 2.

Ekklēsia

The New Testament calls the gatherings of Jesus' disciples the *ekklēsia*, "perhaps to distinguish their group from the Jewish *synagogue*."[9] Both words referred to a gathering or assembly. *Ekklēsia* means literally "those called out" (Gk. *ex kaleo*). In secular Greek the term was political rather than religious; it referred to citizens assembled for some representative function or legislative purpose. The Septuagint adopted the word *ekklēsia* to translate the Hebrew *kehal*, as in *kehal Yahweh* or "community of the Lord" (cf. Num 16:3; Deut 23:2). The English "church" derives ultimately from the Greek *kuriakē oikia*, "belonging to the house of the Lord."

There are several things to note about the word *ekklēsia*. First of all, it refers to a people called together or gathered by God, thus an assembly or congregation. This divine gathering of a people is beautifully expressed in a famous passage in 1 Peter where the author, without using the word *ekklēsia*, says to the communities in Asia Minor that God has "called you out of darkness into his wonderful light" (1 Pet 2:9). In the Septuagint, *ekklēsia* most often has a religious and cultic meaning, and sometimes an eschatological sense. In popular English, the word church is most often used for the building where the *ekklēsia*/church meets; theologically it is better understood as a "house for the Church."

Secondly, the use of *ekklēsia* is widespread in the New Testament. It appears in the Pauline and Deuteropauline letters (65 times), the Acts of the Apostles (23 times), 3 John (vv. 6, 9, 10, 20), the Apocalypse (over 20 times), and James 5:14. It does not appear in the gospels, with the exception of two times in Matthew (16:18; 18:17). In all these cases it means an assembly of the followers of Jesus. Other names for this assembly include "household of God" (Eph 2:20; 1 Tim 3:15), "sheepfold" (John 10:1 ff.) and "synagogue" (James 2:2).

Thirdly, *ekklēsia* can mean the local congregation or Church as well as Church in a universal sense. Paul refers several times to a house church or church in "their" (Rom 16:5; 1 Cor 16:19) or "your" (Phlm 2) house. The early Christians would assemble for worship and fellowship in the home of one of the more prosperous members of the community. In the patriarchal Greco-Roman household (*oikia*)—an extended family that included servants and slaves—the male head of the house would be the host, perhaps presiding in the absence of the apostle or Church founder, though this remains an hypothesis. An interesting early text, Colossians 4:15, refers to Nympha and "the church in her house," though this must have shocked

[9] Harrington, *The Church According to the New Testament*, 49.

later copyists as in some manuscripts the feminine Nympha has been changed to the masculine Nymphas and "her" to "his." John Zizioulas insists that these house churches were not multiple but one in each place, the one gathering of the Church for Eucharist in each city.[10]

Paul's most common use of *ekklēsia* is for the local church, the church in a particular place. Thus he refers to "the church of the Thessalonians" (1 Thess 1:1), "to the church of God that is in Corinth" (1 Cor 1:2), or sometimes to "the churches of God" (1 Cor 11:16) or "all the churches of Christ" (Rom 16:16). Thus there are a number of local churches. As is evident from a careful reading of 1 Corinthians, the local church there was a diverse community of Jews and Greeks, slaves and free persons, men and women (1 Cor 1:26; cf. Gal 3:28). Acts, 3 John, and the Apocalypse also use *ekklēsia* for local churches.

Occasionally Paul uses *ekklēsia* in the absolute or universal sense, for example, referring to the order "God has designated in the church" (1 Cor 12:28; cf. Gal 1:13). In Colossians and Ephesians, later letters in the Pauline tradition, this usage is common.

What is the relation between the local church or congregation and the whole Church? The New Testament does not spell this out in juridical or theological terms. Each local church is more than a manifestation of the Church; it *is* Church. Paul's expression, "the church of God that is in Corinth" (1 Cor 1:2) makes this clear. The Church in its essential fullness is realized in the local church. At the same time, the universal or "catholic" Church is more than the sum of all the local churches. Cyprian refers to "the whole Church, whose members are scattered throughout all of the various provinces."[11] Or as *Lumen gentium* expressed it, the particular churches "are modelled on the universal church; it is in and from these that the one and unique catholic church exists" (LG 23).

Thus the *ekklēsia* is both individual community and universal Church, local particularity and catholic fullness. Catholics since the Second Vatican Council are used to both usages. We speak of the Church of Los Angeles, or the Church in Chicago, each a "local" or, more correctly, a "particular" Church. We speak also of the Church in the United States or the Church in Latin America. The revised 1983 Code of Canon Law has given us a consistent vocabulary; it speaks of the "whole church" and of the diocese as the "particular church," though one finds in some scholars

[10] John D. Zizioulas, *Eucharist, Bishop, Church: The Unity of the Church in the Divine Eucharist and the Bishop During the First Three Centuries*, trans. Elizabeth Theokritoff (Brookline, MA: Holy Cross Orthodox Press, 2001) 89–93.
[11] *Epist.* 36, 4.

such as Henri de Lubac the term "local church" used for groupings of particular churches.[12]

People of God

The most comprehensive metaphor for Church is people of God, a metaphor basic to the self-understanding of ancient Israel,[13] the people of the first covenant. Jesus presumed it in his ministry. In choosing "the Twelve," he claimed for his movement the status of a renewed or eschatological Israel. Finally, people of God is "the oldest and most fundamental concept underlying the self-interpretation of the ekklēsia."[14] While implicit throughout the New Testament, it finds particular expression in Paul, 1 Peter, and Hebrews.

Israel as God's People

In the Hebrew Scriptures, Israel and God's people are virtually interchangeable terms. The notion is rooted in God's promise to Abraham to make of him "a great nation" through whom all the communities of the earth would be blessed (Gen 12:2-3). Symbolic definition to this people is given in the story of Jacob, whose name God changes to Israel (Gen 32:28) and whose twelve sons become the ancestors of Israel's twelve tribes (Gen 35:23-26). Migrating to Egypt because of a famine, God delivers them under Moses from their Egyptian slavery and leads them into the land of promise under Joshua, though the actual history of Israel is considerably more complicated. Thus the Exodus story is the root metaphor for Israel's establishment as a people. God's election of Israel was confessed in creedal statements in the Pentateuch such as "you are a people sacred to the LORD, your God; he has chosen you from all the nations on the face of the earth to be a people peculiarly his own" (Deut 7:6; cf. 26:5-9).

The theological foundation for Israel as God's people is provided in the story of the covenant of Sinai, specifically in the Decalogue (Exod 20:1-17). But being God's people could not be reduced to some kind of national or racial ideology; what became Israel was a group of migrant workers and

[12] Joseph A. Komonchak, "The Local Church," *Horizons* 28 (1989) 322–23; also "The Local Church and the Church Catholic: The Contemporary Problematic," *The Jurist* 52 (1992) 416–47.

[13] See N. T. Wright, *The New Testament and the People of God* (Minneapolis: Fortress Press, 1992).

[14] Küng, *The Church*, 119.

slaves led out of Egypt, joined by a "crowd of mixed ancestry" (Exod 12:38). Israel's unity was in its covenant relationship with Yahweh, thus in its worship, which placed on them the demands of moral living. The placing of the two tablets of the Decalogue within the Ark of the Covenant symbolized this union of Temple and Torah.[15] Israel as a people was to be "a kingdom of priests, a holy nation" (Exod 19:6). The prophets never tired of reminding Israel of the inseparability of justice and worship (Isa 1:10-26; Jer 7:3-7). When Israel's infidelity led to disaster, Isaiah, Jeremiah, and Ezekiel foretold "the gathering of Israel from those who were scattered" (Isa 11:12-13; Jer 23:7-8; Ezek 37:21-22).[16] Thus salvation was always communal, not individualistic.

The Jesus Movement

As a man deeply formed in the religious tradition of his people Jesus was keenly aware of God's eschatological promise to "gather" and restore Israel. Recent research in Christology has coined the term "Jesus movement" to describe those who followed him.[17] Some envision a radical social movement, for example John Dominic Crossan, who describes Jesus' followers as "itinerants . . . like Jesus himself, primarily dispossessed peasant freeholders, tenants, or sharecroppers. They were not invited to give up everything but to accept their loss of everything as judging not them but the system that had done it to them."[18] But others like Richard Horsley find little evidence for this "itinerant" thesis; he argues that the Jesus movement was based in the towns and villages of Galilee and ordered to the renewal of the Jewish communities there.[19]

Those that followed Jesus are distinguished by the evangelists into the "multitude" or "crowd" to whom he ministered (Mark 6:34), "the disciples" (Mark 14:12-16), other friends, and supporters who traveled with him, with some women prominent among them (Luke 8:1-3), and an inner

---

[15] Gerhard Lohfink, *Does God Need the Church: Toward a Theology of the People of God* (Collegeville, MN: The Liturgical Press, 1999) 84; Lohfink argues that for God's people Torah represented a model for a new society; 74–77.

[16] Ibid., 52.

[17] For example, Elisabeth Schüssler Fiorenza, *In Memory of Her: A Feminist Reconstruction of Christian Origins* (New York: Crossroad, 1985) 107; Richard A. Horsley, *Sociology and the Jesus Movement* (New York: Continuum, 1994); Harrington, *The Church According to the New Testament*, 1–12.

[18] John Dominic Crossan, *The Birth of Christianity: Discovering What Happened in the Years Immediately After the Execution of Jesus* (HarperSanFrancisco, 1998) 281–82.

[19] Horsley, *Sociology and the Jesus Movement*, 115–21.

group known as "the Twelve." The disciples of Jesus shared in his ministry; he sent them out to heal the sick, to cast out demons, and to proclaim that the reign of God was at hand (Mark 6:7-13; Luke 10:2-12). There is also evidence that Jesus spoke of a new kind of family, based not on traditional bonds of kinship, clan, and patriarchy, but on doing the will of God (Mark 3:33-35).[20]

The choice of "the Twelve" from the larger group of the disciples has particular eschatological significance. In Jeremiah and Ezekiel and more clearly in postexilic Judaism the anticipation of a regathering of the twelve tribes in God's future, and thus, the hope of a restored or eschatological Israel, appears frequently (cf. Luke 22:30). Even the sectarian community of Qumran shared this hope.[21] But Jesus was not a sectarian; his message was addressed to all. Hans Küng notes that he never bases his preaching on the idea of a remnant; his mission was to the *whole* of Israel.[22] Against this background, Jesus' choice of the Twelve takes on new meaning. Placing at the center of this movement a group of twelve, representing the twelve tribes, would have been immediately understood by the Jews of his day; it was a symbolic act, a prophetic action on the part of Jesus to establish a renewed or eschatological community of Israel.[23] By appointing the Twelve as a sign of the immanent restoration of Israel Jesus was challenging Israel to a decision of faith.[24]

The Jesus Movement and the Church

While much of liberal theology, from its classic expression in nineteenth-century Protestant liberalism to its modern appearance in the Jesus Seminar, has sought to drive a wedge between Jesus and the Church, such a separation is difficult to sustain.[25] Jesus called together a group of disciples to share in his own mission to Israel and placed "the Twelve" at their center, thus establishing symbolically a renewed community of salvation, an

---

[20] See Thomas P. Rausch, *Who Is Jesus? An Introduction to Christology* (Collegeville, MN: The Liturgical Press, 2003) 69–70.

[21] John P. Meier, *A Marginal Jew: Vol. III; Companions and Competitors* (New York: Doubleday, 2001) 148–53.

[22] Küng, *The Church*, 72.

[23] N. T. Wright, *Jesus and the Victory of God* (Minneapolis: Fortress Press, 1996) 300; Lohfink, *Does God Need the Church*, 162, speak of "the eschatological restoration of Israel."

[24] Ben F. Meyer, *The Aims of Jesus* (London: SCM Press, 1979) 154.

[25] In his *Christus Faber: The Master Builder and the House of God* (Allison Park, PA: Pickwick, 1992) Ben F. Meyer refers to "the 1880 consensus" in biblical scholarship that there were no ties between Jesus and Church; 149.

eschatological Israel. No ecclesiology should ever lose sight of the fact that the Church, at its root, is the community of the disciples of Jesus, the men and women who loved him, followed him, and sought to live according to his teachings.

In addition to the important place of the Twelve, together with Peter as their spokesman, Jesus gave to his community certain ritual actions that the Church would know as baptism and Eucharist. The practice of baptizing as a sign of repentance was carried out by Jesus' disciples (and very possibly Jesus himself) at least in the early days of their ministry, an inheritance from their time with John the Baptist (John 3:22). The "table-fellowship tradition," so important in the ministry of Jesus, was a sign of the inclusion of all in the reign of God that Jesus proclaimed, particularly the "tax collectors and sinners." This table-fellowship tradition took on new meaning at the Last Supper and after Jesus' death was carried on by the early Christian communities as the "Lord's Supper" (1 Cor 11:20).

Can we say then that Jesus "founded" the Church? Not in the sense of establishing an institution with a clear structure and a constitution. But there is clear continuity between the Jesus movement and the early Christian communities. According to Daniel Harrington "in their beliefs (about God's kingdom and Jesus as its prophet), personnel (the Twelve, Peter, the women), and practices (shared meals, freedom vis-à-vis Jewish legal traditions), those who gathered around Jesus in the Jesus movement constituted the basis for 'the Church.'"[26] Gerhard Lofink states, "What Jesus founded, when he appointed the Twelve, was not the Church but the eschatological people of God. But in that act of foundation the basis for the Church was prepared. The Church goes back to the actions of Jesus himself."[27]

The Church and the Reign of God

The kingdom or reign of God is at the center of Jesus' preaching. It is both a present and a future reality. God's reign, God's power is *presently* breaking into people's lives through Jesus' ministry—healing, liberating, reconciling, and forgiving men and women. It is evident in his miracles and exorcisms, his proclamation of the forgiveness of sins, and his table fellowship. The still *future* dimension of God's reign is evident in the petition "thy kingdom come" of the Our Father (Matt 6:10; Luke 11:2), in the sayings about the Son of Man coming in judgment, and in the parables

---

[26] Harrington, *The Church According to the New Testament*, 22.
[27] Lofink, *Does God Need the Church?* 163.

of the kingdom (Matt 13:1-53). The reign of God means that the divine activity is present in the midst of the human.

The tension between the present and future dimensions of the reign of God is evident in later expressions in Paul, in the Gospels, and in the Church today. Paul stresses the present dimension of the kingdom when he says, "the kingdom of God is not a matter of food and drink, but of righteousness, peace, and joy in the holy Spirit" (Rom 14:17). His "co-workers for the kingdom of God" (Col 4:11) are fellow missionaries and Church workers. At other times his emphasis falls on the eschatological future, on the immoral and unjust not inheriting the kingdom (1 Cor 6:9-10; Gal 5:21). Matthew tends to identify what he generally calls the "kingdom of heaven" with the Church. Peter holds the keys to the kingdom (Matt 16:19), the scribe learned in the kingdom (Matt 13:52) and those who teach these commandments (Matt 5:19) are Church leaders, while John the Baptist is less than the least in the kingdom (Matt 11:11; cf. Luke 7:28). "Kingdom of God" appears only twice in John (John 3:2, 5). He refers much more often to "eternal life" to express God's salvation in Jesus, and again it is both present and future (John 5:24; 6:54; 11:25-26).

What is the relation between the reign of God and the Church? The kingdom of God cannot be identified with an ideal earthly political or social order. But neither should it be identified with the Church. The Church's role is to proclaim the reign of God and to foreshadow it in the reconciliation and communion of peoples that must be expressed in its life. According to the Second Vatican Council, the Church "receives the mission of proclaiming and establishing among all peoples the kingdom of Christ and of God, and is, on earth, the seed and the beginning of that kingdom" (LG 5). The concern for social justice, peace, and a genuine community of peoples, so evident in *Gaudium et spes*, is evidence of the council's vision of the Church at the service of the kingdom. For the Church, like each Christian, must walk the path of discipleship, expressing Jesus' concern for enacting the reign of God, if it is to be faithful to its mission.

The Church today cannot afford an individualistic doctrine of salvation that ignores the historical ministry of Jesus and the social dimensions of his proclamation of the kingdom. To do so transforms Jesus' "messianic praxis of discipleship" into a "bourgeois religion," as Johann Baptist Metz charges.[28] Liberation theologians have placed the Church on the side of the

---

[28] Johann Baptist Metz, *The Emergent Church*, trans. Peter Mann (New York: Crossroad, 1986) 27.

poor and committed it to the struggle for liberation.[29] Feminist theologians have stressed that salvation means liberation from all forms of dehumanization and oppression, whether sexual, racial, or economic.[30] If the Church is to be faithful to its mission of proclaiming the kingdom, it must address issues of justice and peace in the world as well as personal and interpersonal relations. Tolerating injustice within the Church is equally contrary to its mission.

The Church as the People of God

While people of God is predicated of the Christian community explicitly in only one place (1 Pet 2:10), the recognition that these communities represent the renewed or eschatological Israel is implicit throughout the New Testament. First, as the earliest Christians were all Jews, there was never any doubt of the Christian community's continuity with Israel. The Church begins as a movement or sect within the first century Jewish community (Acts 24:5; 28:22). The word *ekklēsia* itself was simply the Greek Septuagint translation of the Hebrew *kehal*, as in *kehal Yahweh* or "community of the Lord," as we have seen. The Christians of Jerusalem continued to gather in the Temple (Acts 2:46) and take part in its services (Acts 3:1). They did not immediately reject either the Law (Matt 5:17-19) or the Temple cult (Matt 5:23). Küng asks, how could the disciples of Jesus claim to be the chosen people of the eschatological age without observance of the Law?[31] Therefore the continuity of the Church with Israel as the people of God would have been assumed; indeed, the early Christians saw themselves as the renewed or true Israel.

Second, the separation between the Church and the synagogue came about only after several generations. The fact that the primitive Church did not immediately undertake a mission to the Gentiles is evidence that it took time to fully understand the implications of the Christ-event. Because the Christians of Jerusalem did not join in the revolt against Rome in 70 C.E. they were persecuted; many fled and the Jerusalem Church lost its influence as the mother Church, while the center of influence shifted to Rome. At the same time, the increasing number of Gentile converts contributed to the emergence of Christianity as a separate religion.

[29] See Sergio Torres and John Eagelson, (ed.), *The Challenge of Basic Christian Communities* (Maryknoll, NY: Orbis, 1981).

[30] See Letty M. Russell, *Church in the Round: Feminist Interpretation of the Church* (Louisville, KY: Westminster John Knox, 1993); Elisabeth Schüssler Fiorenza, *Discipleship of Equals: A Critical Feminist-Ecclesiology of Liberation* (New York: Crossroad, 1993).

[31] Küng, *The Church*, 108.

It was only in the period between 85 and 130 that the synagogues began excluding the remaining Jewish Christians from their worship (John 9:22; 12:42). The sometimes very negative, anti-Jewish language in Matthew's and John's gospels reflected this conflict, taking place at the time the gospels were written. At stake was the question, reflected in both traditions, who was the true Israel? For example, Matthew's version of the parable of the vineyard, a symbol for Israel (Isa 5:1-7), shows not the destruction of the vineyard but a change of ownership (Matt 21:41-43). A curse against "heretics and Nazarenes" was added to the daily rabbinic prayers somewhere in the second century. Jeffrey Siker argues that this contributed to a process of Jewish self-definition that was, in part, "a conscious reaction against the Christian appropriation of Jewish traditions."[32] He shows that while Paul included the Gentiles as children of Abraham, within a hundred years Justin Martyr was excluding the Jews from that status. That the early Christians saw themselves as part of or successors to Abraham's descendants as the people of God is particularly evident in Paul's letters, the first letter of Peter, and Hebrews.

Corinthians, Galatians and Romans

Paul's letters were written to mixed churches of Jewish Christians and their Gentile converts. In 1 Corinthians he draws a parallel, mixing Jewish and Christian symbols, between Israel and the Church. The ancestors of the Corinthian Christians were baptized into Moses in the cloud and the sea; they ate the same spiritual food and drank the same spiritual drink from the rock, Christ (1 Cor 10:1-5). He warns them against the temptations that will come, lest they fall into idolatry like "Israel of the flesh" (1 Cor 10:18). In 2 Corinthians he contrasts the ministry of the old covenant as a ministry of death with the ministry of a new covenant, not of the letter but of the spirit (2 Cor 2:14-3:18).

In Galatians 3:6-29 Paul explains how the traditional divisions between Jews and Gentiles have been broken down by faith in Christ and baptism, and so the Gentiles have been included among the people of the promise, the people of God. He argues that the true children of Abraham are those who have faith (Gal 3:7), for the justification of the Gentiles was foreseen in Scripture (Gal 3:8). Much of the letter is an argument against imposing circumcision and the observance of the Law on converts from paganism, a requirement urged by those often called "the Judaizers." For Paul, the unity

[32] Jeffrey S. Siker, *Disinheriting the Jews: Abraham in Early Christian Controversy* (Louisville, KY: Westminster/John Knox Press, 1991) 195.

of all in Christ becomes a basic principle: "There is neither Jew nor Greek, there is neither slave nor free person, there is not male and female, for you are all one in Christ Jesus. And if you belong to Christ, then you are Abraham's descendant, heirs according to the promise" (Gal 3:28-29). At the end of the letter, he greets the Galatians as "the Israel of God" (Gal 6:16).

Paul returns to the theme of the incorporation of the Gentiles in his letter to the Romans, but in a much more systematic way. Much of the letter is an argument that both Jews and Gentiles are justified by faith, not by works of the Law. But in a long and very moving section (Romans 9–11) he reflects on the mystery of Israel's rejection of Christ, even wishing that he "might be separated from Christ for the sake of my brothers, my kin according to the flesh" (Rom 9:3). After enumerating God's gifts to Israel, "the adoption, the glory, the covenants, the giving of the law, the worship, and the promises," even the Messiah according to the flesh (Rom 9:4-5), he says, "not all who are of Israel are Israel" (Rom 9:6). For the children of the promise are also descendants of Abraham, those "he has called, not only from the Jews, but also from the Gentiles" (Rom 9:24) who according to the prophets will share in Israel's gifts. He speaks of the Gentiles as a wild shoot, grafted into the rich root of Israel, the olive tree (Rom 11:17-24), an image used by the Second Vatican Council to express the relationship of the Church to Israel (DH 4). As Harrington says, "The root of God's people . . . remains Israel as the historic people of God."[33] Finally, Paul expresses his belief that all Israel will be saved (Rom 11:26), for "the gifts and the call of God are irrevocable" (Rom 11:29).

1 Peter

The first letter of Peter, written to largely Gentile Christians in Asia Minor, addresses them explicitly as the people of God. First, the author applies to them prerogatives taken from the story of the covenant in the Old Testament, telling them that they are "a chosen race, a royal priesthood, a holy nation, a people of his own" (1 Pet 2:9; cf. Exod 19:6). Then he makes it explicit:

> Once you were "no people"
> But now you are God's people;
> You "had not received mercy"
> But now you have received mercy.
> (1 Pet 2:10)

---

[33] Harrington, *The Church According to the New Testament*, 79.

This letter, rich in baptismal imagery, sees these Christians as "called out of darkness into his wonderful light" (1 Pet 2:9). Just as in Paul's letters, the Gentile Christians have been joined with those from a Jewish background to constitute the people of God, the people of the promise.

Hebrews

The letter to the Hebrews parallels Israel as the people of God with the Church as the new people. Christ Jesus is worthy of more glory than Moses, for he has been placed as a son over God's house (Heb 3:3-6) and leads the people of God into God's Sabbath rest (3:7-4:11). He is the new high priest who has established a new covenant (Heb 8-9); his perfect sacrifice fulfills all others (Heb 10). Note how the institutions of Israel are applied to the Christian community as the people of the new covenant, the new people of God.

Some scholars see Hebrews as a letter written to the church of Rome out of concern for a renewed interest in the Jewish cult in this largely conservative Jewish/Gentile Christian community.[34] Thus it argues that the levitical priesthood, Temple sacrifice, and cult have been superseded by the priesthood and sacrifice of Christ. One can argue that in Hebrews 10:9 this "replacement theology" becomes explicit: comparing the sacrifice of Christ with those of the Law the author says, "He takes away the first to establish the second."

Body of Christ

Paul's most powerful metaphor for Church is Body of Christ. Scholars are not able to establish the origin of this metaphor; they "have sought its roots in the image of the city as the 'body politic' in Greco-Roman philosophy, in the idea of the universe as a gigantic body, in the notion of Adam as the archetype of all human persons, and in the Hebrew notion of corporate personality."[35] Küng notes that "body" was commonly used in Hellenistic culture to express the unity of anything made up of many members such as the State, the cosmos, even a speech. Since the "blood of Jesus," that is, his saving death, had already been invested with a saving effect for the post-Easter community, it was possible for Paul to use

interesting

---

[34] For example, Raymond Brown in Raymond E. Brown and John P. Meier, *Antioch and Rome: New Testament Cradles of Catholic Christianity* (New York: Paulist, 1983) 139–58.

[35] Harrington, *The Church According to the New Testament*, 65.

"Body of Christ" in reference to Christ's body on the cross, made present in the Lord's Supper, and finally to the Church.[36]

The metaphor originates in his first letter to the Corinthians, a Church founded by Paul around the year 51 in the course of his second missionary journey (Acts 18:1-18). But the Church at Corinth was a Church divided. It had fractured into a number of competing factions or groups (1 Cor 1:12). The Corinthian Christians were self-consciously identifying themselves with different charismatic figures, saying "I belong to Paul" or "I belong to Apollos" or "I belong to Kephas" (Peter) or "I belong to Christ" (1 Cor 1:12). The divisions in the Corinthian community no doubt mirrored the social and cultural differences present in the community. Some may also have reflected different approaches to the Gentile mission, from a conservative "traditionalist" approach that stressed full observance of the Mosaic Law at one extreme, to a radical Hellenistic group that saw no abiding significance in Jewish cults and feasts at the other. Raymond Brown placed Peter on the less extreme side of the conservative group and Paul on the less radical side of the liberal group.[37] Knowing that these different approaches were present in the early Church helps us to better understand the divisions at Corinth.

Those claiming allegiance to Paul would have followed his approach, dispensing Gentile converts from Mosaic observance but not preventing Jewish Christians from their practice. They would have represented a moderate, mainstream approach, willing to accommodate what we call today cultural difference. Probably the majority in the community, Paul described them as lacking in education, influence, and social status (1 Cor 1:26). Some of them apparently were slaves (1 Cor 7:21). Another group, most probably the more traditionalist Jewish Christians, looked to Kephas or Peter for leadership. They may have argued for a more Law-observant expression of the Christian life. Another group identified with Apollos, a former disciple of John the Baptist from Alexandria who was an eloquent orator and trained exegete. Some of the better educated became attached to him during the time he spent in Corinth (Acts 18:24-28). Paul's protestations that he "did not come with sublimity of words or of wisdom" (1 Cor 2:1) and his emphasis on the very different wisdom of the gospel (1 Cor 2:2-13) may have been in reaction to the more liberal and culturally sophisticated who followed Apollos. Finally there is the mysterious "Christ party." Many scholars see this group as having Gnostic tendencies,

---

[36] Küng, *The Church*, 226.
[37] Brown, in *Antioch and Rome*, 2–8.

claiming a unique relation to Christ on the basis of a special revelation or ecstatic experience. G. F. Snyder suggests that they were members of a house church.[38] Claiming special knowledge, they seemed to have thought that they were not dependent on the community leaders; indeed, they apparently tried to justify their lack of restraint in sexual matters by throwing back at Paul his principle of Christian freedom (1 Cor 6:12 ff.).

Nor were these the only divisions in the community. The practice of some of bringing lawsuits in the Roman courts against others in the community was an offense against unity (1 Cor 6:1-2). So were the divisions evident in the community's celebration of the Lord's Supper, fracturing the community into different groups based on wealth and social status (1 Cor 11:17-22). Finally, the tendency of some to privilege the more dramatic *charismata* in the assembly of the Church, particularly the gift of tongues, was yet another (1 Cor 14).

In response to these divisions in the community Paul developed his theology of the Body of Christ. His vision is rooted in the unifying effects of baptism and the Eucharist, making the community one by replacing divisions and difference with communion. Particularly it was the Lord's Supper as he calls it, the meal of the Body of Christ, which may have provided the metaphor.

> The cup of blessing that we bless, is it not a participation (*koinōnia*) in the blood of Christ? The bread that we break, is it not a participation in the body of Christ? Because the loaf of bread is one, we, though many, are one body, for we all partake of the one loaf (1 Cor 10:16-17).

His metaphor here is based on the unity of the many in the one loaf of bread and their participation or communion (*koinōnia*) with Christ and each other through their participation or communion in the bread and cup of the Lord's Supper.

After addressing some problems in the liturgical assembly in chapter 11, he returns to his image of the one body in chapter 12, though now he relates it to baptism:

> As a body is one though it has many parts, and all the parts of the body, though many, are one body, so also Christ. For in one Spirit we were all baptized into one body, whether Jews or Greeks, slaves or free persons, and we were all given to drink of one Spirit (1 Cor 12:12-13).

---

[38] Graydon F. Snyder, *First Corinthians: A Faith Commentary* (Macon, GA: Mercer, 1991) 21–22.

Having pointed to the unifying function of baptism, he develops his famous comparison of the Christian community to the human body, with its many members, all of which are necessary, working together in unity (1 Cor 12:14-26). As the one body of Christ, the community is rich with a diversity of gifts and ministries (1 Cor 12:27-30). Then he concludes: "Now you are Christ's body, and individually parts of it" (1 Cor 12:27). Note, not one body *in* Christ, but the one Body *of* Christ ("you are Christ's body"). After another famous passage, his celebration of love in chapter 13, he takes up the subject of the spiritual gifts (which we will consider later), showing how these are not to distinguish their bearers, but to build up the Church (1 Cor 14). In Romans he returns to the metaphor of the body: "For as in one body we have many parts, and all the parts do not have the same function, so we, though many, are one body in Christ and individually parts of one another" (Rom 12:4-5).

Colossians and Ephesians further develop the metaphor, applying it explicitly to the Church. Paul is represented as "filling up what is lacking in the afflictions of Christ on behalf of his body, which is the church" through his sufferings (Col 1:24). Christ is the head of the body, the Church (Col 1:18; 2:19; Eph 5:23), the source of its growth (Col 2:19; Eph 4:16), building it up through ministry (Eph 4:12), loving it as husbands must love their wives (Eph 5:25). It is important to note that in Colossians and Ephesians, where the word *ekklēsia* is used in the sense of the whole or universal Church as we saw earlier, the Body of Christ should be understood in the same sense. In other words, the Body of Christ is not just the local congregation; it is the whole Church,[39] something that has important ecumenical implications.

Temple of the Spirit

It can be argued that a "desacralization" of worship took place among the early Christian communities as the locus of God's presence shifted from Temple and priesthood to the community itself. Remembering the death and resurrection of Jesus through symbolic expression became more important than the Temple cult. David Power speaks of this as an assimilation of images attached to ritual and its significance into a non-ritualistic context, "thus changing the meaning of the holy."[40] What was holy was the community itself, the Church, which Paul speaks of as the Temple or

---

[39] Cf. Küng, *The Church*, 230.
[40] David N. Power, *Unsearchable Riches: The Symbolic Nature of Liturgy* (New York: Pueblo, 1984) 37.

household of God, the dwelling place of God in the Spirit (Eph 2:19-22; cf. 1 Cor 3:16). For the Spirit dwells in the community of the disciples of Jesus, empowering them, creating the Church, a theology evident in Luke/Acts and John as well as Paul.

Paul

Just as "spirit" in the Old Testament is frequently used to personify the presence and activity of God, so for Paul the risen Jesus is present and works through "the Spirit of God" or "the Spirit of Christ" or simply "the Spirit" (Rom 8:9-11). Jesus, the "new Adam," has become "a life-giving spirit" (1 Cor 15:45).

Paul's theology of the Spirit is rooted in experience. To be "in Christ" is to have new life "in the Spirit" which enables Christians to know God's love poured out (cf. Rom 5:5), to call on God as Abba, "Father" (Rom 8:15), as Jesus did, to pray from the heart (cf. Rom 8:26-27), and to look forward to a share in his resurrection (Rom 8:11). The Spirit is the source of faith, for "no one can say 'Jesus is Lord,' except by the holy Spirit" (1 Cor 12:3). In other words, it is the Spirit that brings us to recognize Jesus as Lord. The Spirit guides the Christian, while "the fruit of the Spirit" can be recognized in our affective life: "love, joy, peace, kindness, generosity, faithfulness, gentleness, self-control" (Gal 5:22-23). The greatest gift of the Spirit is love (1 Cor 13). Thus, even if the Spirit is not yet understood as a distinct personal expression of the divine, Paul identifies it with the presence of the risen Jesus.

The Spirit is particularly important for Paul's ecclesiology, for the Church is a community in the Spirit. Christians have been united by baptism in the Spirit into the one body of Christ (1 Cor 12:13), empowered with different gifts and ministries. Ephesians speaks of the community as members of the household of God, a structure built upon the foundation of the apostles and prophets, with Christ Jesus himself as the capstone, a temple sacred in the Lord and dwelling place of God (Eph 2:20-22). The Spirit is the source of the Church's charismatic structure and its ministry (1 Cor 12). We will consider Paul's theology of the charisms in a later chapter.

Luke/Acts

Among the many names for Luke's Gospel is the "Gospel of the Spirit," for he shows how the Spirit guides the life of Jesus. But it is in Luke's second work, the Acts of the Apostles, that the Spirit is the major player. From the moment of the Ascension the Spirit guides the community of disciples in the expansion of the Church "to the ends of the earth." Jesus promises the coming of the Holy Spirit to enable them for their mission (Acts 1:8) that begins with the descent of the Spirit at Pentecost (Acts 2:1-4).

The Spirit is bestowed on those baptized (Acts 2:38; 8:16-18; 9:17; 10:44; 15:8; 19:2, 6) and manifested in the gifts of tongues and prophecy (10:46; 19:6). It discloses dishonesty within the community (Acts 5:3), dispatches Paul and Barnabas for what will become the great mission to the Gentiles (Acts 13:2), and enables the mother church of Jerusalem, under the leadership of the "apostles and presbyters," to reach a decision about Gentile converts and the Mosaic law which is communicated with the statement, "It is the decision of the holy Spirit and of us" (Acts 15:28). While the Spirit is portrayed as guiding the decision of church leaders, Acts is eloquent testimony to the working of the Spirit in all the members of the Church.

The Johannine Communities

John's Gospel also emphasizes the Spirit working in and through Jesus and given to his disciples in his glorification. In his last discourse Jesus promises his disciple that he will send "another Advocate," the Spirit of truth who the world cannot see (John 14:16-17), the Spirit who proceeds from the Father (John 15:26) and who "will teach you everything and remind you of all that [I] told you" (John 14:26). After the resurrection he bestows the Spirit on the disciples, with the commission to forgive and retain sins (John 20:22-23).

From the standpoint of ecclesiology, the Fourth Gospel presents the Church as a community of disciples guided by the Spirit; it lacks the emphasis on the developing structures of church life and authority evident in other, even earlier New Testament documents. Daniel Harrington observes that the ideal characteristics of the Christian community in John 13-17 may be more appropriate for a small group or sect than for the larger "catholic" Church.[41] The word "apostle" does not occur, the Beloved Disciple seems more important than Peter, and rather than emphasizing the authority of church leaders, the gospel appeals directly to the role of the Advocate.

According to Raymond Brown, this over-emphasis on a Spirit-guided community, with its lack of a clear teaching authority—what he calls a "Paraclete-centered ecclesiology"—was to lead to a schism within the

---

[41] Harrington, *The Church According to the New Testament*, 127.

later Johannine communities, and the beginning of the end for their existence as a distinct community.[42] The larger part of the community seems
to have moved in the direction of Gnosticism, developing such a high
Christology that they lost sight of the saving significance of the human life
of Jesus and ultimately disappeared from Christian history. Indeed, Brown
sees the final chapter of John's Gospel, the so-called Johannine Appendix
in which Jesus commissions Peter as shepherd of the flock (John 21:15-
17), as material added by the Johannine redactor precisely in order to
recommend to the Johannine Christians their acceptance of the pres-
byteral-episcopal structure emerging in the other churches.[43]

Theological Models

If the New Testament uses metaphors to express communal life in
Christ, modern theology employs models, an approach made popular by
Avery Dulles. Dulles adopted the term model from the physical and social
sciences where it has been used to provide an imaginative point of reference for physical or social reality that cannot be directly experienced. The
term refers to an image, analogy, or symbol which, when reflected upon
and critically analyzed becomes a model. Since theological models are
often symbolic as well as theoretical, they speak to our hearts as well as
to our heads. Here we can only summarize briefly Dulles' models.[44]

The Church as Institution

The institutional model defines the Church in terms of its visible, hierarchical structures, with a strong emphasis on the authority of its office
holders. Such an institutional or juridical ecclesiology had dominated
Catholic theology since the Reformation, reaching a high point in the First
Vatican Council's draft for a constitution on the Church. The schema described the Church as a "perfect society" (*societas perfecta*), a term used
in post-Reformation Catholic theology and given classic expression by
Robert Bellarmine (1542–1621). In Reformation polemics the image was
used to argue that the true Church is a visible society, distinct from and superior to other societies, and lacking nothing for its own completeness. Its
symbol was the pyramid, with all authority descending from above. Its

---

[42] Raymond E. Brown, *The Community of the Beloved Disciple* (New York: Paulist
Press, 1979) 146.

[43] Ibid., 161–62.

[44] See Dulles, *Models of the Church, Expanded Edition.*

bonds of union are external, based on union in doctrine, authority, and sacraments. The role of ordained ministry is to teach, rule, and sanctify.

While this institutional ecclesiology had dominated Roman Catholic thinking on the Church from 1600 to about 1940 and was frequently appealed to in magisterial documents, it does not find strong support in the New Testament and patristic tradition. The institutional model gave Catholics a clear sense of ecclesial identity; yet its approach to the Church was rigid, authoritarian, clerical, and not open to ecumenism; furthermore, it left little room for the charismata.

Church as Mystical Communion

The symbol for the Church as mystical communion is community. The Church is a community of people united by their shared life in the Holy Spirit; thus the interior bond of *communio* is more important than external, juridical ones. In harmony with the biblical metaphors of the Church as people of God and Body of Christ, this model also has strong support from the Church fathers. Johann Adam Möhler and others in the Tübingen school contributed to a revival of this ecclesiology in the nineteenth century, and Pope Pius XII developed it explicitly in his 1943 encyclical on the mystical body, *Mystici corporis*. It can be found in the works of Yves Congar, Jerome Hamer, and Vatican II, particularly in its emphasis on the Church as the people of God. The role of ministry in this model is to foster communion.

The model has strong biblical support, the theme of communion (*koinōnia*) plays an important role in the early Christian centuries, and the interpersonal and communal dimensions of the model appeal strongly to people today. It stresses a community based on organic rather than juridical elements. Yet Dulles argues that in slighting the organizational elements of the Church it risks lapsing into an ecclesiological dualism; if union is in the Spirit, the point of organizational elements is less clear. It does not support a clear sense of mission, and it risks romanticizing the Church as the ideal community.

Church as Sacrament

The sacrament model sees the Church as the sacrament of Christ and of the union of all humankind. It defines the Church in terms of its visible and symbolic elements, so that the Church itself becomes a sign of grace present in history. The bonds of union are all the visible, social signs of grace, the Church's witness, worship, and sacraments. The role of ministry is to be a sign. Henri de Lubac's recovery of patristic theology played a major role in popularizing this model; it was further developed by Karl Rahner, Otto Semmelroth, Edward Schillebeeckx, and Yves Congar, among others.

A strength of this model is its ability to integrate theologically the inner and outer aspects of the Church, its institutional and structural elements with its symbolic ones, including the unity between particular churches and its continuity with the apostolic Church which enables the Church today to make visible God's grace and communion revealed in Christ. Thus it mediates between the institutional and mystical communion models. Its emphasis on sacramentality calls for the renewal of Church life and ritual, for an inadequate sign is less efficacious. Sacramentality presumes the visibility of the Church. Less positively, there is the danger of a narrow sacramentalism, a loss of a sense of mission, and the fact that it has found little response in Protestant thought.

The Church as Herald

If the last model stresses the sacraments, the Church as herald is a kerygmatic model, based on the Word of God. This model is strongly congregational; each local community is fully the Church. It sees the Church as gathered in response to the Word and missioned to proclaim it, and it draws a sharp distinction between the Church and the Kingdom of God that the Church announces or heralds. Thus it represents a typically Protestant ecclesiology, particularly strong in Martin Luther, Karl Barth, Rudolph Bultmann, and represented in Roman Catholic theology by Hans Küng. The primary bond of communion in this model is faith, while the basic role of the ministry is proclamation. In Lutheran theology, ordained ministry is defined as a preaching office (*Predigamt*). Sacraments are considered "visible words."

Positively, the model has firm support in the prophetic tradition and in Paul, and it supports a rich theology of the Word. If it encourages the Church's evangelical mission, it is much less strong on the social dimensions of evangelization and neglects the doctrine that grace brings new life. Faith must result in a communion of life and love. Its congregational approach risks making the local congregation completely self-sufficient. Finally, it risks reducing Christian soteriology to an individualistic message of salvation and often excludes from salvation those who do not believe or come to faith in Christ.

The Church as Servant

The Church as servant model reflects the new attitude towards the world evident in the Pastoral Constitution on the Church in the Modern

World; rather than being a refuge from the world, the Church is at its service. This attitude can also be found in Dietrich Bonhoeffer's posthumous *Letters and Papers from Prison*, in Teilhard de Chardin, Harvey Cox, and in the liberation theologians. The bond of union in this model is the sense of communion and solidarity so often experienced by those who work for justice, a communion that often cuts across ecclesial affiliations. Ministry is seen as an agency of change and liberation.

A strength of this model is its ability to relate the Church to the world in which it dwells and to give it a new sense of mission, enacting the values of the Kingdom of God. Negatively, Dulles fears that this model might threaten the distinctive mission of the Church and secularize ecclesiology. He does not see any direct biblical foundation for understanding the Church's mission as service or the transformation of society, though he recognizes an "indirect foundation."

The Church as Community of Disciples

In his expanded edition of *Models of the Church*, Dulles said that writing when all institutions were under critical scrutiny, he "may have been somewhat too severe in the institutional model."[45] In order to harmonize the differences among the five previous models, he proposed a new model, that of "community of disciples." He sees this model as rooted in the New Testament and in the earthly ministry of Jesus, particularly his constituting his disciples as a community or alternative society. As symbol of a new and renewed Israel, this community was differentiated, with an inner core, constituted by the Twelve, a frequently named group of three: Peter, James, and John, and with Peter always named first. In the post-Easter period, the group of disciples was enlarged to accommodate those who came to faith in the risen Jesus and the Church itself was called the community of disciples (Acts 6:2). If the more heroic aspects of discipleship were occasionally lost as Christians accommodated themselves to their societies, the ideal of discipleship did not entirely disappear.

The community, formed by Word and sacrament, remains bound to the life of discipleship and to the Church's worship and sacramental life. Dulles sees this model as helping bridge the gap between the institutional and community models, particularly by calling Church leaders to imitate the Good Shepherd in their pastoral care of the faithful and to work closely with a larger body of lay ministers. The limitations of this model include that it seems to overemphasize the contrast between Christians and others

---

[45] Dulles *Models, Expanded Edition*, 205.

in the world, to make extravagant demands on the average Christian, and to imply that the Church is a free association of individuals volunteering for service. Yet it effectively brings out the idea of what Dietrich Bonhoeffer called the "the cost of discipleship"[46] and stresses the vocation that each Christian has in Christ.

Dulles argues that no single model is fully adequate for describing the Church, while each brings out important dimensions that enrich our understanding of Church.[47] For evaluating the models he proposes the following criteria:[48]

- Basis in Scripture.
- Basis in the Christian tradition.
- Capacity to give Church members a sense of their corporate identity and mission.
- Tendency to foster the virtues and values generally admired by Christians.
- Correspondence with the religious experience of people today.
- Theological fruitfulness.
- Fruitfulness in enabling Church members to relate successfully to those outside their own group.

Conclusion

In this chapter we have considered the New Testament term *ekklēsia*, as well as the metaphors people of God, Body of Christ, and temple of the Spirit. Common to each of them is the communal dimension of the Church as an assembly, the people of God, united in baptism and Eucharist as the Body of Christ, and animated by the indwelling Spirit. One cannot be a Christian in isolation from other Christians. To be "in Christ" is to be incorporated into his Body, the Church. From the beginning, the disciples of Jesus came together for preaching/proclamation (*kerygma*), teaching (*didachē*), fellowship or communion (*koinōnia*), ministry (*diakonia*), and worship (*leiturgia*). These metaphors also make evident the Trinitarian nature of life in the Church.

The actual word for "Church," *ekklēsia*, was used in the Septuagint for the *kehal Yahweh*, the "community of the Lord." Church means not a structure or building, but a people, called out or gathered by God. Used in

---

[46] Dietrich Bonhoeffer, *The Cost of Discipleship*, trans. R. H. Fuller (New York: Macmillan, 1960).

[47] Dulles, *Models of the Church, Expanded Edition*, 206.

[48] Ibid., 191–92.

the New Testament for the local congregation as well as for the whole Church, it suggests that the Church is a communion of churches.

The metaphor, people of God, expresses the mystery of God's election of a people to be his own. In placing "the Twelve" at the center of his movement, Jesus symbolized it as constituting a renewed or eschatological Israel. The Church has its origins in the actions of Jesus. After the resurrection, the earliest Christians, all Jews, continued to think of themselves as the people of God.

As the communities grew apart, the resulting conflict between the Church and the synagogue becomes evident in some of the later New Testament documents. Too often Christians, ignorant of this history, have seized on the often negative, anti-Jewish language in Matthew and John and used it to argue God's rejection of the Jews, resulting in a long and tragic history of Christian anti-Semitism. The Church today recognizes people of God as an inclusive metaphor, for it does not exclude the people of the first covenant, the Jews. Like Paul, the Church maintains that "God does not take back the gifts he bestowed or the choice he made" (NA 4).

The idea of the Christian community as the Body of Christ comes from Paul. While the image of body was a common metaphor for any diverse group in Hellenistic culture, there is good reason for thinking that Paul found his inspiration for this image in the Eucharist (cf. 1 Cor 10:16-17). In any case, he clearly roots it in the unifying effects of baptism, with its gift of the Spirit, and in the Lord's Supper, making the community the one Body of Christ. In the more developed ecclesiology of Ephesians and Colossians, Christ is said to be the head of his body, the Church, used in a universal sense (cf. Col 1:24; Eph 1:22-23).

For Paul, the Church is a temple or dwelling place of the Spirit. Both Paul and Luke emphasize the guiding role of the Spirit in the life of the Church, but the initial failure of the Johannine communities to develop structures of authority resulted in a schism and loss of the greater part of the community. A Spirit-guided community needs structures of authority, a subject to be addressed in greater detail later.

Avery Dulles' book, *Models of the Church*, has become a classic, a seminal work that neatly captures different theological visions of Church, providing both a useful reference point for different ecclesiologies and introducing a method that has proved helpful in other areas of theology.

The Church as people of God, Body of Christ, and temple of the Spirit express our share in the life of the Trinity. That shared life in God and with one another is summed up by the concept of *koinōnia*, communion. We will consider *koinōnia* in the next chapter.

CHAPTER 4

Communion in the Body of Christ

T he Acts of the Apostles follows the story of Peter's great Pentecost sermon with a short passage which summarizes the life of the primitive Church of Jerusalem: "Those who accepted his message were baptized. . . . They devoted themselves to the teaching of the apostles (*didachē tōn apostolōn*) and to the communal life (*koinōnia*), to the breaking of the bread and to the prayers" (Acts 2:41-42). While admittedly an idealized sketch, Luke's summary suggests that the essential elements of Church include baptism, apostolic teaching (or tradition), communal life, Eucharist, and prayer.

Paul's basic metaphor for the Christian community is the Body of Christ. Introduced in his first letter to the Corinthians (1 Cor 10:15-17; 12:11-28), the metaphor also appears in Romans (12:4-5), Colossians, and Ephesians. Paul tells the Corinthians that by their participation (*koinōnia*) or communion in the body and blood of Christ they, too, become one body.

> The cup of blessing that we bless, is it not a participation in the blood of Christ? The bread that we break, is it not a participation in the body of Christ? Because the loaf of bread is one, we, though many, are one body, for we all partake of the one loaf (1 Cor 10:16-17).

These few verses are heavy with ecclesiological meaning. In the Lord's Supper or Eucharist, Christians have a communion in the body and blood of Christ and are constituted as the Body of Christ.[1] For both Roman Catholic and Orthodox ecclesiology the Eucharist is crucial; "where the

---

[1] This was Augustine's view; see Roger Haight, *Christian Community in History*: Vol. I: *Historical Ecclesiology* (New York: Continuum, 2004) 226.

Eucharist is, there is the Church."[2] Also evident here is the notion of *koinōnia* or communion, so important in the life of the Church.

To better understand Paul's ecclesiological vision of life in Christ through communion in his Body, the Church, we will consider the rich concept of *koinōnia* or communion. Then we will look at baptism and Eucharist, which unite Christians in the Spirit as one body in Christ and equip them with a diversity of gifts and ministries. Finally, we will consider an ecclesiology of communion.

The Concept of Communion

For pre-Vatican II Catholicism, Christian unity meant the return of those who had separated from Rome to their original home in the "one true Church." The Church was too often conceived as a single, unified institution, with too little attention paid to the ecclesial status of the local or particular churches. The notion of *koinōnia* has been present from the outset of the work of the Faith and Order Commission, thus long before the organization of the World Council of Churches in 1948.[3] Since the council, it has moved to the center of Roman Catholic ecclesiology. The report of the 1985 Extraordinary Synod of Bishops in Rome stated that the Roman Catholic Church has fully assumed its ecumenical responsibility on the basis of the ecclesiology of communion.[4] To understand the Church as *koinōnia* is to understand the essential nature of its life.

The Greek *koinōnia* means a sharing or participation in something else. Appearing 19 times in the New Testament, it is generally translated as "communion" (Lt. *communio*) or "fellowship." Roman Catholics, sensitive to its spiritual and sacramental implications, often translate it as communion; Evangelicals prefer fellowship.[5]

The New Testament employs *koinōnia* in a number of senses. First of all the term has the soteriological sense of "the communion of the redeemed with God through Jesus Christ in the Holy Spirit."[6] It describes the sharing or

[2] Susan Wood, "Communion Ecclesiology: Source of Hope, Source of Controversy," *Pro Ecclesia* 2 (1993) 425.

[3] See J. M. R. Tillard, "Koinonia: V. Dan La Vie Chrétienne Aujourd'hui" in *Dictionnaire de spiritualité* (Paris: Beauchesne, 1974) 1759; I'm grateful to Catherine Clifford for bringing this to my attention.

[4] Extraordinary Synod of Bishops, Rome 1985; published as "A Message to the People of God and the Final Report" (Washington: USCCB, 1986) 20–21.

[5] See Catholic Church, World Evangelical Alliance, "Church, Evangelization and 'Koinonia'," (no. 1); *Origins* 33/19 (2003) 311.

[6] Herman J. Pottmeyer, *Towards a Papacy in Communion: Perspectives from Vatican Councils I & II*, trans. Matthew J. O'Connell (New York: Crossroad, 1998) 119.

participation in the life of Christ that comes from God as a gift: "God is faithful, and by him you were called to fellowship (*koinōnia*) with his Son, Jesus Christ our Lord" (1 Cor 1:9). This communion in Christ takes place through sharing (*koinōnia*) in the gospel (Phil 1:5), in faith (Phlm 6), in the sufferings of Christ (Phil 3:10; 2 Cor 1:7), and in his Spirit (2 Cor 13:13). There is a profoundly Trinitarian dimension to *koinōnia*. At the end of 2 Corinthians Paul greets the community with a threefold benediction: "The grace of the Lord Jesus Christ and the love of God and the fellowship (*koinōnia*) of the holy Spirit be with all of you" (2 Cor 13:13; cf. Phil 2:1). The author of 2 Peter, using particularly strong language, says that through God's promises "you may come to share (*koinōnoi*) in the divine nature" (2 Pet 1:4).

Therefore *koinōnia* means more than simply fellowship; it is a participation in the divine life which itself is a communion of Father, Son, and Spirit. The eastern fathers of the Church speak of this as a process of divinization (*theosis*). Vatican II's Decree on Ecumenism describes the Church as "the sacred mystery of the unity . . . . in the Trinity of Persons, of one God, the Father and the Son in the holy Spirit" (UR 2).

Second, there is a sacramental dimension to *koinōnia*. Communion is both symbolized and effected by the rituals of baptism and Eucharist. For Paul especially, the members of the community, united by their communion in the body and blood of Christ, themselves become his Body (1 Cor 10:16-17). Avery Dulles notes that the original meaning of the term *communio sanctorum* in the Apostles Creed seems to have meant, not the "communion of saints" but rather "participation in holy things," the sacraments.[7]

Finally, *koinōnia* has an ecclesial sense, rooted in the Eucharist.[8] To be "in Christ" for Paul is profoundly ecclesial. Life in Christ cannot be conceived individualistically. Communion with God in Christ means that Christians are also in fellowship or communion with each other. Acts 2:42 uses *koinōnia* to describe the "communal life" of the primitive community of Jerusalem as we have seen. John uses it to describe the community's shared life with God and with each other:

> what we have seen and heard
> we proclaim now to you,
> so that you too may have fellowship with
> us;

[7] Avery Dulles, "The Church as Communion," in *New Perspectives on Historical Theology: Essays in Memory of John Meyendorff*, ed. Bradley Nassif (Grand Rapids, MI: William B. Eerdmans, 1996) 126.

[8] See I. Riedel-Spangenberger, "Die Communio als Strukturprinzip der Kirche und ihre Rezeption im CIC/1983," *Trierer Theologische Zeitschrift* 97 (1988) 230–32.

for our fellowship is with the Father
and with his Son, Jesus Christ
(1 John 1:3; cf. 6,7)

There is then both a vertical and a horizontal dimension to communion.[9] For *koinōnia* is rooted in a shared life in the Spirit.

Baptism

Christian baptism derives from the practice of John the Baptist who washed those who came to him at the Jordan with water as a sign of repentance. Jesus himself had been baptized by John, and his own public ministry began in association with John. It is very likely that Jesus and some of his first disciples had been for a time part of John's movement, and there is evidence that Jesus himself baptized in the early days of his ministry (John 3:22).[10]

The New Testament offers various theologies of baptism. The Synoptic gospels stress that while John baptized with water for repentance, Jesus would baptize with the Holy Spirit (Mark 1:8 & plls.). The risen Jesus commands his disciples to "make disciples of all nations, baptizing them in the name of the Father, and of the Son, and of the holy Spirit" (Matt 28:19). A more developed theology of baptism appears in the Acts of the Apostles. Baptism is a response in faith to Christian preaching and a rite of initiation into the Christian community (Acts 2:41); it confers on the believer the forgiveness of sins and the gift of the Holy Spirit (Acts 2:38; cf. 8:16-18; 9:17; 11:16), sometimes accompanied by the gifts of tongues and prophecy (10:44-47; 19:2). As baptism presumes faith, adult baptism should be the norm, though infant baptism makes sense if the child is truly being received into a community of faith, a Christian family or "domestic church" (LG 11).

According to the fourth gospel, "no one can enter the kingdom of God without being born of water and Spirit" (John 3:5); thus baptism is new life, necessary for salvation. Evangelicals have seen in the words of Jesus, "no one can see the kingdom of God without being born from above" (John 3:3) as requiring one to be "born again." The author of 1 Peter compares baptism to the Ark that saved Noah and his family through water

[9] See Susan K. Wood, "The Church as Communion," in *The Gift of the Church: A Textbook on Ecclesiology in Honor of Patrick Granfield, O.S.B.*, ed. Peter C. Phan (Collegeville, MN: The Liturgical Press, 2000) 160.

[10] See John P. Meier, *A Marginal Jew: Rethinking the Historical Jesus*, Vol. II: *Mentor, Message, and Miracles* (New York: Doubleday, 1994) 118–22; also N.T. Wright, *Jesus and the Victory of God* (Minneapolis: Fortress Press, 1996) 168–69.

(1 Pet 3:20-21). Common to these theologies of baptism is the idea that the one baptized is <u>incorporated</u> into salvation in Christ and thus into his community, and that baptism mediates or testifies to the Spirit.

These same themes appear also in Paul, who has the most developed theology of baptism. Baptism incorporates one symbolically and mystically into the Paschal Mystery of Christ, his life, death, and resurrection, so that freed from sin, he or she might live a new life and look forward to union with Christ in the resurrection (Rom 6:3-23). The one baptized has been washed, sanctified, and justified (1 Cor 6:11; cf. Titus 3:5).

Most importantly for Paul, baptism, mediating the one Spirit, incorporates those baptized into the one Body of Christ: "For in one Spirit we were all baptized into one body, whether Jews or Greeks, slaves or free" (1 Cor 12:13). This unifying effect, breaking down barriers and divisions, is basic to Paul's whole ecclesiological understanding of baptism and Eucharist. In 1 Corinthians, baptism initiates one into the Body of Christ. In Galatians, it makes one a descendant of Abraham, and thus a member of the people of God, bringing together Paul's two root metaphors for Church. In both cases, it reconciles and unites people previously divided, and so rules out any divisions based on race, sex, or social status in the Church:

> For all of you who were baptized into Christ have clothed yourself with Christ. There is neither Jew nor Greek, there is neither slave nor free person, there is not male and female; for you are all one in Christ Jesus. And if you belong to Christ, then you are Abraham's descendant, heirs according to the promise (Gal 3:27-29).

This theme of the unity of people in Christ and thus in the Church runs as leitmotif throughout the Pauline letters (cf. Rom 10:12; Eph 2:14-16).

The section on baptism in the World Council of Churches' consensus statement *Baptism, Eucharist and Ministry* (*BEM*)[11] seeks to mediate between two traditions, those who practice infant baptism and those who insist on believers' baptism. While noting that the possibility of infant baptism from the apostolic age cannot be excluded, it reminds those who practice it today that the most clearly attested pattern in the New Testament is baptism upon a personal profession of faith (no. 11) and that therefore, baptism should not be practiced indiscriminately, as it seems to be in many European and North American churches today (Commentary, 21).[12]

[11] *Baptism, Eucharist and Ministry* (Geneva: World Council of Churches, 1982).
[12] The 1983 Code of Canon Law notes that if the hope that a child will be brought up in the Catholic faith "is altogether lacking, the baptism is to be put off according to the prescriptions of particular law and the parents are to be informed of the reason" (Can 868, 2).

Eucharist

Paul's metaphor of the Church as the Body of Christ is rooted in the unifying effects of baptism and in his experience of what he calls the "Lord's Supper" (1 Cor 11:20). From the time of the *Didache* (c. 100) and Ignatius of Antioch (110), the Lord's Supper has been known as the Eucharist, from the prayer of thanksgiving (Gk. *eucharistia*) offered by the presider.[13] Other names include the Mass or liturgy (Catholics), the Divine Liturgy, or sometimes the Synaxis (which means union—Orthodox Christians), the Lord's Supper or simply the Supper (Protestants) or Holy Communion (Anglicans).

The tradition of the meal in Jesus' ministry is rich in symbolism. An Old Testament archetype is the image of the great eschatological banquet provided by the Lord in the age of salvation (Isa 25:6-8), an image found also at Qumran. Jesus adopted this metaphor as a sign of the kingdom (Matt 8:11; 22:1-14; Luke 14:15-24; 22:16,30) and his tradition of table-fellowship offered a share in the kingdom to all. No one was excluded. Jesus shared meals with his disciples, with the multitude (Mark 6:34-44 and plls.), with leading members of the Jewish community (Luke 7:36-50), and especially with the ritually impure and the marginalized, the "tax collectors and sinners" for which he was so frequently criticized (Mark 2:16; Matt 11:18-19). In the Jewish tradition of his day, the distinctions between the clean and the unclean as well as between sinners and the righteous determined one's table companions,[14] for a meal was always a sign of fellowship and communion. Jesus' inclusive practice was a sign that all were welcome in God's reign, reversing the usual pattern of conversion and then repentance by offering them the communion that brought about repentance.[15]

The Last Supper

At his final meal with his disciples the night before he died, Jesus gave new meaning to his table-fellowship tradition. His words over the bread and the cup are heavily colored by the liturgical tradition of the early Christian communities, identifying the bread and wine of the table with his body to be broken and blood poured out. However, one saying in the midst of the narrative did not become a part of the later liturgical tradition

---

[13] Justin Martyr, *First Apology*, nos. 66–67.
[14] Ben F. Meyer, *The Aims of Jesus* (London: SCM Press, 1979) 159.
[15] Ibid., 161.

and therefore is most probably authentic.[16] Jesus says, "Amen, I say to you, I shall not drink again the fruit of the vine until the day when I drink it new in the kingdom of God" (Mark 14:25; cf. Luke 22:16-18). In other words, conscious of his coming death, Jesus was promising his disciples a renewed fellowship with them beyond it. After his death, the disciples continued to gather for meals in his memory, and came to recognize him present among them in a new way; they recognized him in the breaking of the bread (Luke 24:35; cf. Acts 2:42; 10:41; John 21:9-13).

Though there are different theologies of the Lord's Supper in the New Testament, just as there are for baptism, few scholars today hold Lietzmann's thesis that originally there were two different meals, one in Paul's communities focused on the death of Jesus, and another joyful eschatological meal celebrated in the original Jerusalem community.[17] Even less successful has been Bruce Chilton's attempt to argue for six stages of eucharistic development.[18]

The four accounts of the institution in Paul and the Synoptic gospels really represent two traditions, one reflected in Mark 14:22-25 and Matthew 26:26-29, the other in 1 Cor 11:23-26 and Luke 22:15-20. While each has unique features, they are remarkably similar in regard to language and meaning. Common elements include the notions of memorial, sacrifice, covenant, communion in the body and blood of Christ, and eschatological hope. The Lord's Supper or Eucharist is a memorial of Christ's sacrificial death, symbolized by his body broken and blood poured out (Matthew 26:28 adds "for the forgiveness of sins"); the institution narrative refers to a covenant established in his blood ("new covenant" in 1 Cor 11:25 and Luke 22:21); the bread and wine are to be consumed as his body and blood; and the meal looks forward to an eschatological fulfillment, new fellowship in the kingdom (when Christ comes again in 1 Cor 11:26).

While John's Gospel has no narrative of the institution, the entire chapter 6 is broadly eucharistic, beginning with the story of the multiplication

[16] See Walter Kasper, *Jesus the Christ* (New York: Paulist Press, 1976) 117; Edward Schillebeeckx, *Jesus: An Experiment in Christology* (New York: Seabury, 1979) 308.

[17] Hans Lietzmann, *Messe und Herrenmahl*, 3rd edition (Berlin: 1955) 249–55; ET *Mass and Lord's Supper*, trans. Dorothea H. G. Reeve (Leiden: E. J. Brill, 1953).

[18] Jesus' original fellowship meal redefining Jewish purity, later offered as a surrogate for Temple sacrifice; a domestic bread breaking in the Petrine circle celebrating Jesus as the new Moses; a once-a-year Seder associated with James; a Hellenistic meal or symposium associated with Jesus' death as a sacrifice for sins, found in Paul and the Synoptics; and the Eucharist as miraculous food, in Paul and John; see Bruce Chilton, *A Feast of Meanings: Eucharistic Theologies from Jesus through Johannine Circles* (New York: E. J. Brill, 1994).

of the loaves (6:1-15) and finishing with the great discourse on the bread of life (6:22-71). Verses 51-58 are explicitly eucharistic:

> I am the living bread that came down from heaven; whoever eats this bread will live forever; and the bread that I will give is my flesh for the life of the world. . . . Amen, amen I say to you, unless you eat the flesh of the Son of Man and drink his blood, you do not have life within you. Whoever eats my flesh and drinks my blood has eternal life, and I will raise him on the last day. For my flesh is true food, and my blood is true drink. Whoever eats my flesh and drinks my blood remains in me and I in him.
>
> (John 6:51; 53-56)

The elements of memorial, sacrifice, communion, and eschatological hope are present here also, and the idea of a new covenant is implied in the comparison of the bread of life to the manna of the desert: "Your ancestors ate the manna in the desert, but they died; this is the bread that comes down from heaven so that one may eat it and not die" (John 6:49-50).

Christ's Eucharistic Presence

When Catholics talk about the eucharistic presence of Jesus, they tend not infrequently to begin with the eleventh century language of "transubstantiation," a second order philosophical language forged in the heat of controversy with Berengar (d. 1088), head of the school of St. Martin at Tours. Berengar seems to have adopted an exaggerated symbolism in regard to the eucharistic gifts, denying any change in the bread and wine. But starting here to talk about eucharistic presence is to short-circuit a long process of theological development. The New Testament does not use the language of miraculous change; it talks about communion and recognition through ritual. We need to review this development.

From the earliest days of the Church, Christians have recognized that they truly encounter the risen Jesus in the Eucharist; they believe that he is truly present in the bread broken and the wine poured out. But there have long been differences between and among Christians as to how this presence should be explained. To gain some insight into Christ's eucharistic presence, we begin as did the early Christians, not with the later doctrine of the Church, but with their experience of recognizing Christ in the meal. Thus, a theological approach to Eucharist should not start "from above," with the doctrine of the real presence, but "from below," with the liturgical gathering of the community where the risen Jesus is recognized in breaking the bread and sharing the cup.

In addition to the institution narratives in the Synoptic gospels, four sets of New Testament texts, two from Paul's first letter to the Corinthians, Luke's story of the two disciples on the road to Emmaus, and John's Bread of Life discourse reflect the eucharistic experience of the early Christian communities.

1 Cor 10:16-17; 11:17-34

Paul argues that by sharing the cup that has been blessed and the bread that has been broken we have a participation or communion (*koinōnia*) in the body and blood of Christ and thus are united with each other as the Body of Christ. The emphasis is on communion through the meal. The Lord's Supper brings about communion with Christ and with one another, so that the community itself becomes the Body of Christ.

A chapter later, instructing the Corinthian community on their practice of the Lord's Supper, Paul brings out the Supper's memorial (*anamnesis*), sacrificial dimension. He says, "as often as you eat this bread and drink the cup, you proclaim the death of the Lord until he comes" (1 Cor 11:26). In proclaiming Christ's death, the community looks forward to the fullness of salvation. Those who fail to recognize the Body of Christ—present both in the gifts and in the community gathered—bring a judgment on themselves; they "will have to answer for the body and blood of the Lord" (1 Cor 11:27).

Luke 24:13-35

In Luke's Emmaus story, the two disciples encounter but do not recognize Jesus on the road; it is only after he opens the Scriptures for them (Luke 24:27) and they invite him to join them at table, where, using the familiar institution narrative, he "took the bread, said the blessing, broke it, and gave it to them," at that "their eyes were opened and they recognized him" (Luke 24:30-31). Note that the language here is of recognition through the meal.

John 6:51-58

In the eucharistic conclusion of the Bread of Life discourse, the language of the Johannine tradition is quite realistic: "Unless you eat the flesh of the Son of Man and drink his blood, you do not have life within you" (John 6:53). Here we have traditional "real presence" language; the bread and wine of the Eucharist are the flesh and blood of Jesus. The question of the Jews, "How can this man give us [his] flesh to eat?" underlines the point (John 6:52). But the real point here is not miraculous change but the believers' share in Christ's salvation through their participation in the eucharistic meal.

What is important to notice is that in each case, these texts focus not on the language of change, so strong in the later Catholic tradition, but on the ritual, liturgical action of the community. In their sharing in the meal carried on in memory of Jesus, they proclaim his death and resurrection and recognize him in the breaking of the bread (*anamnesis*). The risen Jesus is present in a new way and intimate manner. They have communion with him and one another in his body and blood (*koinōnia*).

Theological Development

From the second century theologians like Ignatius of Antioch, Irenaeus, and Justin used realistic language in referring to the body and blood of Christ.[19] Ignatius of Antioch wrote that the Docetists "hold aloof [from worship], because they do not confess that the eucharist is the flesh of our Savior Jesus Christ" (Smyr. 6.7). Irenaeus attempted to explain the transformation of the bread and wine by referring to the union of earthly and heavenly realities in the sacrament, not unlike the incarnation.[20] Justin makes the comparison to the incarnation explicit: "Just as Jesus Christ our Savior was made flesh through the word of God and took on flesh and blood for our salvation, so too through the word of prayer that comes from him the food over which the thanksgiving has been spoken becomes the flesh and blood of the incarnate Jesus, in order to nourish and transform our flesh and blood."[21] In the post-Nicene Church, the mystery of the transformation of the bread and wine was often compared to Christ's transformation in the Spirit through his resurrection; David Power notes that "The more robust language of eating and drinking the flesh and blood of Christ has to be placed alongside this appeal to the power of the Spirit or of God's word."[22]

The term "transubstantiation" was used against Berengar's overly symbolic approach to affirm that while the appearances of the bread and wine (the "species") remain the same, the substance of both really changed. The confession of faith imposed on Berengar by the Council of Rome (1079)

---

[19] For the patristic texts, see *The Eucharist*, Daniel J. Sheerin (Wilmington, DE: Michael Glazier, 1986).

[20] David N. Power, *The Eucharistic Mystery: Revitalizing the Tradition* (New York: Crossroad, 1992) 119; in the following section I am indebted to Power's work.

[21] Apologia I, 66.2; cited by Power, *Eucharistic Mystery*, 119.

[22] Power, *Eucharistic Mystery*, 160.

strikes us today as overly literal: in David Power's words it "is crudely physicist, for who today would care to state that communicants chew on the body of Christ?"[23] Later, Martin Luther was to use similar literal or "physicalist" language.

The language of transubstantiation was adopted to safeguard the Church's faith in the reality of Christ's presence in the Eucharist. Unfortunately, it led to an increasing focus on "the elements," the bread and wine, and on the notion of substantial change, rather than on the sacrament itself.[24] This emphasis is very much present in Aquinas, though as Power notes, all questions on the sacrament are placed within the context of the eucharistic action.[25] In other words, Aquinas does not separate presence from rite.

The Reformers

While Luther and Calvin had difficulty with the Catholic notions of Eucharist as sacrifice and the mediating role of the priest, they did not intend to deny the tradition of the real presence. Their problem was with the term transubstantiation, thus with theological language. Luther taught that Christ was present "in, with, and under" the elements of bread and wine, which has often been interpreted as "consubstantiation." But more accurately, he saw sacraments in relationship to the Lordship of Jesus, giving him power over all things, and thus allowing him to be present wherever the sacraments are celebrated ("ubiquity"). Ola Tjørhom reports that "Luther excommunicated two priests . . . for defending and practicing what the vast majority of today's Lutheran pastors do every time they celebrate the Eucharist: putting consecrated bread back in the box together with unconsecrated bread as if nothing had happened to it. To Luther, such an attitude and practice put the Real Presence in jeopardy."[26]

John Calvin's concern was to avoid overly physical language. For him, Christ is in heaven; we are made spiritually present to him in the Supper by way of the Spirit. Arguing from Augustine, Calvin writes that Christ is present through "that marvelous communion of his body and blood—provided we understand that it takes place by the power of the Holy Spirit,

---

[23] Ibid., 244; cf. DS 690.

[24] See Edward J. Kilmartin, *The Eucharist in the West: History and Theology*, ed. Robert J. Daly (Collegeville, MN: The Liturgical Press, 1998) 145.

[25] Power, *Eucharistic Mystery*, 217.

[26] Ola Tjørhom, *Visible Church—Visible Unity: Ecumenical Ecclesiology and 'The Great Tradition of the Church'* (Collegeville, MN: The Liturgical Press, 2004) 13.

not by that feigned inclusion of the body itself under the element."[27] But it is not just a spiritual communion. "I am not satisfied with those persons who, recognizing that we have some communion with Christ, when they would show what it is, make us partakers of the Spirit only, omitting mention of flesh and blood. As though all these things were said in vain: that his flesh is truly food, that his blood is truly drink [John 6:55]."[28]

Some ambiguities remain in Calvin's eucharistic theology, as Kilian McDonnell points out. Calvin wants to move from the philosophical notion of substance, even though he uses that term frequently, to that of person. His concept of substance is soteriological; there is a real encounter with Christ the Mediator and Redeemer in the Lord's Supper.[29] Other Reformers were more radical. For Zwingli, the Eucharist was only a sign, an aid to memory to remember Jesus in his passion; it was a recollection or remembering of a past event: "Therefore our eucharist is a visible assembling of the church, in which together we eat and drink bread and wine as (*veluti*) symbols, that we may be reminded of those things which Christ has done for us."[30]

The Council of Trent

The Council of Trent (1545-63) reaffirmed the doctrine of transubstantiation against what it understood to be the Reformers' errors in regard to Christ's eucharistic presence:

> But since Christ our Redeemer declared that which he offered under the form of bread to be truly his own body, it has therefore always been a firm belief in the Church of God, and this Holy Council now declares it anew, that by the consecration of the bread and wine a change is brought about of the whole substance of the bread into the substance of the body of Christ our Lord, and of the whole substance of the wine into the substance of his blood. This change the holy Catholic Church properly and appropriately calls transubstantiation (DS 1642)

Trent's language, like all our theological and doctrinal language is important. But it is always a "second order" language. It remains limited, re-

---

[27] Calvin, *Institutes*, 4,17,26; See John Calvin, *Institutes of the Christian Religion*, Library of Christian Classics, Vol. XXI, ed. John T. McNeill, trans. Ford Lewis Battles (Philadelphia: Westminster Press, 1960) 1394.

[28] Ibid., 4,17,7; 1366–67.

[29] See Kilian McDonnell, *John Calvin, the Church, and the Eucharist* (Princeton, NJ: Princeton University Press, 1967) 246–48.

[30] Cited by W. P. Stevens, *The Theology of Huldrych Zwingli* (Oxford: Clarendon Press, 1986) 239–40; Z IV 938/16–23.

moved by one or more levels of abstraction from the mystery of God's self-disclosure that it seeks to describe. As Yves Congar says, a doctrine simply expresses the meaning of that which is done within the Church.[31]

A Shared Eucharistic Faith?

More important than a particular theological formulation is the affirmation arising from the experience of Christians since the beginning of the Church; Christ is truly encountered in the Eucharist. Through the action of the Holy Spirit in the liturgy he is present in the bread and wine. Through our sharing in the gifts we enter into a profound communion with the Lord and with one another. We receive his Body and Blood.

But even this apparently very literal language recognizes that the presence of the risen Jesus is not physical; it is sacramental. That is to say, the risen Jesus is present in the sacramental action and remains with us, not in his discrete body and blood understood in a physical sense, but personally, in his glorified humanity. Catholics have long been taught that to receive "under one species" is to receive not just the Body or just the Blood of Christ, but both: it is to encounter and receive the risen Jesus. In other words, it is to receive the whole Christ. In the more traditional language of Trent, under the form of the bread or the wine exists "the true body and the true blood of our Lord, together with his soul and divinity" (DS 1640).

By communion in the Body and Blood of Christ, Christians become themselves Christ's Body for the world (1 Cor 10:16). Since the earliest days they have recognized his presence in the breaking of the bread. While Church fathers have used realistic language in referring to the Body and Blood of Christ since the second century, the emphasis on transubstantiation in the Middle Ages was to result in a one-sided focus on the change in the elements.

Ecumenical dialogues in the last forty years have led to a new appreciation of a shared eucharistic faith, in spite of the different theological languages used by our different traditions. If Luther and Calvin rejected the philosophical implications of the language of transubstantiation, they did not intend to deny that Christ was truly present and that his Body and Blood were received in the meal. Particularly important has been the recovery of the biblical notion of *anamnesis* or memorial (cf. 1 Cor 11:24), recalling the saving events of Christ's life, death, and resurrection in the eucharistic prayer. When the Church does this, Christ's once for all sacrifice

---

[31] Yves M.-J. Congar, *Tradition and Traditions: An Historical and a Theological Essay*, trans. Michael Naseby and Thomas Rainborough (New York: Macmillan, 1966) 354.

on the cross is made present through narrative and ritual and Christ himself becomes present in the eucharistic gifts. Speaking of the Eucharist as the memorial of the crucified and risen Christ, the WCC BEM text says "Christ himself with all that he has accomplished for us . . . is present in this anamnesis, granting us communion with himself."[32]

It remains important today to help ordinary Catholics and Protestants understand how much they have in common, and to work towards the restoration of full communion between their separated churches.

Spiritual Gifts and Ministries

The Spirit given in baptism empowers the Christian community with a rich diversity of gifts and ministries to build up the Church as the one Body of Christ and fulfill its mission. Thus baptism, not ordination, is the basic sacrament of ministry.

Paul's term *charisma*, usually translated as "spiritual gift," is derived from the verb *charizesthai*, "to grant freely as a favor." The Greek *charisma* means literally "favored" or "gifted." Paul develops a rich theology of the Church's pneumatological or charismatic structure in 1 Corinthians 12.

> There are different kinds of spiritual gifts (*charismata*) but the same Spirit; there are different forms of service (*diakoniai*) but the same Lord; there are different workings (*energēmata*) but the same God who produces all of them in everyone. To each individual the manifestation of the Spirit is given for some benefit (1 Cor 12:4-7).

He sees the Christian community as richly endowed with a variety of service gifts and more permanent ministries. Each is a manifestation of the inner life of the Spirit; each is given for some benefit, for the building up of the Church (1 Cor 14:5, 12). He then gives several lists of the charisms: the first includes wisdom, knowledge, faith, healing, mighty deeds, prophecy, discernment of spirits, tongues, and the interpretation of tongues (1 Cor 12:8-11). Then after stressing how all the different members of the human body have to work together, he concludes:

> Now you are Christ's body, and individually parts of it. Some people God has designated in the church to be, first, apostles; second, prophets; third teachers; then, mighty deeds; then gifts of healing, assistance, administration, and varieties of tongues. Are all apostles? Are all prophets? Are all teachers? Do all work mighty deeds? Do all have gifts of healing? Do all

---

[32] *Baptism, Eucharist and Ministry*, E. no. 7.

speak in tongues? Do all interpret? Strive eagerly for the greatest spiritual gifts (1 Cor 12:28-31).

He also names both marriage and celibacy for the sake of the kingdom as among the charisms (1 Cor 7:7).

The lists of charisms given in 1 Corinthians contain some more dramatic manifestations of the Spirit, for example, healing, mighty deeds, and tongues. Mighty deeds (*energēmata dunameōn*) is the expression used for the miracles of Jesus in the Synoptic gospels. Tongues, familiar to Pentecostal and charismatic communities, is a form of praise that overflows the boundaries of language. A similar list of charisms in Romans is much more ordinary and commonplace.

> For as in one body we have many parts, and all the parts do not have the same function, so we, though many, are one body in Christ and individually parts of one another. Since we have gifts (*charismata*) that differ according to the grace (*charis*) given to us, let us exercise them: if prophecy, in proportion to the faith; if ministry, in ministering; if one is a teacher, in teaching; if one exhorts, in exhortation; if one contributes, in generosity; if one is over others (*proistamenos*), with diligence; if one does acts of mercy, with cheerfulness (Rom 12:4-8).

Notice how both this passage and the one in 1 Corinthians 12:27-30 join Paul's vision of the Church as the body of Christ with his discussion of the Church's charismatic structure, listing both activities (giving assistance, discernment, exhorting, contributing or alms-giving) and emerging offices (prophet, teacher, administrator, presider or leader [*proistemenos*]). Prophecy means speaking a word of exhortation or comfort in the name of the Lord; it is sometimes identified with preaching. Prophets and teachers are local church leaders who preach and instruct the community; they may also have presided at the Eucharist (cf. Acts 13:2; Didache 10:7). The gift of faith, in one sense common to all believers, suggests a gift that builds up the faith of others. Mother Teresa is an example of this kind of faith. Administration continues to remain an important role in the Church. Other lists of charisms can be found in Ephesians 4:7, 10-12 and 1 Peter 4:10.

Why the more dramatic gifts in 1 Corinthians? The Church at Corinth was characterized by a certain "enthusiasm" for more dramatic manifestations of the Spirit. Some members of the community were contributing to the divisions that caused Paul's letter by priding themselves on their gifts, as Paul's careful instruction on tongues in chapter 14 indicates. The only mention of tongues in all of Paul's letters is in 1 Corinthians. He makes it clear that while he values this gift, he would rather have the members of the community strive for more important gifts such as prophecy that build up the church. Finally, he emphasizes that "everything must be done properly and in order" (1 Cor 15:40), since God is a God not of disorder but of peace.

Paul's vision of the Church is of community richly endowed and structured by the Spirit with a variety of gifts and ministries. Each member had something to contribute for the building up of the Church. We saw earlier how the Second Vatican Council recovered this theology of the charisms, juxtaposing them to the "hierarchical" gifts of the ordained (LG 4, cf. 12). But it is interesting to note that the emergence of the Church's office of leadership in the Church of the sub-apostolic age corresponded with the tendency to restrict the language of charism to certain leading ministries. In 1 Peter 4:10, a letter probably written in the early 80s, the reference seems to be to a twofold ministry of preaching the word and the works of charity. In 1 and 2 Timothy, written even later, charism is used only of the gift received by the laying on of hands (1 Tim 4:14; 2 Tim 1:6). Timothy and Titus are apostolic delegates, supervising churches. In these later letters, the rich diversity of gifts in Paul's churches is not evident.

Conclusion

As we have seen, the term *koinōnia* or communion is a rich theological concept that lies at the heart of the nature of the Church. It applies first to our share in the divine life, and thus, through baptism and Eucharist, to the communion we share with one another. It also refers to the communion between churches, expressed through visible signs, as we will see later, for the Church itself is a communion of churches.

It has never been easy for the Church to be what it must be; a community of disciples reconciled by God's work in Christ (Gal 3:28), made one Body in Christ through baptism and Eucharist, living in his Spirit. Paul makes the breaking down of barriers through these sacraments, bringing about the unity of Jews and Gentiles, slave and free, even male and female, a leitmotif of his letters. Communion is primarily a spiritual reality that is ours through our sharing in the Spirit. But because communion is expressed through visible and institutional signs, it admits of degrees. When ecclesial communion was lost between churches in the eleventh and sixteenth centuries, the sense of spiritual communion was lost as well. Churches today are divided by differences in doctrine, authority, and structure.

The life of the Spirit is manifested in the community through a rich diversity of gifts and ministries; thus for Paul, the Church's fundamental structure is pneumatological or charismatic. As a more developed structure of ministry began to emerge in the later New Testament, this sense for the diversity of the charisms seems to have been lost.

Today the Church has gained a new appreciation for the gifts of the Spirit. Office and authority in the Church presupposes charism (cf. 1 Cor 12:28). One ordained to the presbyteral office should have gifts for pastoral ministry, for example, a charism for preaching, presiding, and leading a community of faith. A bishop should have the charism of being a good shepherd for the local church. Unfortunately, the process of discerning such charisms is imperfect at best, and sometimes fails. A charism is recognized, not created, by the laying on of hands, and that includes a charism for celibacy.

[handwritten margin note: ordination concerns]

The metaphor of the Church as the Body of Christ is unique to Paul and he uses it to express the unity of the community. Though he once uses the expression "Body of Christ" without the article (1 Cor 12:27), he usually says "one body" or "one body in Christ."[33] To be "in Christ" for Paul is not just a christological reality; it is also profoundly ecclesial. It cannot be understood individualistically. Being in Christ means being a part of the Body of Christ, the Church (cf. Gal 1:22; 3:28; Rom 16:7; 1 Thes 2:14).[34]

Men and women enter and become the Body of Christ through those rituals or acts of the Church that the Church came to call sacraments. They are baptized into one body (1 Cor 12:13), blessed with a diversity of gifts and ministries (1 Cor 12:27-30), becoming one body through their sharing in the Eucharist. Though Christians have long been divided by different understandings of the sacraments, the ecumenical dialogues of the last forty years have brought the churches closer together and moved them nearer to the goal of entering into full communion with one another.

If the metaphor of the Church as the Body of Christ is ancient, it is also surprisingly contemporary. Body is the medium for the expression of spirit. Anyone sensitive to "body language" knows this instinctively, for our eyes, facial expression, tone of voice, bodily posture disclose our inner spirit. As the saying goes, "the eyes are the windows of the soul," for body makes spirit visible.

The metaphor is particularly appropriate for the Church today in a secular world. Jesus in his risen existence is no longer visible as he was when he walked the dusty roads of Galilee or preached in the Temple of Jerusalem.

---

[33] Hans Küng, *The Church*, trans. Ray and Roseleen Ockenden (New York: Sheed and Ward, 1967) 228–29.

[34] Küng, *The Church*, 229.

The risen Jesus is spirit (Paul's "spiritual body," 1 Cor 15:44). He is visible only through his Body, the Church, which hands on the Jesus tradition in its Scriptures and its teaching, proclaims and celebrates the mystery of Christ's presence in word, worship, and communion, and ministers to others in his name. Without the Christian community, the Church in its preaching, teaching, fellowship, ministry, and worship, no one could encounter the risen Jesus or come to know him. Through the Church as the Body of Christ the risen Christ is present to the world.

CHAPTER 5

The Church's Apostolic Ministry

I n the last chapter we saw how the Spirit empowers the Church for its mission with a diversity of gifts (*charismata*) and ministries (*diako-niai*) (1 Cor 12:4-7). Contemporary theology rightly sees baptism as the source of all ministries in the Church, and thus, the Church's fundamental structure as pneumatological or charismatic. At the same time, the Second Vatican Council reaffirmed the hierarchical nature of the Church. The Church's apostolic office, exercised by the bishops, is of dominical institution, rooted in Jesus' choice of "the Twelve" (LG 18). Therefore the Church's ministry also has a christological foundation.

Catholic theology from the sixteenth century up to Vatican II has emphasized the hierarchical structure of the Church and its ministry. Protestant theology has tended to stress the charismatic. While these two emphases are not necessarily in contradiction, liberal Protestant theologians[1] as well as contemporary Roman Catholic theologians such as Hans Küng, Leonardo Boff, and Sandra Schneiders have argued for a fundamentally charismatic understanding of ministry and authority. The Church is understood as an egalitarian community that should rid itself of structures derived from cultural or political models. Ordained ministry is not necessarily rejected, but ordained ministers are understood as doing by profession what others can and should be able to do. Preaching and sacramental celebration should not be reserved to a small, clericalized group.[2]

The response of the World Evangelical Fellowship (now Alliance) to the WCC *Baptism, Eucharist and Ministry* text objected particularly to

---

[1] See Avery Dulles, *A Church To Believe In: Discipleship and the Dynamics of Freedom* (New York: Crossroad, 1982) 23.

[2] See Thomas P. Rausch, *Authority and Leadership in the Church: Past Directions and Future Possibilities* (Wilmington, DE: Michael Glazier, 1989) 33–36.

what it called *BEM*'s "sacramentalism."[3] Specifically, it found problematic *BEM*'s statement that ordained ministry is "constitutive for the life and witness of the church," with its implication that the ordained minister represents Christ to the community in a way "*essentially* different from the way in which any believer is called and gifted to represent Christ" or that the ministerial priesthood is distinct from that of all the faithful or that the authority of Jesus is conferred by ordination on the minister.[4] George Vandervelde sees these divergent Roman Catholic and Evangelical views of the nature of ministry as constituting "a crystallization point of divergent ecclesiologies."[5] The Free Church tradition is even more radical in respect to the question of Church office. While office "may indeed be desirable for church life, either in apostolic succession or not, it is *not necessary for ecclesiality*. Ordained office belongs not to the *esse*, but rather to the *bene esse* of the church."[6]

While it is easy to contrast charismatic and hierarchical approaches to ministry and authority in the Church, the separation between the pneumatological and the christological is more difficult to sustain. The real issue is this: does the community simply generate its own ministry or is the community "ordered" (hierarchical) from the beginning, founded upon the apostles, which emphasizes the divine initiative? In this chapter we will consider the role of the apostles, the development of leadership in the early communities, the emergence of the threefold ministry, and the later clericalization of the Church's pastoral office.

Founded on the Apostles

In the first decades of the life of the Church, the various communities were established and developed under the guidance of a group of missionaries and witnesses to the resurrection of Jesus, known from the earliest days as apostles. Paul places them first in the Church (1 Cor 12:28) which the New Testament sees as founded upon the apostles (Apoc 21:14). But it is more difficult to define the concept of the apostle precisely because the New Testament does not provide a unified understanding of the

---

[3] See Paul Schrotenboer, (ed), "An Evangelical Response of *Baptism, Eucharist and Ministry*," *Evangelical Review of Theology* 13 (1989) 312; see WCC, *Baptism, Eucharist and Ministry* (Geneva: WCC, 1982).

[4] Ibid., 306.

[5] George Vandervelde, "Ecclesiology in the Breach: Evangelical Soundings," *Evangelical Review of Theology* 23/1 (1999) 43.

[6] Miroslav Volf, *After Our Likeness: The Church as the Image of the Trinity* (Grand Rapids, MI: William B. Eerdmans, 1998) 152.

apostle's role.[7] Besides the portrait of the Twelve in the Gospels, both Paul and Luke-Acts present different conceptions of the apostle.

Paul's understanding of the apostle is developed largely on the basis of his own experience: an apostle is one who has seen the risen Lord and been sent to preach the gospel. But another, earlier and broader concept of the apostle can be discerned in his writings; apostles are the early Christian missionaries (Rom 16:7; 1 Thess 2:7; 1 Cor 9:5; 15:7). This view represents the original concept of an apostle, common among the early Christian communities. The exclusive identification of the Twelve as apostles is a later Lukan reflection. Luke recognizes the broader extension of the title in the early Church, as Paul and Barnabas are called apostles in Acts 14:1-4; yet it is the Twelve, chosen by Jesus from within the wider circle of his disciples, which constitutes for him the paradigm of the apostle. Matthew also tends to identify the apostles with the Twelve.

The existence of the Twelve is attested to by independent sources such as Mark, John, and probably the special Lukan material and Q, as well as by one of the earliest forms of the Easter kerygma (1 Cor 15:5).[8] The later Church no longer remembers all their names consistently, and they were not the only apostles in the primitive Church. But "the majority of scholars still find persuasive the evidence that the Twelve disciples of Jesus were considered apostles of the Church from the beginning."[9] In this traditional view the apostles, among whom the Twelve held pride of place, exercised roles of leadership in the primitive Church. Edward Schillebeeckx acknowledges that the local church leaders were "ultimately under the oversight of the apostles" and would refer to them when difficulties arose which they were unable to resolve."[10]

What was the source of the apostles' authority? An apostle etymologically is one who has been "sent" (*apostellein*, "to send"). Applying the word to an individual is virtually a unique New Testament usage, though recent research has returned to the view that the Christian understanding of apostle

---

[7] For a survey of opinions on the meaning of "apostle" and bibliography see Rudolph Schnackenburg, "Apostolicity: the Present Position of Studies," *One in Christ* 6 (1970) 243–73; Francis H. Agnew, "The Origin of the NT Apostle-Concept: A Review of Research," *Journal of Biblical Literature* 105 (1986) 75–96; also Francis A. Sullivan, *From Apostles to Bishops: The Development of the Episcopacy in the Early Church* (New York; Paulist Press, 2001) 17–38.

[8] See John P. Meier, *A Marginal Jew*: Vol. III; *Companions and Competitors* (New York: Doubleday, 2001) 141.

[9] Raymond E. Brown, *Priest and Bishop: Biblical Reflections* (New York: Paulist, 1970) 49.

[10] Edward Schillebeeckx, *Ministry: Leadership in the Community of Jesus Christ* (New York: Crossroad, 1981) 9.

(as well as the rabbinic concept of the *saliah*) derives not from Christian experience but has its roots in the Jewish "sending convention" observable in the Old Testament.[11] The Twelve were chosen by Jesus during his historical ministry. Paul attributes his authority as an apostle to his experience of the risen Lord (Gal 1:1). The "apostles of the churches" (2 Cor 8:23; cf. Phil 2:25) were sent by early communities, sometimes for a specific task. Wayne Meeks describes their authority as derivative and limited.[12] But what is common to all the notions of apostle in the New Testament is that of the sending: "All from the community apostles to the apostles of Jesus Christ are commissioned agents sent to act in the name of others/another."[13]

The Role of the Twelve

What kind of a role did the Twelve actually exercise? The New Testament does not provide a great deal of information. There is no evidence that they served as leaders of local churches or carried out a worldwide missionary effort. Francis Sullivan contends that, like Peter, they understood themselves as "apostles to the circumcised" and judging from the evidence that at the time of Paul's last visit to Jerusalem they no longer resided there, "it seems likely that they had left to preach the Gospel to predominantly Jewish communities."[14]

Not all commentators today are willing to grant a unique leadership role to the apostles. Some feminist scholars use an egalitarian model to interpret the early Christian communities.[15] From this perspective, they tend to describe the role of the Twelve as eschatological, symbolizing the twelve tribes of the renewed Israel, rather than actual historical leadership. Elisabeth Schüssler Fiorenza takes this position, though she states that Luke seems to have historicized the apostles' function in regard to the mission to Israel.[16]

---

[11] See Agnew, "The Origin of the NT Apostle-Concept," 91.

[12] Wayne A. Meeks, *The First Urban Christians: The Social World of the Apostle Paul* (New Haven: Yale University Press, 1983) 133.

[13] Ibid., 94.

[14] Sullivan, *From Apostles to Bishops*, 26.

[15] See Sandra M. Schneiders, "Evangelical Equality," *Spirituality Today* 38 (1986) 301; Elisabeth Schüssler Fiorenza, *In Memory of Her: A Feminist Theological Reconstruction of Christian Origins* (New York: Crossroad, 1983) 140.

[16] Elisabeth Schüssler Fiorenza, "The Twelve," in *Women Priests: A Catholic Commentary on the Vatican Declaration*, ed. Leonard Swidler and Arlene Swidler (New York: Paulist, 1977) 117–20; see also Schuyler Brown, "Apostleship in the New Testament as an Historical and Theological Problem," *New Testament Studies* 30 (1984) 474–80.

But important as the eschatological significance of the Twelve is for the Church, other commentators emphasize as well the important role they played as leaders in the early Christian community. Both Paul and Luke show the Jerusalem apostles involved in a decision that was decisive, not just for the mission to Israel, but for the future of the entire Church, the decision concerning Gentile converts and the Mosaic Law. Luke's account of the apostolic "council" of Jerusalem in Acts 15 represents an idealized picture, but his emphasis on the role played by Peter is confirmed indirectly by Paul's own account of going up to Jerusalem to explain "privately to those of repute" how he presented the Gospel to the Gentiles (Gal 2:2). His somewhat begrudging admission that he received the handclasp of fellowship from "James and Kephas and John, who were reputed to be pillars" (Gal 2:9) testifies to the importance of the Jerusalem leadership, two of whom, John and Kephas (Peter) were members of the Twelve.

Bengt Holmberg analyzes authority in the primitive Church from an historical and sociological point of view. He acknowledges the "eschatological uniqueness" of the Jerusalem apostles, especially the Twelve. Precisely because they linked the community with the historical Jesus, he stresses that Paul felt he had to consult them and maintain fellowship with them.[17] He states that Gal 2:1-10 leads to the conclusion that Paul and the Gentile mission of Antioch "is in fact dependent on what decision is taken by the Jerusalem authorities."[18] The appointment of the Seven in Acts 6:2-4 is another example. Though the role of the Twelve is unique, as the number of Hellenist Jewish Christians in the community increased, the Twelve shared their ministry with seven men with Greek names, appointing them to office to serve the Hellenists. While the story is often associated with the institution of the diaconate because Luke says they were appointed to serve at table, in subsequent chapters of Acts we see them exercising the same ministry of the Word that the apostles were said to have reserved for themselves (Acts 6:4). The story witnesses to an early sharing of the original apostolic leadership.[19]

Raymond Brown summarizes the evidence as follows: "there is the image of a collective policy-making authority for the Twelve in the NT; and in the case of Peter . . . the memory of pastoral responsibility. Otherwise the NT is remarkably vague about the kind of supervision

[17] Bengt Holmberg, *Paul and Power: The Structure of Authority in the Primitive Church as Reflected in the Pauline Epistles* (Philadelphia: Fortress, 1980) 27.

[18] Ibid., 28.

[19] Sullivan, *From Apostles to Bishops*, 42; also Joseph A. Fitzmyer, *The Acts of the Apostles*, The Anchor Bible, Vol. 31 (New York: Doubleday, 1997) 345.

exercised by members of the Twelve."[20] Thus there is some evidence that at least some of the Twelve were remembered as exercising an authoritative role in the earliest days of the Christian community. But this is not to suggest that they were involved in all important decisions or that the subsequent growth of the Church took place entirely under their direction.

Leadership in the Early Communities

The New Testament shows a variety of names for those exercising leadership roles in the local communities. The terminology is somewhat fluid, particularly in the earlier documents, though by the end of the New Testament period an emerging pattern can be seen as the various communities began a process of institutionalizing their ecclesial lives.

In the first place are the apostles, followed by prophets and teachers (1 Cor 12:28). Paul also mentions rulers or leaders (*proistamenoi*: 1 Thess 5:12; Rom 12:8), overseers and ministers/deacons (*episkopoi kai diakonoi*: Phil 1:1), and ministers (*diakonos*: Rom 16:1). He also refers to the hosts or heads of house churches (1 Cor 16:19; Rom 16:5; Philemon 2; Col 4:15). Ephesians refers to apostles, prophets, evangelists, pastors and teachers (Eph 4:11). Leaders (*hēgoumenoi*) are mentioned in Hebrews 13:7, 17, 24 and Luke 22:26. Prophets and teachers are still visible in later books (Acts 13:1-3; *Didache* 15:1). Matthew speaks of prophets and scribes (or wise men, Matt 13:52; 23:34). Presbyters (literally "elders") are frequently mentioned in later books (James 5:14; Acts 11:30; 14:23; 20:17; 2 John 1; 3 John 1) or presbyter-bishops (1 and 2 Timothy; Titus; 1 Peter 5:1-4) and deacons (1 Tim 3:1-13; *Didache* 15:1). The *Didache* (c. 100) and 1 Clement (c. 96) are contemporaneous with some of the later New Testament books; *Didache* 15:1 mentions prophets and teachers as well as bishops and deacons. First Clement 42:4 refers to bishops and deacons when speaking of their appointment by the apostles; otherwise he refers to the leaders of the Corinthian Church as presbyters (1:3; 21:6), "perhaps because he knew that Paul had used these terms (Phil 1:1)."[21] In these last two passages he also uses the term *hegoumenoi* (leaders).

---

[20] Raymond E. Brown, "*Episcope* and *Episkopos*: The New Testament Evidence," *Theological Studies* 41 (1980) 325.

[21] Sullivan, *From Apostles to Bishops*, 97.

Diakonia

The concept which underlies all the terms for Church leadership is *diakonia*, service or ministry. Since H. W. Beyer's article in Kittel's *Theological Dictionary of the New Testament* scholars have held that the term came from Hellenistic secular life, with the simple meaning of "service," as in service of table. However John N. Collins has challenged this interpretation. In his book, *Diakonia: Re-interpreting the Ancient Sources*, he argues that the term comes from religious or formal language and carries the implication of authorization or divine representation. On this basis he argues that ministry is not for all the baptized, as many would argue today, but is based on the word and restricted to those to whom it has been given by the community or by the Lord.[22]

The word *diakonia* was adopted even before Paul as a term to describe those who exercised roles of leadership and service in the community; it finds its origin in the example of Jesus who saw his own life and death as a service on behalf of others (Mark 10:45). Edward Schillebeeckx sees the Last Supper as the place of origin for this tradition.[23]

A Variety of Ministries

The apostles were not the only leaders in the early Church. The Christian communities grew considerably between 30 and 50 C.E. as a result of the great missionary effort. Elisabeth Schüssler Fiorenza has contributed to our knowledge of this period by recovering an earlier history from the New Testament which shows that in the early missionary movement women worked with men as partners, founding and playing a leading role in early churches.[24] There is still evidence of this in Paul's letters, where women who played important roles are mentioned frequently. At the end of Romans, Paul commends to the community Phoebe, *diakonos* or minister of the church of Cenchreae (Rom 16:9). He sends greetings to Prisca, along with her husband Aquila, his "fellow workers" and leaders of a house church in Rome (Rom 16:3-5). It is quite possible that many of the early missionaries were partners, husbands and wives working together (cf. 1 Cor 18:1-17). Paul asked that the community leaders or presiders at

[22] John N. Collins, *Diakonia: Re-interpreting the Ancient Sources* (New York: Oxford University Press, 1990) 258–59; see also his, *Are All Christians Ministers?* (Collegeville, MN: The Liturgical Press, 1992).

[23] See Edward Schillebeeckx, *Jesus: An Experiment in Christology*, trans. Hubert Hoskins (New York: Seabury, 1979) 303.

[24] Schüssler Fiorenza, *In Memory of Her*, 160–84.

Thessalonica be shown special respect (1 Thess 5:12), which Schille-beeckx sees as indicating at least a latent opposition towards what some apparently perceived as "non-egalitarian attitudes" in an originally egali-tarian Church.[25]

It is difficult to speak of *office* in Paul's churches, if by office is under-stood a position of authority received through appointment to exercise a permanent public ministry within the community. This is usually termed an "institutional ministry," in contrast to a "charismatic ministry," arising spontaneously through the Spirit to address immediate needs in a commu-nity. Paul uses the term *charism* to refer to those various gifts or manifes-tations of the Spirit that enable a person to perform some service for the common good of the community (1 Cor 12:7), as we have seen.[26] The roles of leadership, recognizable among the charisms, have not yet been "insti-tutionalized," for Paul does not mention any ritual or sign of appointment to what would then be called an office. In this period, ministerial vocabu-lary is still fluid and functional.

But it would be inaccurate to conclude that the theology of the various charisms that Paul develops was actually the structuring principle of the Pauline churches, particularly the church at Corinth.[27] Holmberg insists that in 1 Corinthians 12-14 Paul was not simply describing the Corinthian church but attempting to reform it: "The primary problem was the Corinthians overestimation of glossolalia (*ta pneumatika*), and the con-comitant belief that some Christians had a special endowment of Spirit, manifesting itself 'pneumatically.'"[28]

Some of the charisms named indicate more permanent leadership roles. The prophets and teachers, named after the apostles, are usually recog-nized as local community leaders. Schillebeeckx calls them "incipient local leaders and pioneers."[29] Wayne Meeks points to the few roles com-mon to all the lists, to Paul's ranking of apostles, prophets, and teachers in 1 Cor 12:28, and to the evidence that some leaders were supported by the congregations from a very early period (Gal 6:6) as evidence "that some degree of formalization had already taken place."[30] In proposing a tripar-

[25] Edward Schillebeeckx, *The Church With a Human Face*, trans. John Bowden (New York: Crossroad, 1985) 60.

[26] For a good discussion of the relation of office to charism see Carolyn Osiek, "Relation of Charism to Rights and Duties in the New Testament Church," *The Jurist* 41 (1981) 295–313.

[27] This is Hans Küng's view; see *The Church*, trans. Ray and Rosaleen Ockenden (New York: Sheed and Ward, 1967) 401–04, 442–43.

[28] Holmberg, *Paul and Power*, 120; cf. 201–03.

[29] Schillebeeckx, *Church With a Human Face*, 79.

[30] Meeks, *The First Urban Christians*, 135.

tite classification of the modes of authority present in the local communities Meeks recognizes the balance between the more dramatic "pneumatic" gifts and those roles which would later be associated with office; he points to "visible manifestations of Spirit-possession, position, and association with apostles and other supralocal persons of authority."[31] All of these could be considered as charisms.

The Emergence of a Pastoral Office

As the original witnesses and missionary founders passed from the scene and the Church moved into its third and fourth generations, an institutionalized office of leadership began to emerge. A number of New Testament books contain material that reflect questions from this period about leadership and authority. Matthew recognizes the authority of local church leaders to a considerable degree but seems concerned about a type of "nascent clericalism" which is evident in his warnings against "ostentatious religious clothing and paraphernalia . . . the desire for first seats at the religious meetings . . . and the desire to be addressed with special titles" (Matt 23:5-10).[32] The dispute over rank in the synoptics (Mark 10:35-45 and plls.) is also concerned with authority. Form criticism recognizes this as a tradition on ministry and church order, rooted in a saying of Jesus about his own role of humble service that was adapted by the early communities as an instruction on the exercise of authority in the Church. A variant tradition in 1 Pet 5:1-4 instructs the presbyters to exercise their authority without "lording it over" others.[33]

As the different communities in the sub-apostolic age faced the threats of heterodoxy and schism, a consolidation of the Church's ministry of leadership began to take place.[34] In the later letters the presbyter/bishops (the two terms were not at first clearly distinguished) are taking over the roles exercised in earlier times by the prophets, teachers, and leaders (*proistamenoi*) and probably by the leaders of the house churches. The office of presbyter, literally "elder," was an institution borrowed from Judaism. Each synagogue had a group of older men or elders who advised the community and represented its traditions. Presbyters are first evident

[31] Ibid, 136.

[32] John P. Meier in Raymond E. Brown and John P. Meier, *Antioch and Rome: New Testament Cradles of Catholic Christianity* (New York: Paulist, 1983) 70.

[33] See John Hall Elliott, "Ministry and Church Order in the NT: A Traditio-Historical Analysis (1 Pt 5.1-5 & plls)," *The Catholic Biblical Quarterly* 32 (1970) 367–91.

[34] See Thomas P. Rausch, *The Roots of the Catholic Tradition* (Wilmington, DE: Michael Glazier, 1986) 130–36.

in communities with strong ties to the Jewish tradition (1 Pet 5:1; James 5:14). The role of *episkopos*, "overseer," also seems to have been inherited from Judaism, as the Qumran community had overseers with responsibilities similar to those of the presbyters in the Pastorals.

The responsibilities of the presbyter/bishops frequently included both community leadership and teaching. The expression "pastors and teachers," introduced by a single article in Ephesians 4:11, indicates an office of pastoral leadership which included both functions. The same dual responsibility is attributed in Acts 20:17-35 and the Pastoral Epistles to the presbyters who must watch over preaching and teaching. In 1 Tim 5:17 such presbyters are awarded a double compensation. According to John Meier, these presbyters represent a group emerging within the presbyteral college, exercising not just supervision, but also the liturgical roles implied by preaching and teaching. It is these specialized presbyters who may have received the title *episkopos* at Ephesus (cf. 1 Tim 3:1-7).[35] The laying on of hands, another practice borrowed from Judaism, emerged in this same period as a sign of appointment to office.

Raymond Brown argues that "in churches associated with the three great apostolic figures of the NT, Paul, James, and Peter, presbyters were known and established in the last third of the century."[36] In the Pastoral Letters the primary responsibility of the presbyter-bishops is to guard against false teaching, encouraging the community to follow sound doctrine. In stressing fidelity to the truth, a more objectified concept of faith begins to appear; faith is described in terms of teaching, doctrine, truths handed down, a deposit of faith (1 Tim 6:20-21; 2 Tim 1:13; 4:3; Titus 1:5-14). The emphasis on church structure, office, authority, and the apostolic tradition in the Pastoral Epistles, 2 Peter, and the Acts of the Apostles has led some Protestant scholars to characterize these writings negatively as an expression of "early Catholicism," representing an attempt to "bind" the Spirit to an institutionalized Church office, and thus, an attempt to limit grace.[37] Many Catholic scholars understand these developments as a necessary process of institutionalization, successfully negotiated, as the early communities began to develop the structures needed to safeguard their faith and ecclesial life.

---

[35] John P. Meier, "*Presbyteros* in the Pastoral Epistles," *Catholic Biblical Quarterly* 35 (1973) 344–45.

[36] Brown, "*Episkope* and *Episkopos*," 336.

[37] See Ernst Käsemann's classic essay, "Paul and Early Catholicism" in his *New Testament Questions of Today* (London: SCM Press, 1969) 236–51.

The Threefold Ministry

At the end of the New Testament period, the threefold ministry of a bishop, assisted by presbyters and deacons, is in place at Antioch and some other churches. By the end of the second century it was in place throughout the Church.

The struggle against Montanism and Gnosticism in the second century served to strengthen the authority of the bishops. Montanus and his disciples Prisca and Maximilla were prophets who claimed that their ecstatic preaching represented a direct revelation. Against this claim for the special authority of the spiritually gifted, the conviction developed that the deposit of revelation had been "closed" with the passing of the apostles. Similarly, to counter the Gnostics' claim of secret, unwritten tradition going back to Jesus, appeal was made to the true apostolic tradition publicly proclaimed and handed on through the churches with apostolic foundation. Writers such as Hegessipus, Irenaeus, and Tertullian used the lists of the bishops of these churches to demonstrate their visible continuity with the apostolic period and in this way the authenticity of their doctrinal tradition.[38] For problems affecting a number of churches the bishops of an area would meet together in council even before Nicaea (325). Thus from the second century bishops were recognized as successors of the apostles, both as leaders of the local churches and as teachers who could authoritatively interpret the apostolic tradition.

For a person to be installed into the episcopal or presbyteral office the election or at least approval by the community was necessary.[39] According to Pope Celestine I (d. 432), "No bishop is to be imposed on the people whom they do not want."[40] Pope Leo I (d. 461) stated, "He who has to preside over all must be elected by all."[41] Edward Schillebeeckx has placed great stress on canon 6 of the Council of Chalcedon (451) which decreed that an ordination without assignment to a particular community was invalid.[42]

Resistance to the Pastoral Office

However not all the communities welcomed the emergence of an institutionalized pastoral office. Some tried to resist this development, apparently

[38] See Sullivan, *From Apostles to Bishops*, 141–55.
[39] See David N. Power, "The Basis for Official Ministry in the Church," *The Jurist* 41 (1981) 320–21.
[40] J. Migne, PL 50, 434.
[41] Ibid., 54, 634.
[42] Schillebeeckx, *Ministry*, 38–48.

preferring the more fluid structuring of an earlier generation. The church at Corinth, the Johannine communities, and the Gnostic movement all provide examples of this resistance.

The letter known as 1 Clement, written about the year 96 C.E. from the church of Rome, was sent to Corinth because of a schism developing there. Some agitators in the community had inspired a revolt against the local presbyters, removing them from their office, apparently without cause (44:6; 47:6). It is interesting to note that this church, which some see as the paradigm of the charismatically structured community, had problems with unity in the time of Paul and was still having them some forty years later. The author of 1 Clement admonishes the Corinthians to respect their duly elected leaders on the basis of their appointment by the apostles, an argument perhaps more theological than historical. But the church at Corinth accepted Rome's intervention; around the year 170 Dionysius, bishop of Corinth, writes to Soter, bishop of Rome, that the letter of Clement is still being read in the liturgical assembly.[43]

The Johannine community provides another example of a gradual acceptance of an institutionalized office of ministry. This community may come the closest to being an egalitarian discipleship. Eduard Schweizer says that in the Johannine ecclesiology "there is no longer any kind of special ministry, but only the direct union with God through the Spirit who comes to every individual; here there are neither offices nor even different charismata" (cf. 1 John 2:20, 27).[44]

Raymond Brown does not go as far as Schweizer. In his study of the Johannine community he argues that Schweizer assumes more than is actually known in regard to ecclesiastical ministry; furthermore, there are "contrary indications" in the Johannine epistles.[45] He describes the Johannine Christians as a community apart, distinguished by their high Christology and their apparent lack of interest in developing Church structures at the very time that other Christian communities were stressing them. In the Fourth Gospel one does not find an emphasis on teaching authority or the apostolic tradition, the technical term "apostle" does not appear, and there are no words of Jesus instituting the sacraments of baptism or the Eucharist as one finds in Matthew 28:19 and Luke 22:19. The Beloved Disciple is portrayed as closer to Jesus than Peter. The community itself is

---

[43] Eusebius, *History* 4.23.11.

[44] Eduard Schweizer, *Church Order in the New Testament*, trans. Frank Clarke (London: SCM, 1961) 127.

[45] Raymond E. Brown, *The Community of the Beloved Disciple* (New York: Paulist, 1979) 87.

a community of disciples guided by the Spirit; what is stressed is the teaching role of the Paraclete who will maintain the community in all truth (John 16:13).[46]

But what is most interesting for our considerations here is the point Brown makes about the subsequent history of the Johannine community. He sees in the Johannine epistles, written around the year C.E. 100, the beginning of a schism that was to split the community and lead part of it ultimately into Gnosticism. Both theological and ecclesiological factors contributed to the breakup. Theologically, the secessionists so emphasized the divinity of Jesus that their Christology became docetic, unable to comprehend the salvific importance of Jesus' humanity, and correspondingly, the importance of ethical behavior in the lives of the members of the community. At the same time, their realized eschatology and a pneumatology which could appeal, not to Church authority but only to the inner experience of each believer, left the community ecclesiologically helpless; their differences polarized the community into two sides, with the members of each claiming to be in possession of the Spirit.[47]

The result was the breakup of the community. Those Johannine Christians associated with the author of the Johannine epistles learned from their experience, Brown argues, and came ultimately to accept the authoritative teaching office of the presbyter-bishops which was becoming widespread in the other churches. He suggests that the final chapter of the Fourth Gospel, with its emphasis on the pastoral role of Peter (John 21:15-17) was added to convince the Johannine Christians that the pastoral authority exercised in the other churches was instituted by Jesus himself.[48] But the secessionists—perhaps the larger part of the community—continued moving towards Docetism and Gnosticism. They brought elements of Johannine theology to these emerging second century movements but were themselves lost to Christian history.

Gnosticism presents a third interesting case for the study of emerging structures of authority. In her study of the Nag Hammadi texts Elaine Pagels maintains that Gnostics were among those who opposed the developing Church hierarchy.[49] At least some Gnostic groups rejected in principle any distinctions within the community based on office or function, including that of clergy and laity.

[46] Ibid., 86–88; Brown discusses the Johannine ecclesiology at greater length in his *The Churches the Apostles Left Behind* (New York: Paulist, 1984) 84–104.

[47] Brown, *Community*, 110–44.

[48] Ibid., 159–62.

[49] Elaine Pagels, *The Gnostic Gospels* (New York: Random House, 1979) 40.

One of the most influential forms of the Gnostic movement was that inspired by Valentinus, who founded a sect in Rome in the second century.[50] According to Pagels, Valentinian Gnosticism taught its initiates to reject all ecclesiastical authority on the basis of its deriving, not from the supreme and utterly transcendent God, but from the "creator" (*demiurgos*), a lesser divine being.[51] These Valentinian Gnostics were egalitarians. Irenaeus describes a group of them in Lyons, the followers of Marcus who claimed that each initiated member was directly inspired by the Spirit (*Adv. Haer.* 1.13.3). In Pagels' interpretation of the text, the traditional ecclesiastical functions were doled out to those present, not unlike some contemporary feminist house churches: "Whoever received a certain lot apparently was designated to take the role of *priest*; another was to offer the sacrament, as *bishop*; another would read the Scriptures for worship, and others would address the group as a *prophet*, offering extemporaneous spiritual instructions."[52]

Pagels' interpretation may be going beyond what the text allows, but Tertullian in his "*Prescription Against Heretics*" describes something similar. He criticizes a heretical group as being "without authority, without discipline," for among them "it is doubtful who is a catechumen, and who a believer," while their women "are bold enough to teach, to dispute, to enact exorcisms, to undertake cures—it may be even to baptize." Furthermore, in allowing everyone to do everything, they overturned the traditional ecclesiastical order:

> Their ordinations, are carelessly administered, capricious, changeable. At one time they put *novices* in office; at another time, men who are bound to some secular employment. . . . Nowhere is promotion easier than in the camp of rebels, where the mere fact of being there is a foremost service. And so it comes to pass that to-day one man is their bishop, to-morrow another; to-day he is a deacon who to-morrow is a reader; to-day he is a presbyter who to-morrow is a layman. For even on laymen do they impose the functions of priesthood.[53]

Pagels is correct in recognizing an egalitarian (and feminist) dimension to some parts of the movement. She describes the Gnostics as elitists who

---

[50] For a general introduction to Valentinus and his followers see Bentley Layton, *The Gnostic Scriptures* (Garden City, NY: Doubleday, 1987) 217–22, 267–75.

[51] Pagels, *The Gnostic Gospels*, 32–39.

[52] Ibid., 41.

[53] *The Ante-Nicene Fathers*, Vol. III, ed. Alexander Roberts and James Donaldson (Grand Rapids, MI: William B. Eerdmans, 1978) 263.

stressed a higher level of understanding and the quality of their personal relationships and she contrasts them with the more inclusive orthodox Christians, among whom membership was determined by objective criteria, such as creeds, ritual, and a strong emphasis on episcopal authority.[54] But her suggestion that both the Gnostics and those she calls the orthodox Christians were legitimate expressions of primitive Christianity is highly problematic.[55] Gnosticism was an aberrant phenomenon that emerged in the mid-second century, often combining philosophical speculations and mythological elements with concepts and images borrowed from Christianity, particularly from the Johannine literature, as we saw above. The Gnostic movement could not sustain itself. Never really unified as a system of thought and without adequate provision for leadership, the movement remained splintered and soon disappeared from Christian history.

Presiding at the Eucharist

The New Testament does not provide much information about who presided at the Eucharist in the primitive communities. From parallels with Jewish practice, it is possible that the householders or heads of the house churches (Rom 16:5; 1 Cor 16:19; Col 4:15) led the communities that gathered in their homes, proclaiming the Word and perhaps presiding at their Eucharists. But this is a suggestion; it cannot be proved. There is some evidence that the "prophets and teachers" included eucharistic presidency among their roles. Luke 22:24-27 seems to link Jesus' role as servant with that of local church leaders who celebrate the Lord's Supper.[56] Acts 13:2 shows the prophets and teachers at Antioch "engaged in the liturgy (*leitourgountōn*) of the Lord." And the *Didache* recognizes the prophets and teachers as eucharistic leaders (10:7); it also urges the community to elect bishops and deacons with the encouragement that "they too conduct (*leitourgousi*) the liturgy of the prophets and teachers" (15:1). From the end of the New Testament period, the term bishop becomes increasingly prominent and by the end of the third century the monoepiscopacy is firmly in place.

When the laying on of hands emerged as the ritual sign of appointment to office, the appointment was to the ministry of community leadership, not to a particular function. The first clear attempt to link the Eucharist

---

[54] Pagels, *The Gnostic Gospels*, 102–06.

[55] For a similar approach, see Bart D. Ehrman, *Lost Christianities: The Battles for Scripture and the Faiths We Never Knew* (Oxford/New York: Oxford University Press, 2003).

[56] Schillebeeckx, *Jesus*, 304.

with Church leadership appears in Ignatius of Antioch, around 110 C.E. Ignatius writes, "You should regard that Eucharist as valid which is celebrated either by the bishop or by someone he authorizes" (*Smyrneans* 8:1).[57] The bishop presided at the Eucharist for the first three centuries; by the middle of the third century, with the emergence of smaller "parishes," the liturgical function was assigned to presbyters.[58] But what is increasingly clear today is that in the early tradition eucharistic presidency was linked to those who presided over the community; the role was not seen as explicitly sacerdotal until the early third century.[59]

The Clericalization of the Pastoral Office

While bishops were particularly important in the area of doctrine, they were not the only ones recognized as having authority. Teachers such as Justin Martyr, Tertullian, Clement of Alexandria, and Origen, though not bishops, had considerable authority. The martyrs possessed authority; so did the confessors, those who had been imprisoned and suffered for the sake of Christ. According to the Apostolic Tradition of Hippolytus (9), a confessor could be considered a presbyter, though if he were to be selected as bishop, he would have to receive the laying on of hands. As the ascetic or monastic movement spread in the third and fourth centuries, others were recognized as having authority on the basis of holiness of life. The practice of appointing monks bishops was one way of trying to deal with the rivalry that sometimes developed between the ascetics and those who exercised the Church's pastoral office, the clergy.[60]

If the clergy, particularly the bishops, were the ordinary authorities, in the second and third centuries they were not yet distinguished from others in the community, either by dress or by special privileges. Certainly the New Testament does not distinguish between "clergy" and "laity." As Yves Congar has written, the tension in the Church of the martyrs was between

---

[57] John H. Elliott suggests that Luke's placing the dispute among the disciples over rank in the context of the institution of the Eucharist (Luke 22:24-27) may represent one of the "early stages of a trend associating ministry and Eucharist which later becomes the basis upon which the post-apostolic church builds." See "Ministry and Church Order in the NT," 385.

[58] See John D. Zizioulas, *Eucharist, Bishop, Church: The Unity of the Church in the Divine Eucharist and the Bishop During the First Three Centuries*, trans. Elizabeth Theokritoff (Brookline, MA: Holy Cross Orthodox Press, 2001) 214–15.

[59] Hervé Marie Legrand, "The Presidency of the Eucharist According to the Ancient Tradition," *Worship* 53 (1979) 427.

[60] See Robert B. Eno, *Teaching Authority in the Early Church* (Wilmington, DE: Michael Glazier, 1984) 19.

the Church and the world, not between the various categories of Christians themselves.[61]

Perhaps more important than anything else in this regard was the transition the Church went through in the fourth century from a countercultural Church persecuted by the Empire to an established Church. With Constantine's Edict of Milan in 313 the Church received legal status and its officials began to assume an official place in the Roman Empire.[62] The Church could now own land and began to acquire buildings. Like the pagan priests, bishops and presbyters were exempted from taxes and civil duties. Bishops began to receive certain honors and privileges. In the fifth century they began to wear the insignia of high officials such as the pallium and the stole. Before long other clergy were wearing distinctive clothing. At the same time the liturgy was becoming more ornate, incorporating processions, rich vestments, gold vessels and furnishings, incense, and ceremonies borrowed from the imperial court.

An increasing emphasis on the cultic aspect of the ordained minister's role also contributed to a growing tension between laity and clergy, with a consequent accumulation of privileges for the latter. Recent studies have described the "sacerdotalizing"[63] and "clericalization"[64] of the Church's pastoral office, turning it into a sacral priestly office. Edward Schillebeeckx has emphasized a number of factors that contributed to this development. One was the growth of the Church in the third and fourth centuries which led to the emergence of the "country priest," really the first of what we today call parish priests. These were pastors who served rural communities. Since one of their primary functions was to preside at the local liturgies, they became "Mass priests." Thus their roles were different from those of the presbyters in the large urban churches who assisted the bishop as members of his presbyteral council and joined him at the liturgy. One consequence of this development was an increasing emphasis on the relationship between the priest and the Eucharist, rather than on the relationship between the Eucharist and the community.[65]

Another factor was the practice of private celebrations of the Eucharist which Schillebeeckx maintains began early in the sixth century in connection

[61] Yves Congar, "The Historical Development of Authority," in *Problems of Authority*, ed. John M. Todd (Baltimore: Helicon, 1962) 135.

[62] Yves Congar, *Power and Poverty in the Church*, trans. Jennifer Nicholson (Baltimore: Helicon, 1965) 111–31; also Schillebeeckx, *Church with a Human Face*, 141–53.

[63] Schillebeeckx, *The Church With a Human Face*, 144–47.

[64] Kenan B. Osborne, *Priesthood: A History of the Ordained Ministry in the Roman Catholic Church* (New York: Paulist, 1988) 145–48.

[65] Schillebeeckx, *Church with a Human Face*, 140–43.

with the veneration of relics.[66] This had the effect of weakening considerably the link between ordained ministry and the community itself. The priest was becoming a sacred person whose identity was defined in terms of a cultic function. A third factor was the law of abstinence from sexual intercourse for married priests prior to celebrating the Eucharist, and ultimately clerical celibacy, which became mandatory in the western Church in the twelfth century (1123).[67]

The Germanic influence making itself felt in the Empire around the time of Charlemagne (d. 814) also contributed to the growth of clerical and episcopal privileges. Congar calls attention to the importance placed on gestures of handing over and touching significant objects, pledging obedience by placing one's hands between the hands of a superior, handing over instruments or insignia to incorporate one into an office. The crozier or pastoral staff appeared in Spain in the seventh century and in Gaul in the eighth. About this same time the episcopal ring appeared in both regions. The practice of genuflecting and the kissing of the feet was borowed from Byzantium.[68] These practices enriched the liturgy, but they also contributed to a growing emphasis on priestly and episcopal power.

Similarly the papacy inherited the insignia of the Roman Empire. The popes began to wear the diadem or crown, the phrygium or round, white miter, the red tunic, and to carry the scepter. Gregory VII (1073–1085) claimed exclusive right to wear imperial insignia in his *Dictatus Papae*. While the papacy took on the symbols and titles of monarchy, based on the imperial model, the Church itself became inculturated in a highly feudal system that it reflected in its ranks of officials, insignia, titles, different lifestyles, and forms of dress. Papal absolutism reached its high point under Boniface VIII (1294–1303) who claimed in his famous bull *Unam sanctam* "that it is absolutely necessary for the salvation of all men that they submit to the Roman pontiff" (DS 875). Boniface introduced the triple-crowned tiara: Congar points out that this tiara, which rises from a wide base to a single point at the top "was an apt expression of the idea of pontifical monarchy and a quasi-pyramidal concept of the Church."[69] The Conciliarist movement which in the fourteenth century grew out of the struggle to resolve the dilemma caused by the "western schism," with its rival claimants to the papal throne, was in part a reaction to papal absolutism and the abuse of power.

---

[66] Ibid., 159–60.
[67] Congar, *Power and Poverty*, 118.
[68] Ibid.
[69] Congar, *Power and Poverty*, 125–26.

Conclusion

In the earliest days of the community the Jerusalem apostles, with at least some of the Twelve among them, were recognized as leaders because of their proximity to Jesus. Paul and Barnabas as representatives of the Gentile mission of Antioch acknowledged their authority and in turn were recognized by the Jerusalem leaders. The obvious evidence of Peter's authority in the earliest days should make one cautious about suggesting that the eschatological role of the Twelve did not include actual, historical leadership. Their authority is not merely grounded in the Spirit, but has historical roots in their call and missioning by the historical Jesus; that is to say, it is not just pneumatological, but also christological in its foundation.

Recent scholarship has recovered the important roles played by women in the early missionary movements. It is evident both that women were active in founding churches and exercising leadership ministries in them in the earliest period and that the later New Testament books reflect a hardening of the communities against women in leadership roles. The openness of the Church to the ministry of women in primitive Christianity has implications for the Church of today and tomorrow.

Just as the New Testament recognizes the diversity of charisms, it also recognizes a Church office that it portrays as linked to the ministry of the apostles. The apostles associated others with them in their ministry. The threefold ministry of bishops, presbyters, and deacons developed under the guidance of the Spirit. On the other hand, a structured office of pastoral leadership developed slowly and not always simultaneously in the different communities. Some resisted it, but those that did not incorporate it lost communion with the other churches and lapsed into heterodoxy, ultimately to disappear from Christian history.

The office of Church leadership has the responsibility to regulate the charisms and provide for their expression, exercising a ministry of oversight (*episkopē*). The ordained minister presides over the community, uniting it around the eucharistic table and expressing its unity with the Church catholic and with the Church of the apostles. An egalitarian ecclesiology which would exclude in principle the reality of an office within the Church is both sociologically naïve and unhistorical. The problem is not office, but the loss of the other charisms. What is important is to provide for equality of opportunity and to recover a proper and equitable balance between charism and office. Vatican II, with its emphasis on what it calls "various gifts, both hierarchical and charismatic," is a step in the right direction (LG 4, 7, 12).

The relation between office and charism is best described as dialectical,[70] rather than one of domination and subordination. Office is rooted in charism; an office bestowed without a discerned charism may be valid, but it is ineffective. Charisms challenge office and institution, but unregulated, they can become divisive, even chaotic. Institutional authority may seem to have the last word, but in the final analysis the decisions and teachings of authority must find reception by the whole Church.

Eucharistic presidency belongs to the function of presiding over the community. The traditional language of priesthood (*hiereus/sacerdos*) for Church leaders, dating from the early third century, has served to underline the nature of the Church as a eucharistic community, but it has also contributed to a one-sided concept of a primarily cultic ordained ministry.[71] Recognition of a ministerial priesthood does not mean a metaphysical clericalism which would place the ordained on a higher level; it means that the ordained has been incorporated into the Church's apostolic office and therefore is authorized to act in the name of the Church and thus in the person of Christ (*in persona Christi*). What has changed in such a relational ontology is the relation of the ordained minister to the community.[72] In this way the divine initiative is emphasized. The ordained priesthood serves the priesthood of all the baptized, particularly when presiding at the Eucharist.

In the light of the original nexus between leading the community and eucharistic presidency, Leonardo Boff's suggestion that lay community coordinators be authorized to preside at the Eucharist for communities lacking ordained ministers may not be so untraditional.[73] Certainly the contemporary Roman Catholic problem of local churches not being able to celebrate the Eucharist would not have arisen in the early Church, for a community would always choose a local leader as presider, who could then be appointed with the help of the heads of neighboring churches.[74]

[70] See Holmberg's discussion of the dialectical nature of authority in the primitive Church in *Paul and Power*, 198–201; also Dulles' theses on the relation between institution and charism in his *A Church To Believe In*, 29–40.

[71] See Thomas P. Rausch, *Priesthood Today: An Appraisal* (New York: Paulist, 1992) 15–22.

[72] Richard R. Gaillardetz, "The Ecclesiological Foundations of Ministry within an Ordered Communion," in *Ordering the Baptismal Priesthood: Theologies of Lay and Ordained Ministry*, ed. Susan K. Wood (Collegeville, MN: The Liturgical Press, 2003) 38–39.

[73] Leonardo Boff, *Ecclesiogenesis: The Base Communities Reinvent the Church* (Maryknoll, NY: Orbis, 1986) 61–75.

[74] See Hervé Marie Legrand, "The Presidency of the Eucharist," 437.

Since the second and third centuries, the bishops have been recognized as authentic teachers whose interpretation of the apostolic tradition was considered normative. For Roman Catholicism, the bishop presides over the local Church, while together with the bishop of Rome, bishops have supreme authority over the universal Church. How that papal-episcopal authority is to be exercised we must consider more carefully later in this work.

CHAPTER 6

Safeguarding the Apostolic Tradition

T owards the end of the first century, a period in which the early churches were struggling with false teachers and heterodox views, the author of the letter known as Jude wrote to a community of Christians, urging them "to contend for the faith that was once for all handed down to the holy ones" (Jude 1:3).

The problem of false teachers, and the responsibility of Church leaders to safeguard the faith "handed down" (*paradotheisē*), a technical term for "tradition" (cf. 1 Cor 11:23; 15:3) or what would later be called the "apostolic tradition," is frequently mentioned in letters from the year 70 C.E. to the end of the New Testament period, including such non-canonical works as the *Didache* (11–13) and the letters of Ignatius of Antioch. Exhortation to Church leaders occur regularly in such books as Colossians and Ephesians, 1 and 2 Timothy and Titus, Acts, Jude, 2 Peter, and the Johannine Letters. In the context of an instruction on the role of overseers and deacons, the author of 1 Timothy speaks of the Church as "the pillar and foundation of truth" (1 Tim 3:15). Because these books emphasize "Catholic" concerns for Church structure—the transmission of office, the teaching responsibility of pastors, and the importance of preserving the apostolic tradition—Lutheran scholar Ernst Käsemann used the expression "early Catholicism" to characterize them.[1] Käsemann of course rejected early Catholicism, seeing it as an effort to bind the Spirit to an emerging institutionalized office, thus, as an attempt to limit grace. James Dunn's position is similar. He does not see any normative value to early Catholicism; it is for him only one of several trajectories, even though he acknowledges that the other alternatives at the end of the first century,

---

[1] Ernst Käsemann, "Paul and Early Catholicism," in his *New Testament Questions of Today* (London: SCM Press, 1969) 235–51.

apocalyptic, Jewish, and Hellenistic Christianity, did not provide a pattern of church life that would endure.[2] Neither Käsemann nor Dunn gives sufficient attention to the fact that it was these early Catholic structures emerging in the second and following centuries that were responsible for safeguarding, canonizing, and handing on the New Testament.

But the Church in every age has been concerned with safeguarding the apostolic tradition. Roger Haight sees the establishment of the canon as the single most important structure for stabilizing and objectifying the foundational faith experience of the Christian community.[3] Roman Catholics and Orthodox Christians have emphasized the role played by the bishops in guarding the apostolic faith. For Catholics, the bishops are successors of the apostles and transmitters of the apostolic tradition (LG 20). Orthodox Christians also see the bishops as successors to the apostles; they have been associated with truth (*veritas*) since the earliest days of the Church. Each bishop functions as the image of Christ for his community, particularly in his role at the Eucharist, and as heads of their communities, they express the Church's unity when gathered in council. "The communities' *unity in identity* is the foundation of conciliar infallibility."[4]

In the sixteenth century the Reformers lifted the Bible up against the teaching authority of the Church, proclaiming "*sola Scriptura*," Scripture alone. They didn't mean to suggest, however, that the Christian tradition had no part to play in shaping the Church's life and teaching. Luther and Calvin drew on the Church fathers, the early councils, and even some of the medieval doctors, but none of this at the expense of what was clearly taught by Scripture. The Free Church approach to teaching authority however is more individualistic. This tradition and Protestantism in general has a different understanding of how the Church functions in transmitting the faith, as Miroslav Volf acknowledges.[5] Though he recognizes that Scripture is always read within the context of an interpretative tradition, he expresses the traditional Free Church nervousness about Church authority, the fear that the "custodians of faith may degenerate into lords of

---

[2] James D. G. Dunn, *Unity and Diversity in the New Testament: An Inquiry into the Character of Earliest Christianity: Second Edition* (London: SCM Press, 1990) 364; first published 1977; he speaks of "the Spirit bottled up in office and ritual," 365.

[3] Roger Haight, *Christian Community in History*: Vol. I: *Historical Ecclesiology* (New York: Continuum, 2004) 103.

[4] John D. Zizioulas, *Being as Communion* (Crestwood, NY: St. Vladimir's Seminary Press, 1985) 116.

[5] Miroslav Volf, *After Our Likeness: The Church as the Image of the Trinity* (Grand Rapids, MI: William B. Eerdmans, 1998) 164.

faith by repressing rather than expressing the genuine *sensus fidelium.*" In the final analysis he argues, the only way to escape the danger of sectarianism is "to trust in the Holy Spirit."[6]

Thus, one result of the Reformation was that the Bible emerged as the fundamental doctrinal authority for Protestant Christianity. Scripture alone was and remains the norm. However, the Scripture principle was weakened considerably by the double challenges of the Enlightenment and the Scientific Revolution. In this chapter we will consider, first, the emergence of the Church's teaching office as well as the special role played by the bishop of Rome in Roman Catholicism. We will then look at the crisis of the Scripture principle. Finally, we will review Catholic and Protestant approaches to teaching authority today.

The Church's Teaching Office

If Catholic theologians focus on the emerging structures of ministry and authority evident in the later New Testament, the "early Catholic" writings mentioned earlier, Protestant scholars tend to privilege the early letters of Paul, particularly 1 Corinthians. Paul, of course, was well aware of his own apostolic authority as a teacher, as his letters show. Nevertheless, it is clear that the later New Testament period is very much concerned with the problem of false teachers and the corresponding responsibility of local Church leaders, frequently identified as presbyter/bishops, to guard the apostolic tradition. By the mid-80s, 1 Peter 5, Acts 20, and the Pastoral Epistles show that churches in the Pauline and Petrine tradition had leaders called either elders (*presbyteroi*) or overseers (*episkopoi*), or frequently both.

In his farewell address in Acts to the presbyters of Miletus, Paul exhorts them to "watch over yourselves and over the whole flock of which the holy Spirit has appointed you overseers [*episkopous*]," protecting them against the false teachers who will come from among them, perverting the truth and attempting to draw the disciples to themselves (Acts 20:28-30). The Pastoral Letters addressed to Timothy urge him repeatedly to guard against false teaching in the Church at Ephesus (1 Tim 1:3-4; 6:2-4). The entire 2 Timothy can be seen as an instruction on handing on the apostolic tradition. Timothy, who is represented as having received the laying on of hands from Paul (2 Tim 1:6), is told to take as his norm "the sound words that you heard from me . . . [guarding] this rich trust with the help of the holy Spirit" (2 Tim 1:13-14). He is to entrust this teaching "to faithful people

---

[6] Ibid., 165; interestingly, the only entry under the subject of authority in his glossary is the negative "authoritarianism."

who will have the ability to teach others as well" (2 Tim 2:2). The bishop must be "able to teach" (1 Tim 3:2), "both to exhort with sound doctrine and to refute opponents" (Titus 1:9). Joseph Fitzmyer remarks that in the Pastoral Letters "the function of the teacher is clearly predicated of the delegates of the apostle and of those whom they appoint as *episkopoi*."[7]

The second letter of Peter is also very much concerned with the problem of false teachers (2 Pet 2:1-3; 17-22). Though it underlines the inspired character of Scripture (2 Pet 1:21), it also cautions in Peter's name against certain Christians who are misinterpreting Paul's teachings in his letters (2 Pet 3:15-16).

Development of the Episcopal Office

By the third quarter of the second century the threefold ministry of a single bishop, assisted by presbyters and deacons, had spread throughout the Church. The twofold charism of pastoral leadership and teaching, already associated with the presbyter/bishops in the late New Testament period (1 Tim 5:17; cf. Acts 20:28), now characterized the role of the bishop. Francis Sullivan notes that bishops are already recognized as the successors of the apostles, not only as leaders but also as church teachers and authoritative exponents of the genuine apostolic tradition.[8] They were not, of course, the only teachers. Justin Martyr, Tertullian, Clement of Alexandria, and Origen were recognized as having authority as teachers, even though they were not bishops. But Sullivan argues that the writings of Irenaeus, Tertullian, and others of this period are evidence that the bishops who led the churches "were also exercising a role of pastoral *magisterium*."[9] He concludes that this development is part of God's design for the Church, for "what the whole Church receives, whether doctrine (as Word of God), writings (as canonical Scripture) or bishops (as successors of the apostles) must indeed be what the Church accepts them to be."[10]

---

[7] Joseph A. Fitzmyer, "The Office of Teaching in the Christian Church According to the New Testament," in *Teaching Authority and Infallibility: Lutherans and Catholics in Dialogue VI*, ed. Paul C. Empie, T. Austin Murphy, and Joseph A. Burgess (Minneapolis: Augsburg, 1978) 206.

[8] Francis A. Sullivan, *Magisterium: Teaching Authority in the Catholic Church* (New York: Paulist, 1983) 49; see chapter 3, "Biblical and Historical Basis for the Teaching Authority of Bishops; also Richard R. Gaillardetz, *Teaching With Authority: A Theology of the Magisterium of the Church* (Collegeville, MN: The Liturgical Press, 1997) 35–39.

[9] Sullivan, *Magisterium*, 50; see also his *From Apostles to Bishops: The Development of the Episcopacy in the Early Church* (New York: Paulist, 2001) 144–70.

[10] Sullivan, *Magisterium*, 44; *From Apostles to Bishops*, 229–30.

What led to the transformation of the originally collegial office of local church leadership into the single, monarchical bishop (monoepiscopacy)? Hermann Pottmeyer suggests several possible answers: the fact that this form proved most effective in the struggle to preserve Church unity against heretical teachings, the typological interpretations that sees the bishop as a representative of God and Christ (Ignatius of Antioch), and the idea of the bishop as successor to the apostles (1 Clement). While the question cannot be answered with certainty, he sees the view of the community as the household of God (Eph 2:19; 1 Tim 3:15) as a significant influence on this development. Since many communities originated in family gatherings, it was natural that the community understood itself as God's household, and as the number of house churches increased, the bishop was seen as taking the role of the father of the family, the *pater familias* (cf. 1 Tim 3:4-5). There is, of course, an analogy here with the position of the father in Jewish and Roman families.[11]

The bishop watched over the life of the local church and presided at its Eucharist. The Eucharist both effected and expressed the unity of the Church, while the bishop was a symbol of the communion between the local church and the communion of churches. The teaching authority of the bishops was enhanced considerably by the role they played in the councils and synods from the early centuries of the Church.

In the first millennium the episcopacy was considered the highest rank of the sacrament of holy orders, though there were early exceptions like Jerome who maintained a "presbyteral" view of the sacrament.[12] However, a number of factors at the end of the first millennium contributed to a shift of focus from the bishop to the presbyter. The growth of the Church meant that the priest became the primary minister of the local community and its eucharistic presider. This change was reflected from 1100 on, as scholastic theologians began to define holy orders, not in terms of the bishop's role as pastor of the local church, but rather in terms of the priest's power to consecrate the Eucharist. The bishop's role was understood as jurisdictional rather than sacramental, with his authority coming from the pope.[13] The distinction made by canon lawyers in the eleventh and twelfth cen-

---

[11] See Hermann J. Pottmeyer, "The Episcopacy," in *The Gift of the Church: A Textbook on Ecclesiology in Honor of Patrick Granfield, O.S.B.*, ed. Peter C. Phan (Collegeville, MN: The Liturgical Press, 2000) 343–44.

[12] Ibid., 344; Jerome, Letter 146:6; *Commentary on the Letter to Titus*, 1:5; esp. 69:3.

[13] See Kenan B. Osborne, *Priesthood: A History of the Ordained Ministry in the Roman Catholic Church* (New York: Paulist Press, 1988) 169–94.

turies between the power of ordination and the power of jurisdiction also contributed to the growing emphasis on the sacred power of the priest.[14]

Bishops and Doctors

The Middle Ages saw the development of a challenge to the bishops' teaching authority as well as the emergence of a new kind of council. From the work of the canonists and the growing prestige of the university *doc-tores*, a new kind of authority emerged, based not on the pastoral role but on scholarship. The canonists of the eleventh and twelfth centuries developed a nuanced ecclesiology which held that the ultimate criteria for determining the validity of an ecclesiastical pronouncement or teaching were to be found, not in its source (whether pope or council) or juridical authority, but rather in the intrinsic truth of the decision and in its reception by the Church.[15] And in the great medieval universities, particularly that of Paris, the authority of the professors of theology was associated with that of the Church fathers and for a time assumed "a debatable primacy."[16]

The university theologians (who were, of course, clerics) collaborated with the hierarchy by serving on commissions to evaluate theological positions, condemning those opinions considered heterodox, even preparing papal censures. In this way they played a considerable role in judging what was to be considered orthodox. Avery Dulles points out that the "doctrinal decrees of several general councils (Lyons I, 1245; Lyons II, 1274; and Vienne, 1312) were submitted to universities for approval before being officially published."[17] The university theologians also advanced theology by their own work, though cautiously, lest they themselves incur papal condemnation.

Thus the place of university theologians in the life of the Church was *Interesting* clearly recognized. Thomas Aquinas distinguished between two types of *magisteria* or teaching authority, that of the bishops and that of the doctors. The word magisterium comes from the Latin *magister*, master, which connoted someone with authority, but was used particularly of teachers.

[14] Edward Schillebeeckx, *The Church With a Human Face* (New York: Crossroad, 1985) 192–93.

[15] See Brian Tierney, "Only the Truth Has Authority: The Problem of 'Reception' in the Decretists and in Johannes de Turrecremata," in *Law, Church and Society: Essays in Honor of Stephan Kuttner*, ed. Kenneth Pennington and Robert Somerville (Philadelphia: University of Pennsylvania Press, 1977) 69–96.

[16] Yves Congar, "Theologians and the Magisterium in the West: From the Gregorian Reform to the Council of Trent," *Chicago Studies* 17 (1978) 214.

[17] Avery Dulles, *A Church to Believe In: Discipleship and the Dynamics of Freedom* (New York: Crossroad, 1982) 109.

The bishops with their supervisory responsibility held the "magisterium of the pastoral chair" (*magisterium cathedrae pastoralis*); the theologians, whose competence was based on learning, held the "magisterium of the professor's chair" (*magisterium cathedrae magistralis*).[18] Congar points out that the word magisterium took on its present meaning (i.e., that of the teaching office exercised by the pope and bishops) only under Gregory XVI, about 1830.[19]

The authority of the doctors or professors continued to grow until it began to conflict with that of the bishops. According to Francis Sullivan, the university faculties of theology dominated the Councils of Constance (1415) and Basel (1439): "Anyone with a doctorate in theology or canon law was given full voting rights, with the astonishing result that at the thirty-fourth session of the Council of Basel (25 June 1439) there were three hundred *doctores* with voting rights, and only seven bishops! This, of course, was an aberration, and the council ended in a fiasco."[20]

Conciliarism

Basel and its predecessor, the Council of Constance, gave expression to the conciliarist theory that developed in the fourteenth and fifteenth centuries because of the Great Western Schism (1378–1417). With two and then three claimants to the papal throne, the Council of Constance raised the question of "whether the authority of the universal church resided in a general council made up of bishops, abbots, doctors of theology and canon lawyers, conceived of as a kind of ecclesiastical parliament, distinct from and ultimately superior to the executive, the pope."[21] In his study of papal primacy Klaus Schatz makes a useful distinction in regard to these medieval councils. He argues that while the councils of the first millennium had been councils of bishops, usually with the emperor presiding, the medieval councils were assemblies not just of the bishops, but of Christendom itself, with representatives of other Church institutions (abbots and members of cathedral chapters), the universities, and the civil rulers included.[22] The central issue was that of authority in the Church, and how it was to be exercised.

---

[18] Yves Congar, "A Semantic History of the Term 'Magisterium'," in *Readings in Moral Theology No. 3, The Magisterium and the Theologian*, ed. Charles E. Curran and Richard A. McCormick (New York: Paulist, 1982) 303; (cf. Quodl. III 9 ad 3).

[19] Congar, "Theologians and the Magisterium," 210.

[20] Sullivan, *Magisterium*, 182.

[21] Ibid., 89.

[22] Klaus Schatz, *Papal Primacy: From Its Origins to the Present*, trans. John Otto and Linda Maloney (Collegeville, MN: The Liturgical Press, 1996) 79.

Constance attempted to answer the question about the superiority of a general council over the pope affirmatively in the decree *Haec sancta*, which espoused the conciliarist teaching, but once the schism was resolved, the conciliarist movement lost much of its power. The Council of Florence (1438–1445) emphasized papal authority, clearly a reaction to the excesses of Basel which, among other problems, divided into two factions and ended up electing another anti-pope.[23] Schatz attributes the fact that so few bishops attended to a lack of a true ecclesial spirit within the national episcopates which was responsible "for the failure of a moderate conciliarism that would have corresponded thoroughly to the ancient tradition of the Church."[24] Since Basel, the Roman Catholic Church has understood a general council as exercising the authority of the universal Church when the assembled bishops act both with and under the pope (LG 22).

Even after Florence theologians continued to play an important role in judging orthodoxy; as Congar and Sullivan note, it was scholastic theologians who examined and developed the critique of Luther's forty-one theses that led to their condemnation in the bull *Exsurge Domine* (June 15, 1520).[25] Thus, as Hugh Lawrence observes, in the past, the teaching Church "had several organs, one of which was the university."[26] As late as the Council of Trent (1545-1563) theologians served on some of the congregations of bishops and were called upon to speak at the plenary sessions.

But in the period from Trent to Vatican II teaching authority in the Roman Catholic Church became increasingly identified with the bishops and more centralized in the papal office. United as a college, bishops exercise their teaching authority in union with the bishop of Rome, particularly at an ecumenical council (LG 22); together they constitute the Church's magisterium or teaching office.[27] At this point we need to consider the special role of the papacy.

---

[23] See Roger Haight, *Historical Ecclesiology*, 357; see Haight's analysis of the issues underlying conciliarism, 377–85.

[24] Schatz, *Papal Primacy*, 111.

[25] Congar, "Theologians and the Magisterium," 217; Sullivan, *Magisterium*, 182.

[26] Hugh Lawrence, "Spiritual Authority and Governance," in *Authority in the Roman Catholic Church: Theory and Practice*, ed. Bernard Hoose (Burlington, VT: Ashgate, 2002) 52.

[27] Sullivan, *Magisterium*; Gaillardetz, *Teaching with Authority*; see also his *By What Authority? A Primer on Scripture, the Magisterium, and the Sense of the Faithful* (Collegeville, MN: The Liturgical Press, 2003).

The Bishop of Rome

If the papacy is Roman Catholicism's most obvious symbol, it has also been a sign of contradiction for many Christians. They see the ministry of the Bishop of Rome, not as a ministry of unity and communion, but rather as an oppressive, non-biblical office that has too often violated Christian freedom in its attempts to rule the Church. To gain an appreciation of the papacy we need to consider briefly the ministry of Peter as reflected in history and Scripture, the development of the Roman primacy, and the papacy in the teaching of the Second Vatican Council.

Peter in History and Scripture

The figure of Simon Peter clearly stands out among the disciples during the historical life of Jesus; he is always named first in lists of the Twelve, he is the first (male) witness to the resurrection of Jesus (1 Cor 15:5; cf. Luke 24:34), and plays the leading role in the primitive community in Jerusalem. Already known as Kephas (Aramaic for "rock") by Paul, it is very possible that he received the name Peter (Greek *petra*, rock) from Jesus himself (Matt 16:18). Three classical texts suggest a special role for Peter; he is the rock upon whom the Church is to be built, the one on whom Jesus confers the keys (Matt 16:13-19); the one Jesus has prayed for, that he might strengthen his brothers (Luke 22:31-34); and in spite of his own betrayal, he is commissioned by Jesus to be the pastor of the flock (John 21:15-17). At the end of the New Testament period, the authority of Peter is invoked to correct certain misinterpretations of the teachings of Paul (2 Pet 3:15-16), as we saw earlier. Most scholars today, Catholic and Protestant, agree that texts such as these point to Peter's special position in both the ministry of Jesus and in the primitive Church; the fact that they were written long after his death "testifies to the primitive Church's abiding interest in the person and function of Peter."[28]

From a historical perspective, few would deny that Peter played a leading role in the primitive community of Jerusalem; both the Acts of the Apostles and Paul's account in Galatians 1:18 witness to this. John Meier argues that Peter won the argument with Paul at Antioch, thus playing a key role in maintaining *koinōnia* between Jewish and Gentile Christians in that church.[29] Finally, there is general agreement that Peter labored in

[28] Schatz, *Papal Primacy*, 1; see also *Peter in the New Testament*, ed. Raymond E. Brown, Karl P. Donfried, and John Reumann (Minneapolis: Augsburg; New York: Paulist, 1973).

[29] In Raymond E. Brown and John P. Meier, *Antioch and Rome: New Testament Cradles of Catholic Christianity* (New York: Paulist, 1983) 39–41.

Rome and was martyred there in the mix-sixties, most probably in a persecution under Nero. But to say this is not to suggest that he functioned as a bishop in Rome, or that the New Testament authors were aware of any continuing office in succession to Peter.

The Development of the Roman Primacy

It is also widely acknowledged that the Roman church was recognized from the beginning as having a special dignity among the churches. While this was due in part to Rome's status as capital of the Roman Empire, even more, it was based on the Roman church's unique apostolic heritage. Both Peter and Paul had worked and died there as 1 Clement (5-6) attests. And by the end of the New Testament period there are examples of the Roman church instructing other churches. The first letter of Peter, written from Rome in Peter's name to a group of Christians in Asia Minor most probably in the 80s, is one example. Another is the first letter of Clement itself, written from Rome to the church at Corinth around the year 96 to admonish the Corinthian Christians for ejecting the Corinthian presbyters from their office (44).[30] Not long after this Ignatius of Antioch wrote to the church at Rome, "You have taught others" (3:1).

But the primacy of the Roman church and its bishop developed slowly.[31] From the earliest days Rome's special dignity was recognized, based on the tradition that the city held the tombs of the two great apostles. In the struggle with Gnosticism, Rome was seen as a privileged locus of the apostolic tradition by Irenaeus (c. 180) and Tertullian (c. 213); it was *the* apostolic see. Referring to its two founding apostles, Irenaeus wrote "it is a matter of necessity that every church should agree with this church, on account of its pre-eminent authority."[32] Towards the end of the second century, Rome's efforts to determine the proper date for the celebration of Easter and to recognize the validity of baptism performed by heretics represented early attempts to decide questions for the whole Church. The Roman bishops Victor and Stephen seemed to presume that the Roman practice was normative. Though the churches, first of Asia and then of North Africa, resisted these efforts, Rome's position ultimately won out. By

[30] Raymond E. Brown argues that Rome may have written other churches because it considered itself heir to the pastoral responsibility Peter and Paul had for their Gentile missions; *Antioch and Rome*, 165–66.

[31] See Schatz, *Papal Primacy*; J. M. R. Tillard, *The Bishop of Rome*, trans. John de Satgé (Wilmington, DE: Michael Glazier, 1983); William J. La Due, *The Chair of Saint Peter: A History of the Papacy* (Maryknoll, NY: Orbis, 1999).

[32] Irenaeus, *Adversus haereses* 3.3.2.

the late fourth century, Roman bishops were claiming their succession to Peter and by the fifth reserving for themselves the title "pope." From the fifth century onward a council had to be in union with the bishop of Rome to be valid. The East was slower to accept Roman claims; yet Rome was recognized as the ultimate norm of ecclesial communion, while a series of witnesses acknowledged that the Roman bishop presided over the churches.[33]

In the period from 500 to 700 the collapse of the Roman administration of the empire meant a period of independence for the churches, particularly in Northern Italy, Spain, and North Africa. But Roman influence increased dramatically in Germany under Charlemagne who looked to Roman liturgy and law to unify his empire. The incredible growth of the power of the medieval papacy "was in great part the result of the non-functioning of other Church structures, and not simply of a Roman will to power."[34] The collegial authority of the bishops in the West was ineffective while the old system of episcopal synods had largely collapsed; in reality the churches were largely controlled by secular rulers, particularly after the strong churches of Spain and North Africa were lost to Arab conquests.

The False Decretals, documents forged in the ninth century in the ecclesial province of Rheims, emphasized the primacy of the pope in matters of jurisdiction. While their real purpose was to protect the bishops from the power of the metropolitans who were controlled by the emperor, they ultimately contributed to growth in the power of the papacy.[35] The papacy had become the head of the Church, at least in the West. The Eastern churches recognized Rome's primacy, not in juridical terms or claims to plenary power, but within the framework of collegiality.[36] But relations continued to deteriorate, with the final break coming in 1054.

The Gregorian Reform

The reform begun by Pope Gregory VII (1073–85) in Haight's view gave birth to the modern papacy, not because what he claimed was new, but because he was so successful in achieving his goals.[37] In his *Dictatus Papae* he claimed exclusive right to depose or absolve bishops, use the imperial insignia, establish new laws, and have his name pronounced in all

---

[33] Schatz, *Papal Primacy*, 60.

[34] Ibid., 72.

[35] La Due, *Chair of St. Peter*, 86.

[36] See Olivier Clément, *You Are Peter: An Orthodox Theologian's Reflection on the Exercise of Papal Primacy* (New York: New City Press, 2003) 39.

[37] Roger Haight, *Historical Ecclesiology*, 320.

the churches. Schatz emphasizes that the Gregory's intention was not to diminish episcopal authority. But because of the weakness of episcopal structures, with the bishops largely co-opted by the emperor, a number of factors contributed to strengthening the power of Rome. In an effort to defend the "freedom of the Church" against secular authorities, more and more appeals were made to Rome and efforts to restore the principle of the election of bishops by cathedral chapters were frustrated by political rivalries, with the result that Rome became increasingly involved in the appointment of bishops.

The exemption from episcopal supervision of reformed monasteries and the new mendicant orders founded by Francis and Dominic and the restricting of the canonization of saints to the pope, beginning with Pope Innocent III (1198–1216), also contributed to the growth of papal power.[38] Innocent claimed for himself the title "vicar of Christ," though previously it had been used for both kings and bishops. Innocent IV (1243–54) developed the idea that the pope was above Church law. The ancient sense of the Church as a communion of local churches gave way to a "universal ecclesiology" which saw the Church as a single organization with the pope at its head.[39]

Both the Conciliarist movement in the fourteenth and fifteenth centuries and the Reformation can be seen as reactions to the absolutizing of papal power and the abuses that accompanied it. The decree *Haec sancta*, promulgated by the Council of Constance (1414–1418), claimed its authority immediately from Christ; it asserted that its power was superior to that of the pope alone. Some use the context of the great western schism to explain *Haec sancta* as an emergency measure, but its doctrinal status continues to be debated.[40]

In spite of the Protestant attacks on the papacy, the question of primacy and the relation between the primate and the episcopacy was still too controversial for the Council of Trent (1545–1563) to address. But in the post-Tridentine period papal authority was strengthened. Trent had shown that genuine reform could be carried out without a restriction of papal authority, (the one exception being the great schism of 1378–1417). Other factors

---

[38] Schatz, *Papal Primacy*, 81–85; John M. Huels and Richard R. Gaillardetz also emphasize that the papacy became more involved in appointing or confirming bishops to protect local churches from powerful metropolitans or interference from secular rules, in "The Selection of Bishops: Recovering the Traditions," *The Jurist* 59 (1999) 364–65.

[39] See Paul McPartlan, "The Same but Different: Living in Communion," in *Authority in the Roman Catholic Church: Theory and Practice*, ed. Bernard Hoose (Burlington, VT: Ashgate, 2002) 154–55; Haight, *Historical Ecclesiology*, 339.

[40] See Schatz, *Papal Primacy*, 106–14.

contributing to the growth of papal authority included the establishment of the Roman Office of the Inquisition (1542), later called the Holy Office, the establishment of permanent nunciatures or papal embassies in many countries, particularly under Pope Gregory XIII (1572–1585), the fact that acceptance of the papal authority in the post-Reformation period became a sign of Catholic identity, and the strong support for the papacy from the new Jesuit order.[41]

Yes

It would be a mistake to attribute the growth of papal authority through the centuries simply to Roman self-aggrandizement. More accurately, it was a result of a complex dialectic between the Roman church, recognized as the center of communion and symbol of unity, and its bishops, some of whom like Gregory VII truly sought reform, and changing social and political conditions. The collapse of the old system of regional synods and powerful metropolitans, interference in Church affairs by powerful secular rulers, bishops unwilling to carry out reform or paralyzed by local rivalries, and the threats to Church freedom and teaching authority in the chaos that followed the French Revolution all contributed to the development of papal primacy.

The First Vatican Council

The doctrinal high water mark in this development was reached at Vatican I (1869–70), though the council, interrupted by war, dealt only with primacy and infallibility. Its dogmatic constitution, *Pastor aeternus*, must be understood against the background of Gallicanism, the Enlightenment, and the struggles of the Church against nineteenth century liberalism. According to *Pastor aeternus*, the Roman Pontiff has a primacy of jurisdiction over the universal Church, not only in regard to faith and morals, but also in those things that relate to the discipline and government of the Church throughout the world, thus over churches, pastors, and faithful (DS 3064). Unable to move to the second session, the council did not address the planned schema on the Church, which would have provided a broader context for its teaching on the papacy.

Still the constitution made clear that the pope's supreme power did not detract from the power of the bishops. A 1998 reflection by the Congregation for the Doctrine of the Faith underlined that the concern of *Pastor aeternus* was to stress that there is no higher authority to which the Roman pontiff must answer juridically: *prima sedes a nemine judicatur*. "This does not mean, however, that the pope has absolute power. Listening to what the

[41] Ibid., 129–33.

churches are saying is, in fact, an earmark of the ministry of unity, a consequence also of the unity of the episcopal body and of the *sensus fidei* of the entire people of God."[42] However, the pope's jurisdiction was not as carefully qualified at Vatican I as was his exercise of the Church's infallibility.

The council declared that the pope when speaking *ex cathedra*, that is, from the chair of Peter, "is possessed of that infallibility with which the Divine Redeemer willed that his Church should be endowed for defining doctrine regarding faith or morals: and that therefore such definitions of the Roman Pontiff are irreformable of themselves (*ex sese*), and not from the consent of the Church" (DS 3074). The often misunderstood *ex sese* clause means only that such definitions do not need a subsequent ratification or confirmation by the Church, as the fourth Gallican Article of March 19, 1682 held.[43]

Even in the occasional exercise of the extraordinary or infallible magisterium, the pope is defining what the Church believes. This was evident in the only two cases of infallible definitions by the extraordinary papal magisterium, the Immaculate Conception of Mary (1854) and her Assumption (1950), both of which were made only after a process of consulting the faith of the Catholic Church through a polling of the bishops.

The Second Vatican Council

In practical terms, papal power continued to increase until the Second Vatican Council (1962–1965). But Vatican II's Dogmatic Constitution on the Church, *Lumen gentium*, marked a shift away from Vatican I's monarchical understanding of papal authority, towards a more collegial one. First, the council taught that the order of bishops, successor to the apostolic college, together with its head, the Roman Pontiff, "is the subject of supreme and full authority over the universal church," particularly at an ecumenical council (LG 22). Second, when united with the pope and with one another, the bishops also share in the infallibility "with which the divine redeemer wished to endow his church," particularly at an ecumenical council, but also when dispersed throughout the world but maintaining unity among themselves and with Peter's successor (LG 25). However, it is sometimes difficult to determine when something has been infallibly taught by "the ordinary universal magisterium," as this second case is

---

[42] CDF, "The Primacy of the Successor of Peter in the Mystery of the Church," (no. 10); *Origins* 28/32 (1999) 562.

[43] For the text, see Schatz, *Papal Primacy*, 189; Schatz reviews the origins of the doctrine of infallibility, 117–23.

called.[44] Finally, in governing the particular churches assigned to them the bishops themselves are vicars of Christ; they are not to be regarded as vicars of the Roman Pontiff "for they exercise a power which they possess in their own right" (LG 27).

J.M.R. Tillard notes that *Lumen gentium* did not change the teaching of Vatican I's *Pastor aeternus*, but placed it in a new context, balancing the office of the Roman Pontiff within the shared mission of the bishops who succeed to the role of the apostles. From this perspective, Church authority must be imagined differently; the Church must balance primacy with collegiality. The old pyramid is gone; the universal Church is not a monolithic structure, divided into administrative units (dioceses), but a communion of all the local churches. For *Lumen gentium*, hierarchical authority is grounded sacramentally, not on delegation from the pope.[45]

In a real sense the council sought to relocate the papacy within the Church, but unfortunately it was not able to spell out the boundaries that would maintain the proper tension between primacy and collegiality. In the view of Francis Oakley, Vatican II attempted to restore an element of constitutional balance to the governance of the Church, but having juxtaposed a sacramental ecclesiology of *communio* with a papalist ecclesiology of jurisdiction failed on both the theoretical and the practical level.[46] Schatz argues that the Church needs to recognize again the authority of supra-diocesan structures, national or regional episcopal conferences, that represent an independent expression of episcopal collegiality. "Only those who think in categories of personal, monarchical, individual power can arrive at the conclusion, foreign to the ancient Church, that supra-diocesan authorities can have no power over individual bishops unless it is given them by the pope."[47] Steps in this direction could restore the necessary tension between primacy and collegiality, enabling the Church to function as a true communion.

---

[44] See Francis A. Sullivan, "The 'Secondary Object' of Infallibility," *Theological Studies* 54 (1993) 536–50, at 549–50.

[45] Tillard, *The Bishop of Rome*, 36–41.

[46] Francis Oakley, "Constitutionalism in the Church?" in *Governance, Accountability, and the Future of the Catholic Church*, ed. Francis Oakley and Bruce Russett (New York: Continuum, 2004) 79–80; see Walter Kasper's discussion of the compromise nature of the term "*communio hierarchia*," in his *Theology and Church*, trans. Margaret Kohl (New York: Crossroad, 1989) 158.

[47] Schatz, *Papal Primacy*, 181.

The Scripture Principle

One of the hallmarks of the Reformation was its replacing the Church's teaching office with the sovereign authority of Scripture, what is often referred to as the Scripture principle. The slogan *"sola Scriptura,"* the Bible alone, is a product of the classical Reformation. We need to consider briefly the Scripture principle within Protestantism, and some of the factors that have undermined that principle in more recent times.

For the first fifteen hundred years of the Church's life, the authority of the Church's tradition and that of Scripture were inseparable. The Bible did not stand alone as an authority; it was not considered sufficient by itself. It was always read and understood within the context of the Church's tradition, particularly its liturgy. Disputed questions were answered by appealing to the fathers and in case of a plurality of opinions, to that which was closest to Scripture. Particularly difficult questions were decided by the bishops gathered in council. George Tavard has called this the "classical conception," the inseparability of "Holy Writ and Holy Church,"[48] or as Jaroslav Pelikan puts it, the concept of authority in which the Scriptures were "only a part—though, to be sure, the supreme part—of an entire system of apostolic authority embracing the creedal tradition and the monarchical episcopate as well."[49]

However the classical conception began to break down at the end of the thirteenth century. Henry of Ghent suggested that in case of a difference between Scripture and Church, the authority of Scripture should be preferred. Marsilius of Padua took a similar position. William of Ockham argued that Scripture, properly interpreted, was superior to the authority of the pope.[50] But what became known as the "Scripture principle" emerged from the insistence of the sixteenth century Reformers that no authority was on a par with Scripture.

In holding the Bible up against the Church, the Reformers made the authority of Scripture supreme. They did not however simply reject tradition, as we noted earlier. Though they believed that Christian doctrine and practice must be based on Scripture, doctrines that could not be established by Scripture alone were rejected. From this perspective what was to become the key issue was how the meaning of Scripture was to be determined in controversial cases, and thus, the question of interpretation or hermeneutics.

[48] George H. Tavard, *Holy Writ or Holy Church: The Crisis of the Protestant Reformation* (New York: Harper, 1969) 244.

[49] Jaroslav Pelikan, *Luther the Expositor: Introduction to the Reformer's Exegetical Writings* (St. Louis: Concordia, 1959) 83.

[50] Tavard, *Holy Writ or Holy Church*, 23–31.

Reformation Hermeneutics

Luther presupposed "the clarity of Scripture."[51] The meaning of Scripture emerged when it was interpreted according to sound principles, foremost among them his own doctrine of justification, the "pure Gospel."[52] Thus, difficult or unclear passages were to be interpreted in light of this principle, throwing Luther's "pure Gospel" on texts that were not clear; "This is the true method of interpretation which puts Scripture alongside of Scripture in a right and proper way."[53] Other Reformers followed him in this; they spoke of "interpreting Scripture from Scripture" (*Scriptura sui ipsius interpres*).[54]

But Luther's approach ultimately meant not only that the Word or Scripture became independent of the Church, but also that Scripture itself became subject to Luther's doctrinal construction of the "pure Gospel." Luther had appealed to tradition, for example, to the fathers of the Church in his arguments with Karlstadt and Zwingli.[55] So did other early Reformers, as Daniel Williams, a Baptist patrologist argues; for them the "Tradition" (as opposed to "false" traditions) included the ecumenical creeds, writings of the early fathers, and the worship of the Church.[56] But unfortunately, recourse to history did not become normative in the subsequent Reformation tradition. Instead, in the post-Reformation period a doctrine of Scripture developed that saw Scripture as an independent dogmatic locus and infallible rule of faith, exclusive of any other authority, including the Church.[57] Furthermore, as Sandra Schneiders argues, the effect of "Luther's emancipation of interpretation from dogmatic tutelage was to assign to the reader the ultimate responsibility for interpreting the text rightly."[58]

---

[51] The best known locus for this position is his *Bondage of the Will* (1525), written against Erasmus; see Erling T. Teigen, "The Clarity of Scripture and Hermeneutical Principles in the Lutheran Confessions," *Concordia Theological Quarterly* 46 (1982) 147–66.

[52] Tavard, *Holy Writ or Holy Church*, 92.

[53] Ibid., 85, citing Luther's *Answer to Goat Emser*, vol. 3, p. 334.

[54] Brevard S. Childs, *Biblical Theology in Crisis* (Philadelphia: The Westminster Press, 1970) 110.

[55] Pelikan, *Luther the Expositor*, 120.

[56] Daniel H. Williams (ed.), *The Free Church and the Early Church: Bridging the Historical and Theological Divide* (Grand Rapids, MI: William B. Eerdmans, 2002), in his "Scripture, Tradition, and the Church: Reformation and Post-Reformation," 105–07.

[57] Ibid., 120–21.

[58] Sandra M. Schneiders, *The Revelatory Text; Interpreting the New Testament as Sacred Scripture* (Collegeville, MN: The Liturgical Press, 1999) 21–22.

Crisis of the Scripture Principle

The Reformation's separation of Scripture from the authority of the Church worked as long as the consensus on the clarity of Scripture prevailed.[59] But that consensus began to break down, particularly in the eighteenth century. Under the influence of Enlightenment biblical theology, hitherto a normative discipline, was transformed into a critical one.[60] Religion was to be investigated "objectively." Schneiders argues that this meant that the Bible was to be interpreted according to the same methods as any other historical text, with the result that for critical biblical scholars the Bible came to be for all practical purposes an exclusively historical document rather than a revelatory or spiritually fruitful one.[61]

Brevard Childs locates the crisis in the fact that for those in what was called the biblical theology movement, the biblical canon was no longer the context for the interpretation of Scripture. This meant that the Scriptures were no longer rooted within the community and life of the Church. Assuming that one came to the biblical text from some point outside it, biblical scholars sought some hermeneutical or interpretative principle on which to base the normative meaning of the Scripture. For some, it was a form of the "canon within the canon" principle.[62] For example, finding himself confronted with a theologically unacceptable "early Catholicism" in the latter books of the New Testament, Ernst Käsemann chose a canon within the canon based on what he considered the Pauline center, as we have seen.[63] Others sought to ground what was normative in Scripture on some ontology, ethical theory, or secular humanism, or in some theory such as Cullmann's "salvation history," Bultmann's "self-understanding," or Ebeling-Fuchs' "linguisticality of being,"[64] in other words, in some hermeneutical principle outside the text. Many liberal Protestants today speak of a continuing revelation that goes beyond the biblical canon, using John 16:13, Jesus' promise that the Spirit will lead the disciples into all truth.

The result of this development was that the meaning of Scripture was to be determined, not by its place in the faith and life of the Church, but

---

[59] Interestingly, according to Teigen, Luther's most explicit statements on the clarity of Scripture come in his discussion of the presence of Christ in the Lord's Supper; Teigen, "Clarity of Scripture," 153–55; cf. Pelikan, *Luther the Expositor*, 137–56.

[60] Cf. Gerhard Ebeling, *Word and Faith*, trans. James W. Leitch (Philadelphia: Fortress, 1963), "The Meaning of 'Biblical Theology'," 79–97.

[61] Schneiders, *The Revelatory Text*, 22–23.

[62] Childs, *Biblical Theology in Crisis*, 102.

[63] Ibid., 70; see Ernst Käsemann, *Essays on New Testament Themes*, trans. W. J. Montague (London: SCM, 1964) 63–134.

[64] Childs, *Biblical Theology in Crisis*, 102.

either on the basis of some canon within the canon that relativized the whole on the basis of a presumed core or "center," or on the basis of some *a priori* hermeneutical principle. The former locates the principle of interpretation within the canon, in some presumed "pure Gospel" or "center," the latter places it outside the canon, risking an arbitrary reconstruction determined by a scholar's particular methods and concerns. Thus, biblical theology has been trumped, whether by philosophical theology or historical criticism, and the Scripture principle itself has been overturned.

The collapse of the Scripture principle has too often left contemporary Protestant theology with two alternatives. One is that represented by liberal theology. The other is some form of biblical literalism or fundamentalism. Many Evangelicals, fearful of the "slippery slope" of Protestant liberalism, have chosen the latter. Without a teaching office, able to rethink and reformulate the tradition, they cling to a doctrine of biblical inerrancy that in the final analysis is philosophical and confessional rather than biblical and attributes an infallibility to the Bible, interpreted literally, that Catholics wouldn't dream of attributing to the pope. Furthermore, as Daniel Williams argues, "the assumption that the New Testament needs no external mediation—such as tradition or Church—to be clearly understood" belongs to the Free Church perspective of the radical reformation. "It is this Free church perspective that tends to govern Evangelical ideologies of church and faith today."[65]

Catholic and Protestant Perspectives

Catholic Perspectives

Roman Catholics consider the magisterium or teaching office as a gift to the Church. They recognize that their understanding of the apostolic tradition grows and deepens through the contemplation and study of believers and the preaching of the bishops who have received the charism of truth (DV 8). Thus, the magisterium does more than simply protect the faith; when functioning properly, it ensures that the Catholic tradition remains a living tradition, able to reinterpret traditional teachings in language more appropriate to the time, address new questions, and occasionally reach new answers. It has helped the Church come to appreciate the value of a historical critical approach to biblical scholarship and to rethink traditional positions on questions such as salvation outside the Church,

[65] Daniel H. Williams, "The Search for *Sola Scriptura* in the Early Church," *Interpretation* 52/4 (1998) 358.

ecumenism, religious liberty, and interreligious dialogue. At the same time many Catholics argue that the contemporary Church's leadership is insufficiently responsive to the sense of the faithful (*sensus fidelium*), that there is little accountability in the Church's government, and that pressing issues and concerns in the Church's life are being ignored.[66]

In the period after the Council of Trent, teaching authority increasingly became centered in the papacy. What was lost was the sense for the dialectical tension between the diverse charisms in the Church.[67] Vatican I, with its definition of papal primacy and infallibility, represents the dogmatic high water mark of this development. But even during this period there was provision to include some who did not hold the episcopal office in the Church's councils. Avery Dulles has pointed out that cardinals, abbots, and general superiors of religious orders took part as voting members at Trent, Vatican I, and Vatican II.[68]

Some Catholics misunderstand the magisterium as a teaching authority placed over the Church rather than an office through which the faith entrusted to the entire Church comes to expression. From this perspective the magisterium was described as the *ecclesia docens*, the "teaching Church," placed over and separate from the *ecclesia discens*, the "learning Church." Similarly, some Catholics continue to imagine the pope as the source, after God, from which all power and authority flow and as the chief decision-maker for contemporary questions. Such people still perceive the Church monarchically. Disputed questions are answered simply by citing what the pope has said. Thus complicated questions are decided on the basis of an appeal to authority, and the whole complex process of doctrinal development is ignored. This approach represents the Catholic version of the fundamentalist attitude, though it is a papal or magisterial fundamentalism rather than a biblical one.

In the real order, the magisterium functions quite differently. The Holy Spirit is active in the whole Church, not just in the hierarchy. The doctrine of the *sensus fidelium* shows that the Church's doctrines and dogmas emerge out of the faith of the entire Church.[69] The formulation of doctrine

---

[66] See *Governance, Accountability, and the Future of the Catholic Church*, ed. Francis Oakley and Bruce Russett (New York; Continuum, 2004).

[67] See Avery Dulles, *The Resilient Church: The Necessity and Limits of Adaption* (Garden City, NY: Doubleday, 1977) 102.

[68] Dulles, *A Church to Believe In*, 111.

[69] See Gaillardetz, *By What Authority?* 107–20; also Francis A. Sullivan, "The Sense of Faith: The Sense/Consensus of the Faithful," in *Authority in the Roman Catholic Church*, 85–93.

is not based on a majority opinion, but develops out of a consensus that under the guidance of the Holy Spirit embraces both pastors and laity (LG 12). At the same time, when Rome continues to defend disputed positions as certain, without discussion on the part of the bishops, against the opinion of the majority of theologians, and without taking into account the views of the laity, many are scandalized.

Dulles has proposed a pluralistic model of authority. Recognizing that authority can only teach what the whole Church believes, he places primary emphasis on the general sense of the faithful, with the important qualification that the views of "committed Christians should be given more weight than those of indifferent or marginal Christians," even though the views of the latter should also be considered.[70] And there are others who speak with special authority. First, professional theologians have an authority based on their competence or scholarship. Secondly, there must always be room for prophetic voices in the Church, men and women who can help the Church discern the truth through prophetic insight. Finally, the bishops speak with an authority based on their sacramental ordination to the Church's pastoral office, assisted by the graces particular to it. These doctoral, prophetic, and pastoral ministries have been present within the Church since biblical times.[71]

Thus, without denying the teaching authority that Vatican II ascribed to the order of bishops as successors to the apostles, there are theological reasons as well as historical precedents for finding ways for others with theological, ministerial, or professional competence to have some part in the exercise of the Church's magisterium. The Church, both Roman Catholic and Orthodox, needs again today to recognize the pluralistic sources of teaching authority with which it has been gifted.

Protestant Perspectives

On the Protestant side, the Scripture principle worked well enough in the first centuries of Protestantism. But the emergence of biblical theology as a critical rather than normative discipline in the eighteenth and nineteenth centuries raised hermeneutical problems about the meaning of Scripture that continue to divide both theologians and churches. Some Protestant churches have been able to move forward on new questions, for example, the ordination of women, and have taken significant steps towards full communion with traditions from whom they have long been

---

[70] Dulles, *The Resilient Church*, 100.
[71] Ibid., 100–01.

separated. Yet positions taken on divisive questions such as divorce, abortion, euthanasia, and the full inclusion of homosexual Christians, including ordaining those living in homosexual relationships, continue to trouble these churches and threaten further divisions.

Conservative Protestants are scandalized by what they see as an abandoning of biblical teaching in the more liberal churches. In response, many have adopted a biblical literalism or fundamentalism. Aware of the charge that they have turned the Scripture principle into a warrant for private interpretation, independent of the great tradition of the Church, some Evangelicals are showing a new interest in the fathers, creeds, and councils of the Church.[72] Daniel Williams is one of them; he calls for a reappraisal of the concept of *sola Scriptura* as it impacts the faith of Protestant and particularly Free Church Protestants.[73]

But the fundamental problem is structural. Without an authoritative teaching office able to assist in rethinking traditional answers and the binding nature of a tradition they do not always acknowledge, most conservative Protestants have been unable to move beyond traditional positions, many based on a literal reading of the text. For example, both the Roman Catholic Church and many mainline Protestants have rethought the traditional "no salvation outside the Church" principle that dates from the early Church. But conservative Protestants insist on what to them are biblical grounds that salvation is impossible apart from an explicit confession of faith in Jesus. Thus they remain locked into a position that hampers them in their efforts to dialogue with other religious traditions.

The fact that some conservative traditions have unacknowledged teaching offices or *magisteria* can cause even more problems. At the same time, the Fourth World Conference on Faith and Order, a meeting at Montreal in 1963 which had some Catholic participants, found considerable convergence on the relation between Scripture and tradition. We will consider both of these issues in chapter ten.

Conclusion

Christians in every age have been concerned about guarding the faith once for all delivered to the saints (Jude 1:3), though they differ about how that is to be done and what is to be the role of the Church. Roman Catholics

[72] See Thomas C. Oden, *The Rebirth of Orthodoxy: Signs of New Life in Christianity* (San Francisco: HarperSanFrancisco, 2003).
[73] Williams, "Scripture, Tradition, and the Church," 124, in his *The Free Church and the Early Church.*

see the bishops teaching in communion with the pope as "witnesses of divine and catholic truth" (LG 25). Orthodox Christians also see the Church's bishops as teaching with authority when gathered in council.

Protestant Christians take Scripture as the norm for all doctrine; teachings that are not demonstrable from Scripture cannot be considered binding. For many Protestants, the isolation of the Scripture from the tradition of the Church has resulted in the hegemony of private interpretation that continues to fragment the Church into a vast multiplicity of denominations. Yet none of these solutions to safeguarding the faith seems fully adequate today.

The contemporary Church needs a credible teaching authority to proclaim its faith authentically and occasionally to update and reformulate its teaching in the light of new understandings and complex problems not addressed in its Scriptures. The development of doctrine is always a complex process, involving the work of theologians, the sense of the faithful, the process of reception, and the authoritative teaching of the Church's pastors, particularly its bishops. The discernment of Christian truth needs to take this complex process into account. It is not discerned simply by citing some magisterial pronouncement, even of a pope. Nor can difficult questions be resolved by appealing to the infallibility of Scripture. Both of these approaches risk falling into a species of fundamentalism, whether of the Bible or the magisterial text.

The Spirit is limited to neither hierarchy nor text; it is present in the whole Church. As a community in the Spirit, all members of the Church are mutually interdependent—pastors, theologians, prophets, and faithful. The Church is a communion in its essential nature.

CHAPTER 7

The Marks of the Church

In reaffirming the christological faith of Nicaea, the bishops gathered at the First Council of Constantinople in 381 added a final article, confessing belief in "one, holy, catholic and apostolic church," four descriptors that would subsequently be known as the marks of the Church.[1] Though not the only marks, they have become traditional. Augustine listed five indicators or characteristics of the Church: security of faith, universal consent, authority, a succession in the priesthood from the seat of Peter, and the name "catholic" itself. He adds, "though all heretics wish to be called Catholics, yet when a stranger asks where the Catholic Church meets, no heretic will venture to point to his own chapel or house."[2] Martin Luther and the later Lutheran confessions refer to baptism, the Lord's Supper, and the preached word of God ("baptism, the bread, and, most importantly of all, the gospel") as signs of the Church,[3] while Luther added the cross and suffering as belonging among the marks.[4] Some Evangelical churches, uncomfortable with having to affirm *credimus catholicam ecclesiam*, have abandoned the word *catholic*, in spite of the fact many of

[1] *Decrees of the Ecumenical Councils*, Vol. One; *Nicaea I to Lateran V*, ed. Norman P. Tanner (Washington: Georgetown University Press, 1990) 24; earlier Cyril of Jerusalem so characterized the Church in his *Catechetical Lectures*. The article, part of what is known as the Nicene-Constantinopolitan Creed, is common to Roman Catholic, Orthodox, and mainline Protestant churches (though the Orthodox omit the *filioque* clause, added to the creed in the West in the eleventh century stating that the Spirit proceeds from the Father *and* the Son).

[2] Augustine, *Contra Ep. Manichaei* 4,5; PL 42:175.

[3] See Gordon W. Lathrop and Timothy J. Wengert, *Christian Assembly: Marks of the Church in a Pluralistic Age* (Minneapolis: Fortress Press, 2004) 17–36, at 27; *WA* 7:720.

[4] See Walther von Loewenich, *Luther's Theology of the Cross* (Belfast: Christian Journals, 1976) 127.

their sixteenth and seventeenth century ancestors had no difficulties with the word.[5]

But what does it mean to confess that the Church is one, holy, catholic, and apostolic? It is fairly obvious that the contemporary Church in its divided state is not one, but many, unless one resorts to an ecclesiology which makes the *ecclesia catholica* invisible. This is the approach of most Pentecostals, who stress the spiritual and invisible nature of the Church.[6] Again, if the Church is holy, it is also a Church of sinners, even a sinful Church, though official Catholicism does not like to use this language. If some churches are still uncomfortable with the word "catholic," none would deny that they are apostolic, though what constitutes the Church's apostolicity has been differently understood and remains a neuralgic question.

At times in Christian history, the "marks" of the Church have been used apologetically, to identify the "one true Church." Others, more sensitive to the difficulty of predicating the marks of the actual Church as it exists in history, have tended to conceive the marks more as gifts of God and tasks to be achieved,[7] or even as eschatological qualities, to be realized only in the fullness of time. Neither the "one true Church" theology nor the ecclesial relativism so popular today represents an adequate approach. The first ignores the role of the Spirit in constituting the Church, while the second too easily overlooks questions of apostolic origin, faithfulness to the tradition, and realization of the Church's fundamental nature. In its complexity, the Church is both visible and invisible, one and many, mystical body and visible assembly, united by the Spirit and expressed in structures of sacraments, ecclesiastical government, and communion (cf. LG 8). In this chapter we will consider the traditional marks of the Church and the different ecclesiological types, Catholic, Reformed, and Restorationist, which reflect the historical origins of the different ecclesial traditions.

The Church Is One

The Church is at once one and many. We saw earlier that Paul uses the word *ekklēsia* in several senses. Most often, he uses it for the local church,

[5] See Timothy George, "Towards an Evangelical Ecclesiology," in *Catholics and Evangelicals: Do They Share a Common Future?* ed. Thomas P. Rausch (New York: Paulist, 2000) 136–37.

[6] See Veli-Matti Kärkkäinen, *An Introduction to Ecclesiology: Ecumenical, Historical and Global Perspectives* (Downers Grove, IL: InterVarsity Press, 2002) 73.

[7] Cf. Hans Küng, *The Church*, trans. Ray and Rosaleen Ockenden (New York: Sheed and Ward, 1967) 268; see also Francis A. Sullivan, *The Church We Believe In: One, Holy, Catholic and Apostolic* (New York: Paulist, 1988) 214–15.

as in "the church of God that is in Corinth" (1 Cor 1:2; cf. Rom 16:16), though he occasionally uses it in an absolute sense (1 Cor 12:28).

In the Deutero-Pauline letters, Colossians and Ephesians, this absolute or universal sense of Church is much more common. Colossians begins by speaking of Christ as "head of the body, the church" (Col 1:18). The author of Ephesians uses a number of metaphors to express the unity of Jews and Gentiles, reconciled in "one body" (Eph 2:16). They are fellow citizens, members of the household of God, built upon the foundation of the apostles and prophets, with Christ Jesus himself as the capstone, a whole structure, a sacred temple, a dwelling place of God (Eph 2:19-22), joined together with Christ, the head, bringing about its growth and building itself up in love (Eph 4:15-16). The first letter of Peter stresses the Church as the People of God (1 Pet 2:5-10). In the fourth gospel Jesus speaks of his intention that there be "one flock, one shepherd" (John 10:16).

In the Introduction we found that Käsemann overstates his argument that the New Testament represents a foundation, not for the unity of the Church but only for the multiplicity of the confessions. While the different churches were able to tolerate considerable diversity, they maintained communion (*koinōnia*) with each other.[8] In the post New Testament period, the local churches were joined into a communion of churches by visible signs such as eucharistic hospitality, letters of communion, communion between the bishops themselves, and as early as the third century, communion with the bishop of Rome.[9] That those bonds were real is evident from the ability of bishops to join together at councils to resolve divisive issues, as they did at the early councils of the fourth and fifth centuries.

Loss of Communion

Unfortunately, the churches were not able to sustain those bonds of communion. Differences in Christology resulted in the loss of communion with East Syrian churches after the Council of Ephesus (431) and again with the Copts and Armenians after Chalcedon (451). The first great division came in 1054 when tensions between Rome and Constantinople led to a loss of communion between the eastern churches and the Latin west. Then the Reformation in the sixteenth century shattered the unity of the western Church. With the charism of unity lost, churches continued to divide. Today over some two billion Christians are divided into a multiplicity

---

[8] See Küng, *The Church*, 295.

[9] See Ludwig Hertling, *Communio: Church and Papacy in Early Christianity*, trans. with an intro. Jared Wicks (Chicago: Loyola University Press, 1972) 23–36.

of churches and denominations (30,000 according to some). Roman Catholics number over a billion; in addition there are some 342 million mainstream Protestants, another 386 million "Independents," made up of Pentecostals, African-instituted and other independent churches, 215 million Orthodox, and 79 million Anglicans.[10]

Can we speak of an originally undivided Church? Congar notes that Protestant theologians reject this idea as a fiction.[11] While seeking to avoid a simplistic idea of original unity, he makes the case for a unity which allows for diversity; it is evident in accepting "the fundamental dogmas of the *regula fidei* and the baptismal confession of faith," and particularly, an understanding of the sacramental nature of the Church which he calls "the common foundation of the ecclesiologies of East and West." It is in this sense that we can speak of the undivided church.[12]

The Roman Catholic and Orthodox churches continue to profess belief in one Church.[13] Vatican II taught that the Church is both a "visible organization" and "spiritual community" (LG 8). To be fully incorporated into the Church one must be united in the visible structure of the Church with Christ "who rules it through the Supreme Pontiff and the bishops" (LG 14). The bishops are the visible source of unity in their own particular churches, constituted after the model of the universal Church, while "it is in and from these that the one and unique catholic church exists" (LG 23). Anglicans also require the episcopate for the unity of their communion.[14] For the Orthodox, the local Church is fully Church, gathered around its bishop and united by the Eucharist,[15] though some Orthodox theologians acknowledge that "the unity of the Orthodox Church is becoming a sort of abstract ideal, with no means of manifesting itself in the real life of the Church."[16]

[10] *World Christian Encyclopedia*, ed. David B. Barrett, George T. Kurian, and Todd M. Johnson (New York: Oxford University Press, 2001) 4.

[11] Yves Congar, *Diversity and Community*, trans. John Bowden (Mystic, CT: Twenty-Third Publications, 1985) 19.

[12] Ibid., 21.

[13] See Kallistos Ware, *The Orthodox Church*, rev. ed. (London: Penguin, 1993), Section I.

[14] The Lambeth Quadrilateral bases Anglican faith and order on scripture, the creeds, the sacraments, and the historic episcopate.

[15] John D. Zizioulas, *Being as Communion: Studies in Personhood and Church* (Crestwood, NY: St. Vadimir's Seminary Press, 1985) 250–51.

[16] Nicholas Afanassieff, "The Church Which Presides in Love," in *The Primacy of Peter: Essays in Ecclesiology and the Early Church*, ed. John Meyendorff (Crestwood, NY: St. Vladimir's Seminary Press, 1992) 143.

Vatican II uses the word Church for the separated "Churches of the East" (UR 14) that are recognized as possessing true sacraments as well as the priesthood and the Eucharist (UR 15). Though the council did not use this language of the separated "ecclesial communities" in the West,[17] it did not go so far as to declare that they are not churches in the proper sense as has sometimes been alleged.[18] They are called ecclesial communities because the Church of Christ is in some way present in them, even if imperfectly; "they are analogous to particular churches of the Catholic Church."[19] Thus according to Vatican II, the one Church of Christ is present in some way beyond the boundaries of the Roman Catholic Church which remains "joined in many ways" in the Holy Spirit to the baptized in other churches and ecclesial communities (LG 15).

The Reformers were greatly influenced by Augustine's Platonic distinction between the visible Church and the true, invisible Church.[20] Luther's view of the visibility of the Church was complex; he saw the Church as visible in its preaching and sacraments, but remaining hidden in its fellowship before God. The Lutheran Augsburg Confession defines the "one holy Christian church" as "the assembly of all believers among whom the Gospel is preached in its purity and the holy sacraments are administered according to the Gospel." This is "sufficient (*satis est*) for the true unity of the Christian church," rather than that "ceremonies instituted by men be observed uniformly in all places" (CA 7). For Calvin the Church is a visible community that includes all the baptized, but he notes that Scripture also speaks of the Church as comprised of all the elect from the beginning of the world, and thus as invisible.[21] In the final analysis, Calvin's distinction between the visible and invisible Church is eschatological.[22] However for many Protestants today, the universal Church is invisible, becoming visible only in the local congregation.

The Free Church tradition has its roots in the Anabaptist movement, often referred to as the Radical Reformation. Its congregationalist ecclesiology privileges 1 Corinthians over later New Testament letters such as the Pastoral Epistles.[23] Many in this tradition follow the ecclesiological principle

---

[17] The council acknowledged the "special place" of the Anglican communion (UR 15).

[18] For example, in the document of the Congregation for the Doctrine of the Faith, "*Dominus Iesus*," *Origins* 30 (September 14, 2000) (no. 17).

[19] Sullivan, *The Church We Believe In*, 54.

[20] See Wallace Alston, *The Church of the Living God* (Louisville, KY: Westminster John Knox, 2002) 53.

[21] Calvin, *Institutes* IV,1,7.

[22] Kärkkäinen, *Introduction to Ecclesiology*, 52.

[23] Ibid., 66; for his review of Free Church ecclesiology, see 59–67.

of the first Baptist, John Smyth, for whom the Church is the gathering of two or three faithful, separated from the world and united by a covenant in Christ.[24] This ecclesiology according to Miroslav Volf "allows us to speak only of a plurality of churches rather than of the *one* church."[25] But such an ecclesiology risks becoming individualistic, separatist, and reductively eschatological; it does not require sacramental relations between churches as a condition of ecclesiality, but only that each church retains an *openness* towards all other churches.[26] Openness however is not communion, a network of relationships uniting the Church of Christ, enabling it to function as "one" in its witness, ministry, and ecclesial life. For Volf, the Church's universality remains a dimension of the local church's eschatological future.[27]

Unity or universality cannot simply be reduced to an eschatological designation. As Richard Gaillardetz says, "the Body of Christ is one and cannot be fragmented. Therefore one must be able to speak of a unity, a communion, existing among all eucharistic communities."[28] To the extent that the Church's unity is impaired, or realized only imperfectly, the one Church itself becomes a less credible sign of the reconciliation of all peoples in Christ Jesus (cf. Eph 2:14-22). Thus all Christians are called to work for the unity of the Church.

The Church Is Holy

When a man addresses Jesus as "good teacher" in Mark's Gospel, Jesus responds, "Why do you call me good? No one is good but God alone" (Mark 10:18). One might say the same thing about holiness; God alone is holy. The idea of holiness, from the Hebrew root *kds*, means separate, set apart. God is the "wholly other," so different from human beings that from the perspective of the early Hebrew tradition coming into God's presence or seeing God's face could be fatal (Judg 6:22; 13:22). When Moses asks to see God's face, God responds "no man sees me and still lives" (Exod 33:20). Rudolf Otto captures this terrifying and yet fascinating character of the numinous in his seminal book, *The Idea of the Holy*, the "*mysterium tremendum et*

---

[24] John Smyth, *The Works of John Smyth*, ed. W. T. Whitley (Cambridge: Cambridge University Press, 1915) 403; see Miroslav Volf, *After Our Likeness: The Church as the Image of the Trinity* (Grand Rapids, MI: William B. Eerdmans, 1998) 10, 175.

[25] Volf, *After Our Likeness*, 157.

[26] Ibid., 156–57.

[27] Ibid., 203.

[28] Richard R. Gaillardetz, *By What Authority? A Primer on Scripture, the Magisterium, and the Sense of the Faithful* (Collegeville, MN: the Liturgical Press, 2003) 67.

fascinans."[29] We are both drawn towards the holy, as Moses is drawn to the burning bush (Exod 3:5), and frightened by its manifestation.

Persons, places, and things are called holy in the Bible from their association with God. Israel is holy because of the covenant relationship with God, spelled out in the Decalogue; they are to be "a kingdom of priests, a holy nation" (Exod 19:5-6). Similarly, objects set apart for use in the cult or liturgy such as the tent of meeting, the temple, the altar, the sacred vestments, the priests, the Sabbath, the sacrifice—all these are considered holy, not in a magical sense, but because of their association with the divine.

The Church can also be called holy in this derivative sense. Though the New Testament does not predicate holiness of the Church, its earliest documents refer to the members of the Church as the holy ones (*hagioi*) or saints (Rom 1:7; 12:13; 15:25; 1 Cor 14:33; 16:1; Phil 4:22; Acts 9:13, 21). Their holiness is God's work (1 Thess 5:23); they have been "sanctified in Christ Jesus, called to be holy" (1 Cor 1:2), "sanctified by the holy Spirit" (Rom 15:16). Because of God's abiding presence, the Church is holy in this derivative sense. The community of Christians is "Christ's body" (1 Cor 12:27), "God's building" (1 Cor 3:9), "a temple sacred in the Lord" and "a dwelling place of God in the Spirit" (Eph 2:21-22).

The Church can also be called holy because God has given it holy gifts: the Word of God (Jas 1:21; 1 Pet 1:23), the Church's ministry (2 Cor 5:18; Eph 4:11-12), the sacraments (John 3:5; 20:23; 1 Cor 6:11; 11:27; Jas 5:14-15), particularly the Eucharist. For Tertullian, a holy Church meant the high moral quality of Christian living which Cyprian and the Donatists demanded at least of Church ministers. With Augustine the holiness of the Church became more objective, grounded in its doctrine and sacraments.[30] As we saw earlier, *communio sanctorum* can mean both a communion in holy things, most likely the orginal meaning, and a communion of holy people. To this day in the Eastern churches the deacon proclaims before Communion "God's holy gifts for God's holy people."

A Church of Sinners

But if the Church is holy, it is also a Church of sinners. Like the Eastern churches, official Catholicism is reluctant to speak of a sinful Church because it understands the Church as a sacrament (cf. LG 1). For Calvin, the Church's holiness is imperfect; "it makes progress from day to day but

[29] Rudolf Otto, *The Idea of the Holy* (New York: Oxford University Press, 1958).

[30] Roger Haight, *Christian Community in History*, Vol. I: *Historical Ecclesiology* (New York: Continuum, 2004) 261.

has not yet reached its goal of holiness" (*Institutes*, 4.1.17). The fathers at Vatican II acknowledged that the Church's holiness is an imperfect one; it remains "at once holy and always in need of purification" (LG 8); its radiance "shines less brightly" because of the sins of its members (UR 4), and as a pilgrim Church on the way it has need of "continual reformation" (UR 6), language similar to the Protestant emphasis on the Church always in need of reform (*ecclesia semper reformanda*). Many Protestants were deeply moved when the council fathers, speaking of sins against unity, asked "pardon of God and of our separated brethren, just as we forgive them that offend us" (UR 7).

For contemporary men and women, more conscious of the lights and shadows in the Church's history, the Church's holiness is not always evident. Indeed, the conduct of the Church has been a scandal for many. Pope John Paul II called for an examination of conscience and "purification of memory" as part of a great Jubilee Year celebration to mark the beginning of the Third Millennium. He repeatedly requested forgiveness for the sins of the Church's members, even sins done in the name of the Church; sins in the Church's efforts to defend the truth, sins against Christian unity, for violations of the rights of immigrants and ethnic groups, including the use of forms of evangelization that did not respect the dignity of other cultures and the conscience of individuals. He asked forgiveness of sins against the Jewish people, for sins against the dignity of women, and others, including the poor, the defenseless, and the unborn.[31] And many other Church leaders followed his example.

If the Church is holy, its holiness is less than perfect, and so all Christians are called to a conversion of personal and ecclesial life, so that the holiness of the Church might more clearly shine forth.

The Church Is Catholic

The catholicity of the Church is claimed by most traditions but there is considerable disagreement about what it means.[32] The Greek *katholikos* is derived from *kat' holos*, "according to the whole." Its basic meaning in the Greek of that period is full, whole, or general. The adjective is first applied to the Church perhaps as early as 110 by Ignatius of Antioch in his letter to the Smyrnaeans. "Wheresoever the bishop shall appear, there let the

---

[31] John Paul II, "Service Requesting Pardon," held at St. Peter's Basilica on the First Sunday of Lent, March 23, 2000; *Origins* 29/40 (2000) 645–48.

[32] See Avery Dulles, "The Concept of Catholicity," in his *The Catholicity of the Church* (Oxford: Clarendon Press, 1985) esp. 13–18.

people be; even as where Jesus may be, there is the universal [*katholikē*] Church" (Smyrn 8:2).[33]

Avery Dulles notes that the "fleeting" appearance of the adjective *katholikos* in Ignatius and later in Polycarp (c. 160) leaves the term open to various interpretations.[34] According to Francis Sullivan, Ignatius contrasts the bishop as head of the local congregation with Christ as head of the whole or universal (catholic) Church.[35] The Church is already understood in a universal sense in Colossians and Ephesians; the Church is the one body of Christ in which divisions between peoples, specifically Jews and Gentiles, have been overcome (Col 1:24-27; Eph 2:16-22). A similar usage appears in the *Didache* (9:4): "As this broken bread was scattered upon the mountains and being gathered together became one, so may Thy Church be gathered together from the ends of the earth into Thy kingdom."[36]

John Zizioulas maintains that the word "catholic" became identified with universal only in the fourth century.[37] Yet the way the word catholic is used in the *Martyrdom of Polycarp* (c. 156) suggests some awareness of its reference to the whole or universal Church in contrast to the local church and it is usually translated that way. Thus the letter addresses "all the brotherhoods of the holy and universal [*katholikēs*] Church sojourning in every place."[38] It describes Polycarp praying for "all the universal [*katholikēs ekklēsias*] Church throughout the world" (8, 1) just as Christ is "the shepherd of the universal Church which is throughout the world" (19, 2).[39]

Sullivan notes an exceptional use of the adjective in which Polycarp is described as "the bishop of the catholic church of Smyrna" (16, 2). He argues "in the course of the second century the orthodox Christians began to distinguish their church from the numerous heretical and schismatic sects on the grounds of the oneness and universality of the true church, in contrast to the multiplicity and locally limited nature of the sects."[40] J.N.D.

---

[33] See *The Apostolic Fathers*, J. B. Lightfoot (Grand Rapids, MI: Baker Books, 1987) 84.

[34] Dulles, *The Catholicity of the Church*, 14.

[35] Francis A. Sullivan, *From Apostles to Bishops: The Development of the Episcopacy in the Early Church* (New York: Paulist, 2001) 120.

[36] Lightfoot, *The Apostolic Fathers*, 126.

[37] Zizioulas, *Being as Communion*, 144, note 3; see also his *Eucharist, Bishop, Church: The Unity of the Church in the Divine Eucharist and the Bishop During the First Three Centuries*, trans. Elizabeth Theokritoff (Brookline, MA: Holy Cross Orthodox Press, 2001) 107–28.

[38] Salutation; Lightfoot, *Apostolic Fathers*, 109.

[39] Ibid., 115.

[40] Sullivan, *The Church We Believe In*, 85; he is citing *The Apostolic Fathers*, Vol. 2, ed. K. Lake (Cambridge, 1961) 334–35.

Kelly takes a similar position; "This then is the dominant meaning of 'catholic' from the second half of the second century onwards in East and West alike; it denotes the one, true Church of Christ as opposed to all heretical and schismatic groups, and points to the universality of the former as the guarantee of its authenticity."[41] This sense appears clearly in Augustine (d. 430), who uses the word catholic to distinguish the great or true Church from heretical groups or movements separate from it, as we saw earlier.[42]

Senses of Catholicity

Thus, the word catholic has been used in a number of senses. First, it refers to the Church in its fullness or totality. The catholicity of the Church implies the inclusion of all those reconciled in Christ and united in the Spirit, as the story of the birth of the Church on Pentecost suggests (Acts 2:5-11). A Church that excluded others on the basis of race, social status, or culture would not be catholic. Second, the term has been used in a geographical or universal sense for the Church present everywhere. Cyril of Jerusalem (d. 387) brought together a number of senses of the word when he described the Church as catholic because it extends to the ends of the earth, teaches all the doctrines necessary for salvation, instructs all peoples, heals every kind of sin, and possesses every virtue.[43] Finally, catholic has been used for the true Church, as opposed to heretical or sectarian communities.

While Roman Catholics stress catholicity as universality, Orthodox Christians understand it, not in reference to the universal extension of the Church, but as adherence to the truth proper to the Church, confessed by the Fathers, the confessors, and the martyrs, witnessed to by the ecumenical councils, and maintained by a living tradition.[44] They hold that the local Church as a eucharistic community is catholic because it represents the wholeness and totality of the one body of Christ.[45] For a community to be a catholic Church it must be both eucharistic and orthodox in doctrine.[46] Luther substituted the German word *christlich* (Christian) for catholic in

[41] J.N.D. Kelly, "'Catholic' and 'Apostolic' in the Early Centuries," *One in Christ* 6 (1970) 278.

[42] *Contr ep. Manichaei* 4.5; PL 42,175.

[43] *Catechesis* 18.

[44] See Vladimir Lossky, *In the Image and Likeness of God* (Crestwood, NY: St. Vladimir's Seminary Press, 1974) 169–81.

[45] Zizioulas, *Being as Communion*, 149; *Eucharist, Bishop, Church*, 107–28.

[46] Zizioulas, *Eucharist, Bishop, Church*, 256–57.

the Creed, though Melanchthon and other Reformers claimed catholicity for their churches on the basis of their adherence to the teachings of the ancient, undivided Church.[47]

From a Free Church perspective, Miroslav Volf distinguishes between qualitative or extensive understanding of catholicity and quantitative or intensive understanding. Though he argues that they are inseparable, he sees the quantitative dimension of catholicity, the universal expansion of the Church, as an eschatological notion to be realized only in the comprehensive reality of the new creation when God will be "all in all" (Eph 1:10; 1 Cor 15:28). The primary notion of catholicity is its qualitative sense, the fullness of salvation. In this way, by making the quantitative or universal sense of catholicity an eschatological notion, he is able to claim that each local Church is catholic in the full sense, for as each Church is constituted in the Spirit it has the fullness of salvation.[48] Yet Volf is aware that his argument could be interpreted in such a way that any group of Christians could claim to be a catholic Church, without any visible relation to a global Christian community. To avoid this, he argues that each Church should exhibit the "*external* marks of catholicity," openness to other churches, loyalty to the apostolic tradition, and a universal openness towards all human beings who profess faith in Christ.[49]

If catholicity can be understood analogously, it should not be defined too narrowly. It cannot be reduced to adherence to the Greek fathers of the fifth century as the Orthodox often suggest, or to the local Church gathered for Eucharist. Neither can it be limited to the "alleged universality of the Roman Catholic Church."[50] Nor can catholicity be reduced to the local Church's embodiment of salvific grace; a Church lacking real relations with other local churches does not adequately image the Church "spread throughout the world."[51]

Catholicity does not necessarily mean universal organization. But it does mean relationship, communion. A catholicity not visible is not real. A local Church shows itself to be catholic if it is in union with the communion of churches; "a Church which is not united with the rest of the Catholic Churches, i.e. with the *one body of Christ in all the world*, cannot

---

[47] Dulles, *The Catholicity of the Church*, 16.

[48] Volf, *After Our Likeness*, 266–67; universality also is an eschatological notion for Volf, 203; Dulles says that the adjective catholic can be predicated of every Christian church "in some measure," *The Catholicity of the Church*, 169.

[49] Ibid., 274–78.

[50] Dulles, The *Catholicity of the Church*, 19.

[51] Cyril of Jerusalem, *Catechesis* 18.

continue to be the Church of God."[52] That communion is both sacramental and hierarchical and for Catholics it includes communion with the bishop of Rome. Vatican II teaches that a fullness of catholicity belongs to the Catholic Church, though it acknowledges that because of the divisions among Christians, "the Church herself finds it more difficult to express in actual life her full catholicity in all its aspects" (UR 4).

Elements of catholicity appear also in other traditions. The rich theological, liturgical, and spiritual traditions of the Orthodox churches belong to the catholicity of the undivided Church. Some traditions express their catholicity through membership in world confessional families such as the Anglican Communion, the Lutheran World Federation, and the World Alliance of Reformed Churches, though each member Church generally remains juridically independent. Some of these Churches, for example the Lutherans and Anglicans in the United States,[53] have moved or are moving towards full ecclesial communion with each other. The World Council of Churches represents a desire for catholicity on the part of its members. The WCC is neither a Church nor a communion, but rather a council of some 347 independent churches or denominations, each of which remains free to disassociate itself from any position or statement taken by the council. If the Roman Catholic Church is to claim a fullness of catholicity, it has a special responsibility to find ways to include other churches in that fullness.

The Church Is Apostolic

The issue of apostolicity is perhaps the most difficult; Joseph Ratzinger calls tradition and the *successio apostolica* "the key question in the Catholic/Protestant debate."[54] While all Christian traditions agree that the Church today must be in succession to the apostles, there has been considerable difference about how apostolic succession should be understood since the Reformation in the sixteenth century. The Roman Catholic, Orthodox, and Anglican traditions have traditionally emphasized apostolicity in terms of succession in the historical episcopal office. Vatican II,

---

[52] Zizioulas, *Eucharist, Bishop, Church*, 259.

[53] See W. A. Norgren and William G. Rusch, (ed.), *Toward Full Agreement and Concordat of Agreement* (Augsburg: Fortress Press, 1991); Episcopalians in the U.S. approved the "Concordat of Agreement" in 1997; after some controversy the Evangelical Lutheran Church in America approved it at its assembly in 1999.

[54] Joseph Ratzinger, *Principles of Catholic Theology: Building Stones for a Fundamental Theology*, trans. Mary Frances McCarthy (San Francisco: Ignatius Press, 1987) 239.

stressing the collegial nature of the episcopal office (LG 22), teaches that the bishops have by divine institution taken the place of the apostles as pastors of the Church (LG 20). Orthodox theology recognizes the historical approach to apostolic continuity, but it places considerable emphasis on the eschatological approach. The Church in its eucharistic structure, with the presbyters surrounding the bishop, expresses God's eschatological gathering in peoples from all times and cultures. Thus it is "a *continuity of communities* and *Churches* that constitutes and expresses apostolic succession in this approach."[55]

The Reformers broke with the episcopally ordered Church in the sixteenth century, though the Lutherans did so only when the bishops showed themselves unwilling to ordain their pastors. Calvin taught that apostolicity meant conformity with the teaching of the apostles (*Institutes* 4.2.2-3). This became the basic position of the mainline Protestant and Evangelical churches; apostolic succession was understood in terms of succession in apostolic faith and life. They find the claim that apostolicity is guaranteed by succession in the episcopal office unconvincing. Pentecostals fear attempts to maintain the apostolic faith through creeds and the *Regulae Fidei* work against unity.[56] They claim that apostolicity is demonstrated by apostolic life, particularly by the charismatic gifts and miraculous powers individual Christians received through the "Baptism in the Spirit."[57] Cecil Robeck argues that "By opening up the possibility that God can chose—today—to use *any individual* in the service of the Church *in any way God chooses to do so*, Pentecostals, Charismatics, as well as many independent denominations have offered a level of personal and corporate empowerment or enablement to their people that seems to be more in keeping with the Apostolic Tradition than that which is held in many other Christian groups."[58]

---

[55] See Zizioulas, "Apostolic Continuity and Succession," in *Being as Communion*, at 177.

[56] See Cecil M. Robeck, Jr., "Canon, *Regulae Fidei*, and Continuing Revelation in the Early Church," in *Church, Word and Spirit: Historical and Theological Essays in Honor of Geoffrey W. Bromiley*, ed. James E. Bradley and Richard A. Muller (Grand Rapids, MI: William B. Eerdmans, 1987) 65–91.

[57] See Kärkkäinen, *An Introduction to Ecclesiology*, 70–72; B. Campos. "In the Power of the Spirit: Pentecostalism, Theology and Social Ethics," *In the Power of the Spirit: The Pentecostal Challenge to the Historic Churches in Latin America*, ed. Benjamin F. Gutiérrez and Dennis A. Smith (Louisville, KY: Presbyterian Church USA, 1996) 42.

[58] Cecil M. Robeck, Jr., "The Holy Spirit and the Unity of the Church: The Challenge of Pentecostal, Charismatic, and Independent Movements," *Bibliotheca Ephemeridum Theologicarum Lovaniensium*, Series 3, 181 (2004) 366–67.

Apostolic Succession

The notion that the Church's pastoral office is linked to that of the apostles is already evident in the New Testament. The story of the appointment of "the seven" in Acts 6:1-6 represents an early example. Though often misinterpreted as the institution of the diaconate, the story represents a sharing of the original apostolic ministry, in order to provide the Greek-speaking Hellenistic Jewish Christians with their own leaders.[59] And there are other examples. On their first missionary journey, Paul and Barnabas appoint (*cheirotonēsantes*) presbyters in each city they visit (Acts 14:23). While this may be a Lukan rejection of later practice, it is evidence of the author's theological concern to show continuity between the apostles and the presbyters. Other examples might include Paul's farewell address to the presbyters of Ephesus (Acts 20:17-38), his instructions to Timothy and Titus to set up presbyteral colleges in each of their churches (1 Tim 5:22; Titus 1:5), and the author of 1 Peter, writing in Peter's name as a "fellow presbyter" to the presbyters of Asia Minor (1 Pet 5:1), claiming for them a continuity with his own ministry.

The first letter of Clement, written around the year 96 by a leader of the church of Rome to the church at Corinth, formulates apostolic succession as a principle. The occasion for the letter was the removal from office of the presbyters at Corinth, apparently without cause (44:6; 47:6) as we saw earlier. In urging them to recognize the authority of the presbyters, Clement argues that the Church order now in place there had been established by the apostles who "appointed their first fruits . . . to be bishops and deacons" (42:4) and provided that when these died "other approved men should succeed to their ministration" (44:2). Thus he establishes what the later Church would recognize as the principle of apostolic succession (42:1-4). While his argument is more theological than strictly historical, the Corinthians accepted it. Yet its historicity cannot be rejected out of hand. There is some evidence to suggest that the apostles appointed leaders who would later be known as presbyter-bishops.[60] On the other hand, it was not the only practice. In the *Didache*, the author instructs the communities to "appoint for yourselves bishops and deacons worthy of the Lord" (15.1).

In the post-New Testament Church appeal was frequently made by writers such as Hegesippus (c. 180), Irenaeus (d. c. 200), and Tertullian (c. 200) to lists of bishops from churches that claimed apostolic foundation.

---

[59] Joseph T. Lienhard argues that the tradition behind this passage is basically historical, "Acts 6:1-6: A Redactional View," *Catholic Biblical Quarterly* 37 (1975) 236.

[60] See Sullivan, *From Apostles to Bishops*, 94–95.

These lists were seen as evidence that these churches were in visible continuity with the apostolic Church and so had preserved the true apostolic tradition through a succession of teachers. Tertullian challenged Marcion to produce one Marcionite Church that could trace its descent from an apostle (*Marc* 1.21.5). Thus by the end of the second century bishops were recognized as successors to the apostles. Irenaeus saw the bishops as inheritors of the teaching office of the apostles, while Tertullian put the emphasis on the apostolic churches as bearers of the apostolic tradition.[61] According to Kelly, by inserting "apostolic" into the creed in the patristic era, Christians "intended thereby to affirm the apostolicity of the Church in the sense that it was continuous with the apostles, not only in the faith to which it witnessed but also in its structure, organization and practice."[62] Walter Kasper argues that in the ancient Church, *succesio* was inseparable from both *traditio* and *communio*.[63]

The Historic Episcopate

In both the Roman Catholic and Orthodox traditions,[64] a new bishop receives the laying on of hands from at least two or three bishops (cf. Canon 4 of Nicaea), preferably from neighboring churches, to show that this new bishop and his Church are in communion with the other churches and in succession to the Church of the apostles. Liturgical evidence for this practice, suggesting the collegial nature of the episcopal office, can be found as early as the late second or early third century in the so-called *Apostolic Tradition* of Hippolytus (2.3).[65] In his study of apostolicity, John Burkhard argues that to be a bishop is not to be an individual successor to an apostle, but to have communion with other pastoral leaders in the Church's apostolic ministry.[66]

Today it is more common to distinguish between the succession of the Church in apostolic faith and life and succession in the historical episcopal office. According to Burkhard theologians generally "point to apostolicity as guaranteeing the identity of the church of a later period with the early

---

[61] Ibid., 170.

[62] J.N.D. Kelly, "'Catholic and Apostolic' in the Early Centuries," 287.

[63] Walter Kasper, *Leadership in the Church: How Traditional Roles Can Serve the Christian Community Today* (New York; Herder and Herder, 2003) 124–27.

[64] Zizioulas, *Being as Communion,* 155.

[65] For a critical study, see John F. Baldovin, "Hippolytus and the *Apostolic Tradition*: Recent Research," *Theological Studies* 64/3 (2003) 520–42.

[66] See John J. Burkhard, *Apostolicity Then and Now: An Ecumenical Church in a Postmodern World,* (Collegeville, MN: The Liturgical Press, 2004) 73.

Christian community,"[67] and he emphasizes that the ecumenical statements of the last forty years agree that primacy is to be given to the apostolicity of the whole Church.[68] For example, the 1982 World Council of Churches text, *Baptism, Eucharist and Ministry* (*BEM*) sees the episcopal succession "as a sign, though not a guarantee, of the continuity and unity of the Church" (M no. 38), and it suggests that those churches that lack it may need to recover the sign (M no. 53b).[69] In this way, it offers a nuanced argument for the recovery of the historical episcopal succession. The only thing it cannot accept is the idea that the ministry of a particular Church is invalid until it enters the line of episcopal succession (M no. 38).[70]

The Roman Catholic Church continues to insist on ordination in the episcopal succession as necessary for valid ministry and the full reality of the eucharistic mystery. Yet few today hold the mechanistic, "pipeline" theory of apostolic succession that prevailed earlier in Catholicism, holding that those not incorporated into this unbroken line of ordinations stretching back to an apostle lack the sacramental power necessary for authentic sacraments. Indeed a theological consensus seems to be emerging since *BEM*'s distinction between the episcopal succession as a sign rather than a guarantee of the unity and continuity of the Church that authentic ministry can be present even if it lacks the sign of continuity. The 1985 international Lutheran-Catholic Joint Commission report, *Facing Unity: Models, Forms and Phases of Catholic-Lutheran Church Fellowship*, co-sponsored by the Lutheran World Federation and the Pontifical Council for Promoting Christian unity, suggests that the "*defectus*" Vatican II found in regard to ordained ministry in the Reformation churches (UR 22) could be understood, not as a simple absence, but as "a lack of fullness . . . which, for the sake of church fellowship, has jointly to be overcome" (no. 124).[71] From an Orthodox perspective, John Zizioulas argues that divided communities should focus, not on each other's

---

[67] Ibid., 25.

[68] Ibid., 236.

[69] World Council of Churches, *Baptism, Eucharist and Ministry* (Geneva: WCC, 1982).

[70] Margaret O'Gara presents a survey of the understanding of apostolicity in several ecumenical statements; see "Apostolicity in Ecumenical Dialogue," *Mid-Stream* 37/2 (1998) 175–212.

[71] Roman Catholic/Lutheran Joint Commission, *Facing Unity: Models, Forms and Phases of Catholic-Lutheran Fellowship* (Geneva: Lutheran World Federation, 1985) 57; David N. Power argues that the question of ministry is not reducible to an issue of the power to celebrate, but to a lack of the fullness of visible communion"; see his "Roman Catholic Theologies of Eucharistic Communion: A Contribution to Ecumenical Conversation," *Theological Studies* 57 (1996) 609.

"orders," but rather they "should try to recognize each other as ecclesial *communities* relating to God and the world through their ministries in the way that is implied in the mystery of Christ and the Spirit."[72]

Ecclesiological Types

The historical location of the churches influences their ecclesiologies. The Catholic and Orthodox churches begin from the perspective of the undivided Church, while churches springing from the Reformation in the sixteenth century begin from the perspective of a Church divided. These different points of departure obviously effect their different ecclesiologies or ecclesiological types. Three basic approaches can be distinguished, Catholic, Reformed, and Restorationist.

Catholic

The Roman Catholic, Orthodox, and some within Anglican and Lutheran churches, though they will nuance it differently, stress an ecclesiology of continuity in which the community founded by Christ has an unbroken succession in faith, sacraments, church order, and authority.[73] If the First Vatican Council understood the Church as a *societas perfecta*, Vatican II reclaimed the image of the Church as the people of God, and indeed, as a pilgrim people. It also reclaimed implicitly the ancient notion of the Church as a communion of churches by seeing the local Church with its bishop as a particular Church (LG 23). The concept of communion is in origin sacramental; the Eucharist makes the Church one (1 Cor 10:16-17). The one, holy, catholic, and apostolic Church "subsists in the Catholic Church . . . although many elements of sanctification and of truth can be found outside of her visible structure" (LG 8).

Reformed

Reformed ecclesiology also stresses continuity with the historic church; Jeff Gros speaks of the "reformed catholicity" of the classical Reformers that finds expression as well in some later Protestant developments, like Methodism and some strains of the Baptist heritage. "The claim is to preserve the same apostolic continuity of faith, forms of worship,

---

[72] Zizioulas, *Being as Communion*, 246.
[73] See Jeffrey Gros, "The Church in Ecumenical Dialogue: Critical Choices, Essential Contributions," *Journal of the Wesleyan Theological Society* 39/1 (2004) 37–38.

church order and authority, but with more serious reforms in sacramental faith and structure than in the first type."[74]

However, the starting point in an already divided Church frequently led to a reinterpretation, often radical, of the traditional marks. The unity of the Church was frequently understood eschatologically, a gift of the Spirit in God's future or as a task to be striven for, while the universal Church became invisible.[75] For some, like Luther, the word catholic was to be replaced by Christian, or understood qualitatively rather than in terms of extension or universality, as we have seen. The loss of bishops for many traditions at the time of the Reformation led to an understanding of apostolicity in terms of succession in apostolic teaching or tradition rather than as a visible succession to the apostolic churches through the succession of bishops.

Restorationist

Restorationist ecclesiology had its roots in the Anabaptist judgment that the Post-Constantinian Church had "fallen" and needed to be restored on the basis of the New Testament Church. Thus discontinuity became more important than continuity. The Restoration Movement itself developed in certain nineteenth century communities in the United States, particularly those influenced by the theology of Alexander Campbell. This perspective generally places more emphasis on pneumatology and restoring the apostolic Church than on historical continuity.[76] Pentecostals and Free Churches "understand the holiness of their churches primarily in the holiness of their members, the oneness of the church as 'spiritual unity' of all born-again Christians, the apostolicity as faithfulness to the apostolic doctrine and life, and the catholicity consequently as self-evident fact."[77] Pentecostals in particular have defined apostolicity in terms of the restoration of the apostolic gifts of the New Testament Church—tongues, prophecy, and miraculous healing. For Kärkkäinen, "the essence of Pentecostalism is to go back to the faith and experience of apostolic times, to live in consistency with the New Testament church." Pentecostals "have claimed

---

[74] Ibid., 40.

[75] See Alston, *The Church of the Living God*, 55–56.

[76] See Richard M. Tristano, *The Origins of the Restoration Movement: An Intellectual History* (Atlanta: Glenmary Research Center, 1988) 80–95.

[77] Veli-Matti Kärkkäinen, "Pentecostalism and the Claim for Apostolicity: An Essay in Ecumenical Ecclesiology," *Evangelical Review of Theology* 25/4 (2001) 324.

continuity with the church in the New Testament by arguing for discontinuity with much of the historical church."[78]

There are a number of problems in approaching the marks from the perspective of the divided Church. First, reformed and restorationist ecclesiologies do not generally find anything binding in the New Testament
evidence for a developing Church office, linked to the ministry of the
apostles, as we saw earlier.[79] Some Protestants are inclined to equate development with decline, as is evident in the discussion of "early Catholicism."[80]

More significantly, the ecclesiological implications of Christology are
generally ignored. The reformed and particularly the restorationist approaches tend to place their emphasis on the eschatological, the pneumatological, and the charismatic. While Jesus did not provide a constitution for
the Church, Catholics and Orthodox see certain ecclesiological implications
that flow from his life and ministry. These include his preaching of the reign
of God and the community of the disciples called to proclaim and embody it;
the constitution of the Twelve as a college or fixed group at its center (LG
19),[81] and the Eucharist. Thus pneumatology cannot be separated from Christology. A restorationist overemphasis on pneumatology at the expense of
christological foundation, or on discontinuity at the expense of continuity in
faith, structure, and practice risks an ecclesiological individualism which
may have more to do with the spirit of modernity than with Christian origins
and the Christian tradition. Hierarchy and charism need to be kept in proper
balance. The Church cannot be reconstituted *ex nihilo* in every generation.

On the other hand, Christians in Pentecostal, Charismatic, Independent,
and African Instituted Churches see the recent emergence of their churches
as testimony to the Spirit's activity in the world; they claim to take pneumatology seriously. They wonder why the episcopal office should be so
privileged, when the New Testament seems to offer many models of
Church.[82] Like John Smyth, they appeal to Matthew 18:20, where Jesus

---

[78] Veli-Matti Kärkkäinen, "The Apostolicity of Free Churches: A Contradiction in Terms
or an Ecumenical Breakthrough?" *Pro Ecclesia* 10/4 (2001) 483.

[79] From Ch. 5 "Apostolic Ministry."

[80] See Avery Dulles, *The Catholicity of the Church*, 96–97.

[81] Zizioulas recognizes the Twelve as a college, but sees the constitution of this college
as an eschatological event, accomplished pneumatologically by the Spirit as the agent of
Christ; thus he seeks to synthesize the historical and pneumatological approaches; *Being as
Communion*, 172–88.

[82] Cecil M. Robeck, Jr., in "The Challenge Pentecostalism Poses to the Quest for Unity,"
in *Kirche in ökumenischer Perspektive*, Peter Walter, Klaus Krämer and George Augustin,
ed. (Friburg: Herder, 2003) 318.

says "where two or three are gathered together in my name, there am I in the midst of them." And they point out that many of the historic churches are declining in membership, while their own congregations continue to multiply. Miroslav Volf suggests that "Protestant Christendom of the future will exhibit largely a Free Christian form," while episcopal churches will have to integrate Free Church elements into their own lives.[83]

Conclusion

While the Church has been described as "one, holy, catholic and apostolic" since the end of the fourth century, how those marks should be understood today continues to be debated. Avery Dulles has observed that the concept of catholicity is analogous and so does not admit of any precise definition.[84] We call the Church catholic in the creed; nevertheless when we say this

> we are going beyond the empirical data. Although something of the catholicity of the Church appears in history, we perceive only the external signs of a far deeper reality, apprehended in faith, which alone can affirm the divine dimension of the Church's life. The adjective 'catholic' in the creed does not express a mere hope or ideal, but a present, though imperfect, reality.[85]

But is it not true that the other marks should also be understood analogically? Dulles calls them "dynamic realities that depend on the foundational work of Christ and on his continued presence and activity through the Holy Spirit."[86] Given the empirical reality of the Church, the constitutive role of the Holy Spirit in bringing men and women to new life in Christ through the community of the Church, and the acknowledgement of the Roman Catholic Church that the one Church of Christ is present in some ways beyond its borders (LG 8), it seems clear that the marks cannot be understood univocally. Kasper suggests that Vatican II, in not stating that only bishops can receive new members into the college of bishops, at least hints at the possibility of "more than one exclusive form and conception of apostolic succession."[87] Or as Burkhard argues, the apostolic succession of bishops is "not an affair of a historically unbroken chain of

---

[83] Volf, *After Our Likeness*, 13.
[84] Dulles, *The Catholicity of the Church*, 167.
[85] Ibid., 168.
[86] Avery Dulles, "The Church as 'One, Holy, Catholic, and Apostolic'," in *Evangelical Review of Theology* 223/1 (1999) 27.
[87] Kasper, *Leadership in the Church*, 135.

episcopal leaders, but of proper, sacramental succession to the leadership of an apostolic community."[88]

Seeing the marks analogically means a broadening of their meaning; they cannot be understood merely from a sectarian perspective, from the point of view of a particular tradition. At the same time, an inability to manifest aspects of the marks important to other traditions might indicate that a particular Church is deficiently one, holy, catholic, or apostolic. The marks stand as a challenge to all the churches.[89] If a Church already shares a unity in the Spirit, it must strive to make that unity visible in its life. If it is holy in spite of the sinfulness of its members, it should manifest God's abiding presence in Word and sacrament as well as in the gifted lives of its members. A Church closed in on itself, completely self-sufficient, lacking communion with other churches would be deficient in catholicity. A Spirit-filled apostolic life is important, but a Church lacking a sense of evangelical mission or failing to celebrate baptism and Eucharist or unable to show its continuity with the apostolic Church and tradition would be deficient in apostolicity.

No Church fully realizes what it means to be one, holy, catholic, and apostolic; each embodies important aspects of these marks. Catholicism and Orthodoxy need to acknowledge the ecclesiality of other churches more effectively and move towards greater communion. Protestant and Evangelical/Pentecostal churches need to find ways of acknowledging the special gifts of Catholicism. These include the episcopal office visibly uniting particular churches into a worldwide communion as well as the Petrine ministry that serves that unity. In his encyclical on ecumenism, *Ut unum sint*, Pope John Paul II encouraged communities to frank dialogue in light of the apostolic tradition: "This leads them to ask themselves whether they truly express in an adequate way all that the Holy Spirit has transmitted through the apostles."[90]

---

[88] Burkhard, *Apostolicity Then and Now*, 38.

[89] Cf. Edward Schillebeeckx, *Church: The Human Story of God*, trans. John Bowden (New York: Crossroad, 1990) 197.

[90] John Paul II, *Ut unum sint*, no. 16; *Origins* 25/4 (1995) 54.

CHAPTER 8

Reception and Communion

In recent discussions on ecclesiology, two terms, reception (*receptio*) and communion (*communio*), regularly appear as key to the future of the Church, and they are in fact closely related. Reception refers to the process by which practices, traditions, and authoritative decisions are accepted into the life of the Church as a community of disciples, sharing God's life in Christ. Communion (*communio*), from the Greek *koinōnia*, describes the relationship brought about by that shared life. Reception describes the process, communion the goal in the search for a truly catholic Church. This chapter will explore the process of reception, the notion of ecclesial communion, and various steps already taken towards full communion.

The Process of Reception

The process of handing on and safeguarding the apostolic tradition cannot be adequately understood without adverting to the ecclesial practice of reception. The concept of reception describes a process through which practices, rituals, and authoritative decisions become effective in the Church's life. The historical or "classical" concept of reception refers to the acceptance by local churches of particular ecclesiastical or conciliar decisions.[1] Today the concept is also used frequently in an ecumenical context, as in the case of a church "receiving" an agreed statement or common confession of faith arrived at through dialogue with another church.

---

[1] John Zizoulas speaks of the "classical idea of reception" in "The Theological Problem of Reception," *Bulletin/Centro Pro Unione* 26 (1984) 3; Richard R. Gaillardetz traces the history of the rediscovery of reception in "The Reception of Doctrine: New Perspectives," in *Authority in the Roman Catholic Church: Theory and Practice*, ed. Bernard Hoose (Aldershot, England/ Burlington, VT: Ashgate, 2002) 95–115.

Behind the Latin words *receptio* and *recipere* lie the New Testament Greek words *lambanein* (to receive) and *deschesthai* (to accept) and their derivates. Paul uses the Greek equivalents for the technical rabbinic terms for the process of handing on (*paradidonai*) and receiving (*paralam-banein*) the tradition. He reminds the Corinthians that they have "received" the Gospel he preached (1 Cor 15:1); similarly, he tells them that they have received the Holy Spirit (1 Cor 1:12). In the parable of the seed the word is accepted (Mark 4:20); in Acts Peter's preaching is accepted by those who are subsequently baptized (Acts 2:41). Those who accept Jesus and his messengers in doing so also accept God (*deschesthai*, Matt 10:40; *lambanein* John 13:20).

The Church itself resulted from the reception of the apostolic preaching by those who became the converts of the apostles and other early Christian missionaries. The same dynamic can be seen in the formation of New Testament canon.[2] Those Christian writings that were accepted by the early communities as expressions of the apostolic faith became through this process of reception part of the Church's canon of Sacred Scripture. Still later the receiving of liturgical practices, church laws, and customs of one church by others further illustrates the process of reception. As examples, Edward Kilmartin points to the fourth century reception of the Spirit epiclesis in the East, to the acceptance of the Roman liturgy in Germany beginning in the sixth century, and to the reception of the Mainz Pontifical by Rome in the tenth.[3] Thus the faith, the biblical canon, the liturgy, and the Church itself are all products of reception.

Although reception as an ecclesial reality has a broad application, the term in its "classical" sense is used more restrictively to refer to the acceptance in the early Church of conciliar decrees and decisions, particularly those of the great ecumenical councils. Ulrich Kuhn points out that recent writers tend to speak of reception in the ancient Church in two main connections. First, in the pre-Constantinian period reception is primarily concerned with the process through which decisions of local or regional synods were made known to and accepted by other churches. He stresses that what underlies this practice is the recognition that a particular Church is authentically Church only if it lives in communion with other churches.[4]

---

[2] Ulrich Kuhn, "Reception—An Imperative and an Opportunity," in *Ecumenical Perspectives on Baptism, Eucharist and Ministry*, ed. Max Thurian (Geneva: WCC, 1983) 166.

[3] Edward J. Kilmartin, "Reception in History: An Ecclesiological Phenomenon and Its Significance," *Journal of Ecumenical Studies* 21 (1984) 41–43.

[4] Kuhn, "Reception," 166.

Secondly, since the time of Constantine, the focus has generally been on the process through which those decisions made by the great "ecumenical" councils were discussed, interpreted, and received by local churches or a later council.[5] An example would be the acceptance of the doctrinal decrees of the Council of Nicaea (325), though only after considerable opposition. Other examples include that of Pope Leo II, who both confirmed the teachings of Constantinople III (681) and asked the Spanish bishops to support it with their own authority, which they did at the regional Council of Toledo XIV (684).[6]

But the process might also lead to non-reception, thus, to a rejection. The Church ultimately did not receive the claim of Boniface VIII in the bull *Unam sanctam* (1302) "that it is absolutely necessary for the salvation of all men that they submit to the Roman pontiff" (DS 875). Similarly, the conciliarist teaching on the supremacy of a general assembly of bishops over a pope, expressed in the Council of Constance's decree *Haec sancta* (1415), was not received by the universal Church, though the validity and intention of this decree still provokes debate among theologians. Other examples might include Pope John XXIII's letter *Veterum sapientiae*, urging the continued use of Latin in seminaries. And one could ask if Pope Paul VI's 1968 encyclical on contraception, *Humanae vitae*, has been received by the Catholic faithful.

The classical concept of reception must be understood as an ecclesiological reality that is evident in the life of the Church of the first millennium. It is most important to note that during this period the Church was understood and functioned as a communion of churches. The concept of reception was still implicit in the ecclesiology of the canonists of the twelfth and thirteenth centuries.[7] But the excessively hierarchical concept of Church that developed in the late medieval and post-Tridentine period tends to reduce reception to a purely juridical category,[8] if indeed it does not so emphasize the role of ecclesiastical authority that the notion of reception is virtually rejected.[9]

---

[5] Ibid., 167.

[6] Kilmartin, "Reception in History," 49.

[7] See Brian Tierney, "'Only the Truth Has Authority': The Problem of 'Reception' in the Decretists and in Johannes de Turrecremata," in *Law, Church and Society: Essays in Honor of Stephan Kuttner*, ed. Kenneth Pennington and Robert Somerville (University of Pennsylvania Press, 1977) 69–96.

[8] Kilmartin, "Reception in History," 35–36.

[9] Yves Congar, "Reception as an Ecclesiological Reality," in *Election and Consensus in the Church*, ed. Guiseppe Alberigo and Anton Weiler (Concilium 77) (New York: Herder and Herder, 1972) 60.

However, if the ecclesiology that developed in the later part of the second millennium was excessively hierarchical, that does not mean that reception as a reality in the life of the Church had entirely disappeared. A study of Church history shows that a number of positions taught by the ordinary magisterium, both papal and universal, and held as Catholic doctrine for centuries ultimately were changed, partly as a result of a development of doctrine, partly as a result of theological critique, and partly because of a lack of reception by the faithful. Luis M. Bermejo gives the following examples; the impossibility of salvation outside the Church, taught by Lateran IV (1215), Florence (1442), and Lateran V (1516); the tolerance of slavery, sanctioned by Lateran III (1179), Lateran IV (1215), Lyons I (1245), and Lyons II (1274); and the justification of the use of torture by Lateran III (1179) and Vienne (1311).[10] Examples from more recent times include Pius IX's position denying the presence of any truth or goodness in non-Christian religions, his condemnation of the proposition that there should be a separation of Church and state, along with the correlative question of religious freedom as an objective right, and Pius XII's exclusive identification of the Roman Catholic Church with the Mystical Body of Christ. These papal teachings were ultimately modified or reversed by the Second Vatican Council because of what J. Robert Dionne calls the "modalities" of their reception by theologians.[11] In other words, theologians did not receive them without critique.

As an ecumenical concept, reception refers to the acceptance of consensus statements or doctrinal agreements and ultimately the ecclesial reality of another Church by churches separated from one another by differences of history and culture, doctrine and structure. But this is a difficult process. It is sad but true, as Anton Houtepen has observed, "More theological consensus is needed to restore unity than to preserve unity."[12]

Reception as an Ecclesial Reality

Reception thus refers to a process that illustrates *how* the Church works. Having considered reception both in the history of the Church and in the present ecumenical sense, a number of conclusions can be drawn.

---

[10] See Luis M. Bermejo, *Infallibility on Trial: Church, Conciliarity and Communion* (Westminster, MD: Christian Classics, 1992) 252–64, 309–40; see also *Rome Has Spoken: A Guide to Forgotten Papal Statements, and How They Have Changed Through the Centuries*, ed. Maureen Fiedler and Linda Rabben (New York: Crossroad, 1998).

[11] J. Robert Dionne, *The Papacy and the Church: A Study of Praxis and Reception in Ecumenical Perspective* (New York: Philosophical Library, 1987).

[12] Anton Houtepen, "Reception, Tradition, Communion," in Thurian, *Ecumenical Perspectives*, 148.

1. *Reception cannot be reduced to a juridical determination on the part of authority; it is a process involving the whole Church*. In the ancient Church ecclesiastical decisions or teachings became normative only when they were received by the communion of churches and ultimately by the faithful themselves. At the same time, reception does not constitute a decision as legitimate. Congar emphasizes that reception "does not confer validity, but affirms, acknowledges and attests that this matter is for the good of the Church." In other words, reception guarantees that a decision or teaching will be efficacious in the life of the Church.[13]

Vatican II teaches that the whole Church is involved in grasping Christian truth; it is not simply the work of authority:

> The whole body of the faithful who have received an anointing which comes from the holy one (see 1 Jn 2:20 and 27) cannot be mistaken in belief. It shows this characteristic through the entire people's supernatural sense of the faith, when, "from the bishops to the last of the faithful," it manifests a universal consensus in matters of faith and morals (LG 12).

Cardinal Johannes Willebrands stressed that reception cannot be understood "as a purely technical or instrumental concept"; he argues that it involves the whole People of God and in this sense "has certain aspects of a sociological process."[14] Thus it involves the research activities of theologians, "the preserving fidelity and piety" of the faithful, and the binding decisions arrived at by the college of bishops.[15] As Richard Gaillardetz writes, "Reception means not mere acceptance, but transformation, both of the receiving community and that which is received."[16]

As a contemporary example of reception, Willebrands points to the reception of the ecumenical movement itself by Vatican II, a reception made possible by earlier developments in theology, in the Christian lives of the faithful, and in some "often hesitant" statements of the magisterium.[17] At the same time, not all initiatives on the part of authority have been received by the faithful. John Long calls attention to the failure of Church authorities in the fifteenth century to translate the agreements between the Eastern churches and the Latin West reached at the Council of Florence

[13] Congar, "Reception," 66.
[14] Johannes Willebrands, "The Ecumenical Dialogue and Its Reception," *Bulletin/Centro Pro Unione* 27 (1985) 5.
[15] Ibid., 6.
[16] Gaillardetz, "The Reception of Doctrine," 98.
[17] Ibid., 5.

into terms intelligible to the clergy and faithful of both traditions, with the sad result that this attempt at reconciliation failed.[18]

2. *Reception also involves formal decisions on the part of Church authorities.* In the classical model of reception the bishop symbolized the link between the local Church and the apostolic Church; the bishop also maintained the communion between the local Church and the universal Church by participating in conciliar gatherings.[19] Sometimes it was the role of the bishops in council to initiate a process of reception through formal conciliar decisions. The creed proclaimed by the Council of Nicaea (325) is an obvious example. Sometimes the authority of the bishops served to give formal approval to a process of reception already underway, thus bringing the process to a juridical close. Thus, the practice of private, frequent confession, brought to the European continent by the Irish missionaries in the sixth and seventh centuries, was only gradually received there. Yet it became the official and universal practice when the Fourth Lateran Council (1215) decreed that every Christian who committed a serious sin should confess it within the year.

Therefore Church authorities have a role to play in the process of reception, but they do not carry out that role simply by making authoritative decisions. Their role is to articulate what is the faith of the Church. Even the dogma of infallibility is essentially a statement about the Church, not about the pope, or the pope and the bishops, apart from the Church. The statement in the constitution *Pastor aeternus* at Vatican I that solemn definitions of the pope are "irreformable of themselves [*ex sese*], and not from the consent of the Church" (DS 3074), means only that papal teachings are not dependent on subsequent juridical approval by national hierarchies, as we have seen.

In saying that "the Roman Pontiff . . . is possessed of that infallibility with which the Divine Redeemer willed that his Church should be endowed," Vatican I was pointing to how the Church's infallibility comes to expression (DS 3074). Vatican II clarified this by saying that the bishops, united with the pope, share in the exercise of the Church's charism of infallibility, at the same time pointing out that the "assent of the church can never be lacking to such definitions on account of the same holy Spirit's influence, through which Christ's whole flock is maintained in the unity of the faith and makes progress in it" (LG 25).

---

[18] John Long, "Reception: Ecumenical Dialogue at a Turning Point," *Ecumenical Trends* 112 (1983) 19–20; Long refers to Joseph Gill's study, *The Council of Florence* (Cambridge: University Press, 1959).

[19] Zizioulas, "The Theological Problem," 5.

3. *Reception cannot be reduced to the acceptance of doctrinal formulations; it involves the recognition and acceptance of a common faith.* Forms of worship, life, and practice emerge out of a living tradition that bears the faith experience of a community. To accept a liturgical practice from another community is to acknowledge a shared faith which comes to expression through a ritual.

The same holds true for doctrinal formulations. When the representatives of churches in dialogue are able to arrive at a statement of consensus or agreement on those issues which have previously divided them, the completion of the dialogue process represents more than the mutual acceptance of a theological formula; it also implies the recognition of a common faith. That common faith is often expressed differently in the various Christian traditions, and no particular expression, no matter how true, completely captures the reality with which it is concerned. There will always be a diversity of expression.[20] But when a consensus based on a common language is reached, the dialogue partners are beginning to discover each other as sharing the same faith.

4. *The norm for recognizing a common faith is not agreement with one's own ecclesial position but agreement with the apostolic tradition.* In his study of reception Edward Kilmartin singles out the work of Herman Josef Sieben as the best description of the relationship between reception and the authority of ecumenical councils, formulated as a *consensio antiquitatis et universitatis* which is grounded in the work of the Holy Spirit.[21] The *consensio universitatis* represented the "horizontal consensus" of the whole Church that the council sought to express and which had to be secured by reception. But the *consensio antiquitatis*, the "vertical consensus" with the teaching of Scripture and the apostolic tradition, had to be demonstrated by the council and tested by the whole Church. Of the two, Kilmartin argues, the vertical consensus, which includes the element of formal authority, has priority and "is ultimately decisive because the truth of faith is, from its essence, a truth handed on."[22] In other words, in receiving the teaching of a council an individual Church was acknowledging that its own life of faith, received from the apostolic tradition, could be expressed by the conciliar decision.

J.M.R. Tillard also stressed the apostolic tradition as a norm. He warns against making the term reception so extensive that it loses any specific

---

[20] Kuhn, "Reception," 169.
[21] Kilmartin, "Reception in History," 48–50; see Herman Josef Sieben, *Die Konzilsidee der alten Kirche* (Paderborn: Schöningh, 1979) 511–16.
[22] Ibid., 146–47.

meaning. The correct approach in respect to any ecumenical accord must be found "in subjecting it to a critical evaluation in the light of the apostolic tradition," for the essential requirement is not merely mutual understanding but rather "a collective conversion to the claims of the apostolic faith *as such*."[23]

Tillard suggests several practical considerations for those willing to implement reception with the conversion it implies, suggestions which have great significance for ecumenism. First, they should beware of accepting only what is already included in their own tradition. Second, there must be a willingness to inquire if an ecclesial element present in another tradition and absent from one's own—even if one's own tradition dates from the earliest Christian centuries—is not a deficiency.[24] Finally, in the case of one tradition lacking something strongly present in another, the question must be asked: "Does this lack arise from a denial of the point at issue, or from an alternative and valid interpretation which also has its roots in the great apostolic tradition?"[25]

Ecclesial Communion

The rediscovery of the biblical concept of communion (*koinōnia*) provides the foundation for understanding the Church as a communion of the faithful in life of the Triune God and with one another. Ecclesial communion is primarily spiritual, based on sharing the divine life, but it is also visibly expressed. Communion in fact flows from reception.

Paul occasionally uses *koinōnia* in the context of visible signs of communion between Christians and between their churches. After Paul and Barnabas met with the leaders of the Church in Jerusalem, James, Kephas (or Peter), and John, about the way they presented the Gospel to the Gentiles, they received "their right hand in partnership (*koinōnia*)" (Gal 2:9). At the same time, when someone's conduct was seen as destructive of the life of the community, Paul orders the community to exclude him, what the later Church would call "excommunication" (1 Cor 5:2). And there are other indications "that refractory Christians were cut off from the community, at least for a time" (Matt 18:15-18; 1 Cor 5:11; 3 John 9-10).[26]

---

[23] J.M.R. Tillard, "'Reception': A Time to Beware of False Steps," *Ecumenical Trends* 14 (1985) 145; Tillard's emphasis.

[24] Tillard, "Reception," 146–47.

[25] Ibid., 148.

[26] John E. Lynch, "The Limits of *Communio* in the Pre-Constantinian Church," in *The Church as Communion*, ed. James H. Provost (Washington, D.C.: Canon Law Society of America, 1984) 165.

Paul's concern to maintain unity and communion among the churches is evident in his letters, visits, dispatching of apostolic delegates (2 Cor 8:18-23), and particularly, in the collection he sponsored for the Church in Jerusalem (1 Cor 16:1-4; 2 Cor 8:2–9:14; Rom 15:25-29). In 2 Cor 9:13, *koinōnia* is used in the sense of sharing material gifts ("the generosity of your contribution [*koinōnias*] to them," cf. 2 Cor 8:4). Schuyler Brown sees efforts such as these to maintain communion among the churches as indicating that the problem of "the Church and the churches" already exists in the New Testament period, even if the term "communion of churches" does not yet appear.[27]

Finally, in the fourth century the expression *"communio sanctorum"* appears in several creedal formulas, first in the *Confession* (378–79) of Jerome. The term is ambiguous, as the Latin can be interpreted in either a personal (communion of saints) or a sacramental sense (communion in holy things). Scholarly opinion today favors the sacramental interpretation as the original meaning, referring to the participation of Christians in Christ's saving grace through baptism and Eucharist.[28] But *communio sanctorum* has also taken on the sense of the communion of saints, the communion in the Body of Christ of the saints in heaven, the souls in purgatory, and the faithful on earth. Protestants tend to identify the *communio sanctorum* with the *congregatio fidelium*, the congregation of the faithful. Fahey comments, "Such an interpretation is not inaccurate dogmatically but it does omit reference to Saint Paul's understanding of *koinōnia* as the most intimate sharing and union of man with God and with one's fellow men accomplished through Christ's salvific actions made sacramentally present in the community."[29]

Signs of Communion

In the post-New Testament period, communion was exhibited through visible signs such as eucharistic hospitality, letters of communion, communion between the bishops themselves, and as early as the third century, communion with the Rome.[30] Eucharistic hospitality was a sign that one

---

[27] Schuyler Brown, "Koinonia as the Basis of New Testament Ecclesiology?" *One in Christ* 12 (1976) 165–66.

[28] See Michael A. Fahey, "Ecclesial Community as Communion," *The Jurist* 36 (1976) 16–17; Fahey refers to the works of Stephen Benko, *The Meaning of Sanctorum Communio* (London: SCM Press, 1964) and Henri de Lubac, "Credo. . . Sanctorum Communionem," *Internationale Katholische Zeitschrift/Communio* 1 (1972) 18–32.

[29] Fahey, "Ecclesial Community," 17.

[30] See Ludwig Hertling, *Communio: Church and Papacy in Early Christianity*, trans. Jared Wicks (Chicago: Loyola University Press, 1972) 23–36.

was in communion with the Church. Bishops gave letters of communion to travelers, whether clerical or lay, identifying them as faithful Christians so that they might be welcomed at their destinations. These letters served as a kind of early passport. At the same time, those guilty of false teaching or serious sin were excluded from the Eucharist in the Pre-Constantinian Church, with the terms *akoinonatos* appearing in the East as early as Nicaea (325) and "excommunication" in the West after the year 400.[31]

Other signs of communion included the practice of having several bishops participate in the ordination of a new bishop, to indicate that he and thus his church were in communion with the other bishops and their churches, making visible the nature of the Church as a communion of churches. This is still the practice in the Catholic and Orthodox traditions. Creeds, synods, and councils that gathered bishops to deal with issues facing their churches were other methods of expressing and safeguarding communion. Even today, the expression *"communicatio in sacris,"* referring to common worship or eucharistic hospitality (UR 8), derives from the Greek *koinōnia*. The Latin *"communicatio"* was one of the words used by Jerome in the Vulgate to translate *koinōnia*.

One of the most interesting signs of communion was that of the *fermentum*, the sending of a particle of bread from the bishop's Eucharist to his priests or to the bishop of a neighboring Church, to be consumed at their Eucharists.[32] The practice, illustrating the sacramental dimension of *koinōnia*, may have originated at Rome; it is mentioned by Irenaeus (d.c. 202) and was still in force as late as the beginning of the fifth century. A vestige of this practice can be seen today in the Catholic liturgy when the presider drops a particle of the host into the chalice just before communion. To this day, the communion between the local congregation and the worldwide communion of the Church is symbolized and maintained in the presidency at the Eucharist of an episcopally ordained priest. Through his presidency, the nature of the Church confessed and lived out as one, holy, catholic and apostolic comes to expression.

Communion as Life in the Spirit

The foundation of communion is always spiritual; it is rooted in our shared life in Christ and in his Spirit. For example, Irenaeus of Lyons in his *Adversus Haereses* uses *koinōnia* some eighty times to describe our

[31] Lynch, "The Limits of *Communio* in the Pre-Constantinian Church" 187–88.
[32] Archdale A. King, *Eucharistic Reservation in the Western Church* (London: A. R. Mowbray, 1965) 8–9.

access to salvation in the Spirit.[33] But this sense for the primacy of the spiritual was not always kept to the fore as communion became increasingly associated with those sacramental and institutional elements we have been considering.

Still, visible signs of communion are important. As Herman Pottmeyer says, "like all forms of life, a living communion cannot develop if it is not given scope, forms, and structures."[34] When visible, ecclesial communion was lost, first between the eastern and western Church in 1054, and again with the Reformation churches in the sixteenth century, all sense of spiritual communion was lost as well. The tragedy of the Reformation was its inability to preserve communion within itself; new churches continued to appear. Thus the importance of the visible aspects of *communio* should not be minimized. Because it designates a real relationship, communion has a visible, public, or even institutional character.

Paul grounds the unity of the Church as the one Body of Christ in baptism (1 Cor 12:13) and the Lord's Supper (1 Cor 10:15-16). John suggests the same ecclesiological foundation in more poetic language when he speaks of Jesus handing over the spirit at his death and calls attention to the blood and water flowing from his pierced side (John 19:30-34).

Moving Towards Full Communion

An ecclesiology of communion, so characteristic of the Church's self-understanding in the first millennium, describes the Church as a communion of believers sharing in the divine life (*communio sanctorum*), as a communion of particular churches (*communio ecclesiarum*) linked by the bonds of communion joining their bishops (*communio hierarchica*) to each other and to the bishop of Rome, and as a wider but still imperfect communion of all the churches and ecclesial communities (*communio christiana*).[35]

How can the broken body of Christ find again its unity as one, holy, catholic and apostolic Church? How can the church truly be "a sacrament— a sign and instrument, that is, of communion with God and of the unity of the entire human race" (LG 1) while it remains fractured and divided? To ask these questions is to ask how tomorrow's Church might be envisioned.

---

[33] Fahey, "Ecclesial Community," 14.

[34] Herman J. Pottmeyer, *Towards a Papacy in Communion: Perspectives from Vatican Councils I & II*, trans. Matthew J. O'Connell (New York: Crossroad, 1998) 131.

[35] See I. Riedel-Spangenberger, "Die Communio als Strukturprinzip der Kirche und ihre Rezeption im CIC/1983," *Trierer Theologische Zeitschrift* 97 (1988) 230–32.

The rediscovery of an ecclesiology of communion has provided a model for the reconciliation of the churches that is the goal of the ecumenical movement. The WCC stated at the 1961 New Delhi Assembly that "The word 'fellowship' (*koinonia*) has been chosen because it describes what the Church truly is."[36] The notion of *koinōnia* is present in Vatican II, though not elaborated thematically.[37] The 1981 Anglican Roman Catholic International Commission's *Final Report* acknowledges that although *koinōnia* is never equated with Church in the New Testament, "it is the term which most aptly expresses the mystery underlying the various New Testament images of the Church."[38] The report of the 1985 Extraordinary Synod of Bishops states that the Catholic Church has fully assumed its ecumenical responsibility on the basis of the ecclesiology of communion.[39] The World Council of Church's 1991 World Assembly at Canberra describes its vision of Christian unity in terms of *koinōnia*:

> The unity of the church to which we are called is a *koinonia* given and expressed in the common confession of apostolic faith; a common sacramental life entered by the one baptism and celebrated together in one eucharistic fellowship; a common life in which members and ministries are mutually recognized and reconciled; and a common mission witnessing to all people to the gospel of God's grace and serving the whole of creation. The goal of the search for full communion is realized when all the churches are able to recognize in one another the one, holy, catholic and apostolic church in its fullness. This full communion will be expressed on the local and the universal levels through conciliar forms of life and action.[40]

And the WCC text, *The Nature and Mission of the Church*, singles out *koinōnia* as the central notion for a common understanding of the nature of the Church and its visible unity.[41] Thus the universal Church sees its ecumenical future in terms of a communion of churches, or perhaps more accurately, a communion of communions.

---

[36] *The New Delhi Report: Third Assembly of the World Council of Churches*, ed. W. A. Visser t'Hooft (London: SCM, 1962) 119.

[37] George Vandervelde, "Koinonia Ecclesiology—Ecumenical Breakthrough?" *One in Christ* 29/2 (1993) 129.

[38] Anglican-Roman Catholic International Commission, *Final Report* (London: CTS/SPCK, 1982), Introduction, (no. 4, 5–6).

[39] Extraordinary Synod of Bishops, *The Final Report*; in *Origins* 15 (1985) 449.

[40] World Council of Churches, Canberra Statement: *The Unity of the Church: Gift and Calling*, (1991) 2.1.

[41] WCC, *The Nature and Mission of the Church: A Stage on the Way to a Common Statement*, Faith and Order Paper, No. 181, (no. 24).

Vatican II's Decree on Ecumenism, *Unitatis redintegratio*, taught that a partial communion already exists between baptized Christians in other churches and the Catholic Church: "For those who believe in Christ and have been properly baptized are put in some, though imperfect, communion with the Catholic Church" (UR 3). The 1993 *Ecumenical Directory* goes further, extending the notion of imperfect communion to other Christian churches; it says that "other churches and ecclesial communities, though not in full communion with the Catholic church, retain in reality a certain communion with it."[42] The challenge facing the Catholic Church is that of finding a way to reestablish full communion with the Orthodox churches and to integrate the Protestant churches as distinct, particular churches, each with its own tradition, spirituality, liturgy, and government, into the wider communion of the *ecclesia catholica*.

The ecumenical dialogues of the last forty years have led to a broad consensus on the theological issues which have divided the churches since the sixteenth century: the doctrine of justification, the nature of the Eucharist, the theology and structure of the ordained ministry, the exercise of authority, episcopacy and even—in the Anglican-Catholic and Lutheran-Catholic dialogues—the question of papal primacy. These agreements have been worked out between Church representatives and theologians, though most have not yet been officially received by the sponsoring churches.

Steps Toward Reconciliation

Since *Baptism, Eucharist and Ministry* was published in 1982,[43] a number of specific proposals for the reconciliation of churches have appeared. John Hotchkin, then executive director of the U.S. bishops' Secretariat for Ecumenical and Interreligious Affairs, sees these proposals for a "phased reconciliation" as constituting the "third stage" in the ecumenical movement."[44] Of the six he reviewed, four have since been realized. In 1997 the Evangelical Lutheran Church in America (ELCA) entered into full communion with the United Church of Christ, the Presbyterian Church (USA), and the Reformed Church in America. In 1998, representatives of the Lutheran World Federation and the Vatican's Pontifical Council for Promoting Christian Unity signed a "Joint Declaration" on justification, stat-

---

[42] *Ecumenical Directory*, (no. 18); *Origins* 23 (1993).

[43] WCC, *Baptism, Eucharist and Ministry* (Geneva: WCC, 1982).

[44] John Hotchkin, "The Ecumenical Movement's Third Stage," *Origins* 25 (1995) 356; the pioneering and organizational work which began in 1910 and was well established by 1961 constitutes the first stage, while the second stage is marked by the stage of dialogue.

ing that they had found "a consensus in basic truths of the doctrine of justification,"[45] and that in light of this consensus, the condemnations of the sixteenth century were no longer applicable. In 1999, the ELCA signed an agreement, "Called to Common Mission," establishing full communion with the U.S. Episcopal Church. The agreement makes possible full eucharistic hospitality and the interchangeability of ministers between the two traditions. Finally, on January 20, 2002, the Consultation on Church Union (COCU), representing nine Protestant denominations, reorganized itself as "Churches Uniting in Christ," pledging to recognize each other's churches and baptisms, share communion with "intentional regularity," and to struggle cooperatively, especially against racism in local communities.

There are still many challenges to be faced by the different churches as they struggle to renew their structures, liturgical life, and commitment to evangelization, and new challenges such as the ordination of women with which some must eventually deal. But the proposals are extremely significant as the churches begin finally to move beyond dialogue to the concrete steps towards reconciliation and full communion that the dialogues have shown to be necessary.

Conclusion

Reception and communion are related concepts. Reception means accepting into one's own life something from another. Communion refers to the bond of unity that results from a shared life.

Reception begins with the acceptance of the divine self-communication, mediated by the apostolic preaching. As an ecclesial process, reception describes the acceptance of practices, liturgical traditions, and customs, particularly the decisions and decrees of Church authority. The modalities of reception by theologians, communities, and churches has played an important role in the clarification of Church teaching and the development of doctrine. The process illustrates "the interrelational foundations of ecclesial life."[46]

The ecclesial practice of reception has much to teach all Christians—Catholics, Orthodox, and Protestants—about how the Church comes to make decisions in questions of doctrine. For churches that emphasize episcopal authority, the process of reception is evidence of a mutuality or interdependence between the authority of the bishops and the body of the

---

[45] Lutheran-Catholic Dialogue, "Joint Declaration on the Doctrine of Justification" (no. 40); *Origins* 28/8 (1998) 124.

[46] Gaillardetz, "The Reception of Doctrine," 111.

faithful in the formulation of doctrine, leading occasionally to the modification or revision of the teachings of the ordinary magisterium, even the papal magisterium.

In more recent times, reception has been used in an ecumenical sense as churches accept agreed statements and ultimately the full ecclesial reality of other churches. The norm for reception in this case is not one's own ecclesial identity but agreement with the apostolic tradition.

The term *koinōnia* or communion is a rich theological concept which applies first of all to our share in the divine life and thus, through baptism, Eucharist, and the indwelling Spirit, the communion we share with one another. It has never been easy for the Church to be what it must be, a community of disciples reconciled and made one by God's work in Christ (Gal 3:28). One of the greatest challenges faced by the New Testament churches was working out the implications of this reconciliation for Jews and Gentiles.

The notion of communion teaches us that the Church itself, the *ecclesia catholica*, is a communion of churches. Each local or particular Church, to be fully Church, must be part of the communion. Thus all the churches are being challenged today to strive for reconciliation and full communion.

Interchurch covenants, agreements between congregations or churches of different traditions, common prayer, and where possible, shared ministry, can help separated churches express their common faith and be a significant step towards reconciliation. But finally those churches must take concrete steps towards the renewal of their theology and ecclesial life for the sake of entering into full communion. It is essential that the churches continue to move in this direction. As Pope John Paul II emphasized in his encyclical on ecumenism, *Ut unum sint*, the question of Christian unity is essential for the Church's evangelical mission (no. 98).[47]

---

[47] John Paul II, *Ut unum sint*, *Origins* 25 (1995) 70.

CHAPTER 9

A Truly Catholic Church

T he Church today is living in a world very different from that of the last century. The ever-growing communication networks which unite peoples around the world, integrating their economies, financial markets, and information systems have contributed to a phenomenon known as globalization, "a shift or transformation in the scale of human organization that links distant communities and expands the reach of power relations across the world's regions and continents."[1] At the same time, a number of theologians see a similar phenomenon affecting the Church, with a world Church already emerging. In this chapter we want to explore some of the implications of globalization for the *"ecclesia catholica,"* a world Church that is truly catholic.

Globalization

Robert Schreiter defines globalization as a compressing of the boundaries of time and space that accelerates the process of modernization.[2] He sees it resulting in a paradox of simultaneous homogenization and particularization. On the one hand, the influence of a rich and powerful culture like that of the United States contributes to common tastes in food, clothing, and entertainment, creating a type of "hyperculture," while a similar homogenization affects science, medicine, and education. The rapidity of communications links people together and creates new possibilities for sharing knowledge and resources. Some sociologists see "an idea of community" as an inevitable aspect of globalization.[3]

[1] David Held and Anthony McGrew, *Globalization/Anti-Globalization* (Cambridge [UK]: Polity, 2002) 1.

[2] See Robert J. Schreiter, "The World Church and Its Mission: A Theological Perspective," *Proceedings of the Canon Law Society of America* 59 (1997) 53.

[3] Roland Robertson, "Religion and The Global Field," *Social Compass* 41/1 (1994) 132.

On the other hand, the disruptive effect this new mass culture with its accompanying values has on traditional cultures leads to "particularization," a reassertion of identity which "include newly (re)constructed cultures, so-called fundamentalisms, and the violent drawing of boundaries to try to keep out the modern world."[4] The disputes over whether Muslim girls may wear headscarves in French primary schools or the violence perpetrated by terrorists in the name of Islam are but the most salient examples. The heightened violence against women in many places is seen by many as a reaction by men who feel that they have lost control of their world. The image of the burning Twin Towers, the result of terrorist attacks on the World Trade Center and the Pentagon on 9/11/2001—twin symbols of American economic and military dominance—has become itself a symbol of a violent rejection of the present world order.

Pope John Paul II has called attention to both the positive and negative implications of economic globalization. Positively, globalization brings with it efficiency, increased production, and links between countries that can bring greater unity among peoples. "However, if globalization is ruled merely by the laws of the market applied to suit the powerful, the consequences cannot but be negative."[5] The problematic aspects of globalization are obvious. Electronic networks have changed the way economies function. Increasingly dependent on "electronic money—money that exists only as digits in computers—the current world economy has no parallels in earlier times."[6] As powerful economic interests push the campaign for global free trade, jobs are "out-sourced" from more affluent countries, while poorer ones, rich in labor but lacking legal and social controls to protect their workers, often see even greater poverty. The rush to develop resources in poorer countries frequently does violence to the environment. Production increases, but their standards of living continue to decline in comparison to more prosperous countries, while the gap between the wealthy and the poor continues to grow.

As the forces driving globalization increase, nation states and their governments seem less able to control their destinies; while they will not disappear, some scholars see their influence as fading.[7] Their economies are subject to powerful agencies beyond their control such as

---

[4] Schreiter, "The World Church," 55.

[5] John Paul II, *Ecclesia in America*, (no. 20); *Origins* 28/33 (1999) 573.

[6] Anthony Giddens, *Runaway World: How Globalization is Reshaping Our Lives* (New York: Routledge, 2003) 9.

[7] See *Transnational Religion and Fading States*, ed. Susanne Hoeber Rudolph and James Piscatori (Boulder, CO: Westview Press, 1997).

banks, multinational corporations, and international organizations (the International Monetary Fund, the World Bank, the World Trade Organization) that function as an "invisible government."[8] The vast number of immigrants on the move is eroding national identities, rooted in a common language, memory, culture, and ethnicity.

At the same time, globalization's perceived threat to cultural and religious identities has led to a resurgence of nationalism and religious fundamentalisms—Islamic, Hindu, Jewish, Christian—and thus, to greater fragmentation. The result has been hostility and confrontation between peoples. In many countries today, Christians are harassed, prevented from evangelizing or making converts, or are the victims of sectarian violence.

A World Church

What does globalization mean for the Church? In some ways it mirrors a similar phenomenon, the emergence of a world Church. Walter Bühlmann was one of the first to foreshadow this development in his book, *The Coming of the Third Church*, first published in 1974.[9] He predicted the movement of the Church towards the Southern Hemisphere, with its center of gravity in the Third World. But if this Third Church was emerging in the newly independent Third World countries, it was a Church facing enormous challenges caused by the gap between the wealthy and the poor, widespread corruption, repressive regimes, and the accompanying institutional violence. While written from a Roman Catholic perspective, he sought to envision a Church for the world characterized by dialogue, subsidiarity, decentralization, collegiality, and participation. He called for an ecumenism, not just with all Christians, but also with non-Christians, stressing the importance of a dialogue focused less on doctrine and more on the kingdom of God.

Karl Rahner has argued that the Second Vatican Council represented the transformation of western Christianity, a Church largely of Europe and North America, into a world Church. "For the first time a world-wide Council with a world-wide episcopate came into existence and functioned independently."[10] Others speak of the globalization of the church, "not so

---

[8] Held and McGrew, *Globalization*, 13.
[9] Walter Bühlmann, *The Coming of the Third Church* (Maryknoll, NY: Orbis, 1978).
[10] Karl Rahner, "Towards a Fundamental Theological Interpretation of Vatican Council II," *Theological Studies* 40 (1979) 718.

much as the globalization of a Euro-American Church but the advent of a new church of the Southern Hemisphere, the Third Church."[11]

The diversity of this global Church, with new expressions of Church appearing in Africa, Asia, and Latin America, has become ever more obvious. Since these churches will be rooted in very different cultures, their social location will give rise to contextual theologies, often different in concept and concern from traditional western theology. But this very diversity brings its own set of challenges. Some are calling for a "new ecumenism," bringing to the table those previously absent, particularly Evangelicals, Pentecostals, new independent churches, and Roman Catholics.[12] But what will such a Church be like? Will it be one or many? Will it be a truly catholic Church, a communion of local churches, living in visible unity? Or will it be a multiplicity of churches, perhaps "open" towards each other but even more divided in faith and life?

For the Roman Catholic Church in particular, integrating different theologies and approaches to pastoral problems will highlight the tensions between local and regional churches and Rome. Nevertheless, globalization means that the Church of Christ has at least the potential of becoming a truly world church, an *ecclesia catholica* embracing an incredible diversity of people. At the same time, some communities, fearful of change and the loss of particular identities, resist the call for a truly catholic Church or even the idea of visible unity. Let us consider briefly some of these challenges.

Non-Western Churches

Philip Jenkins' book *The Next Christendom* gives concrete evidence of the Church's incredible growth, particularly in the global South where the growth has been most dramatic in its Evangelical and Pentecostal expressions, though also for the Catholic Church.[13] This "new" Christendom that Jenkins addresses is primarily a non-western, non-white phenomenon.

While both the Roman Catholic and Anglican churches have experienced great growth in Africa, the continent has also witnessed an explosion of new churches radically different in ecclesial life and theology.

---

[11] Ian T. Douglas, "Globalization and the Local Church," in *The Local Church in a Global Era: Reflections for a New Century*, ed. Max L. Stackhouse, Tim Dearborn, and Scott Paeth (Grand Rapids, MI: William B. Eerdmans, 2000) 204.

[12] Cecil M. Robeck, Jr., "The New Ecumenism," in Stackhouse, *The Local Church in a Global Era*, 170–71; Mark S. Heim, "The Next Ecumenical Movement," *The Christian Century* 112/24 (14–21 August 1996) 780.

[13] Philip Jenkins, *The Next Christendom: The Coming of Global Christianity* (Oxford: Oxford University Press, 2002) 7.

Many are identified as African Initiated Churches, African Instituted Churches, or African Independent Churches (AICs); others are Pentecostal or charismatic in inspiration.[14] By some estimates, forty to sixty percent of African Christians belong to these churches.[15]

The African Independent Churches are not merely offshoots of traditional western missionary churches; many commentators see them as an authentic expression of African religious impulses and culture. Where the missionary churches brought with them a western, even European theology, the AICs have sought to root African Christianity in a traditional African worldview.[16] They are communitarian in style, pneumatological in ecclesiology, and more comprehensive in regard to their doctrine of salvation. First, the AICs reflect in their ecclesial life the communal, even clan-based structure of African society. Their worship is known for "its exuberance, spontaneity, free expression, and corporate reverence."[17] Second, great emphasis is placed on the possession and work of the Holy Spirit, particularly in prophecy, visions, dreams, and other spiritual gifts, to the extent that they are often known as "spiritual churches."[18] The animism of indigenous African sensitivity is evident in their more comprehensive understanding of salvation. More than liberation from original sin, salvation "involves whatever contributes to the reinforcement of life in the here-and-now. This includes good health, ability to ward off evil, prosperity, peace of mind, human and animal fertility, mutual relationship, and success in one's occupation."[19] This emphasis on the essentially communal dimension of life in Christ and the comprehensive understanding of salvation in the context of the Church is a valuable corrective to the individualistic soteriology of so much of western, particularly Evangelical, Protestantism.

China has also seen a great growth of Christian communities, though estimating the number of Christians is extremely difficult and controversial.

---

[14] See Veli-Matti Kärkkäinen, *An Introduction to Ecclesiology: Ecumenical, Historical and Global Perspectives* (Downers Grove, IL: InterVarsity, 2002) 194–201; also Jenkins, *The New Christendom*, 47–53, 147–50.

[15] Rufus Okikiolaolu Olubiyi Ositelu, *African Instituted Churches: Diversities, Growth, Gifts, Spirituality and Ecumenical Understanding of African Instituted Churches* (New Brunswick and London: Transaction Publishers, 2002) 33.

[16] Ositelu, *African Instituted Churches*, 47.

[17] See Cephas N. Omenyo, "Essential Aspects of African Ecclesiology: The Case of the African Independent Churches," *PNEUMA: The Journal of the Society for Pentecostal Studies*, 22/2 (Fall 2000) 241.

[18] Ibid., 239.

[19] Ibid., 244; see also J. S. Mbiti, "Some Reflections on African Experience of Salvation," in *Living Faiths and Ultimate Goals* (Geneva: WCC, 1974)

Chinese academics say that the country has at least 45 million Christians, most of whom are Protestant, though some Western researchers put the number closer to 60 million, many of whom worship in unregistered churches. Some scholars estimate that within the next thirty years between 20 and 30 percent of China's population could be Christian.[20] Much of the Protestant growth takes place through "house churches" that continue to spring up, to the frustration of the government, which seeks to control all religious expression. Exact numbers are difficult to obtain, as the Evangelicals claim as Christians anyone who has had a "born again" experience, though not all persevere. The 50,000 officially recognized Protestant churches with some 16 million members subscribe to what is called the "Three-Self Patriotic Movement," a nondenominational Church, unified by the government, that seeks to be self-administering, self-supporting, and self-propagating.

The Catholic Church, with 115 Chinese dioceses, is divided between the official or open Church (usually affiliated with the Chinese Catholic Patriotic Association) and the "underground" Church, though the differences should not be overemphasized. There are also some open churches that technically belong to neither group; they have bishops appointed by the pope and approved by the government-recognized Bishops' Conference of the Catholic Church in China. At least two bishops in this group are in their early forties. Estimates put the Catholic population at about 12 million, of whom about 6 million are members of the official government-recognized Church. Catechesis is difficult, as those under 18 years of age cannot be publicly evangelized. Yet lay Catholics are becoming more evangelical, taking on increasing responsibility to spread the faith themselves.

Since April 1989 the pope has been acknowledged as the spiritual head of the Chinese Church and most priests and bishops remember him at Mass.[21] Some have contact with the Rome through electronic mail. Cardinal Roger Etchegaray, who frequently served as a special envoy for Pope John Paul II, has said that the different groups constitute "two faces of the same community, which seeks to be both faithful and at the same time patriotic."[22] There is also evidence that even among the Protestants the lines between the registered and unregistered churches are becoming blurred.

---

[20] David Aikman, *Jesus in Beijing, How Christianity Is Transforming China and Changing the Global Balance of Power* (Washington, DC: Regnery Publishing, 2003) 285.

[21] Jean-Paul Wiest, "Catholics in China: the Bumpy Road Toward Reconciliation," *International Bulletin of Missionary Research* 27/1 (January 2003) 3; according to Aikman, between two-thirds and three-quarters of the seventy-two CPA bishops are said to have formally but privately sworn allegiance to Rome, *Jesus in Beijing*, 217.

[22] Cited in *China Church Quarterly* 56 (Fall 2003) 4.

While not all the Asian Catholic churches are new churches, they emerged as a new force, willing to argue for their own pastoral vision against Roman centralism at the 1998 Synod of Bishops for Asia. The Federation of Asian Bishops' Conferences (FABC), established in 1972, includes Bangladesh, Taiwan, India-Nepal, Indonesia, Japan, Korea, Laos-Cambodia, Malaysia-Singapore-Brunei, Myanmar, Pakistan, the Philippines, Sri Lanka, Thailand, Hong Kong, and Vietnam. Significantly, the bishops of China with the exception of Hong Kong are not members. Rooted in the culture of Asia, the style of the Asian bishops is often different from their western counterparts. According to Tom Fox, they are more informal at home, for example, rarely wearing their Roman clerical clothes.[23] In the very different culture of Asia, their theological reflection is necessarily contextual.

Contextual Theologies

In the struggle to address their own problems local churches and disadvantaged groups have begun to theologize from their own particular contexts. The result is what has become known as "contextual" theologies. In part, this reflects a growing awareness that all theology is ultimately local, a reflection on praxis, Christian life as it is lived out in communities and churches.[24] And in part it reflects the influence of a postmodernist ethos, with its emphasis on the construction of knowledge on the basis of social location. Thus contextual theologies of necessity take into account the social, political, economic, and cultural factors of the areas from which they spring and are critical of any claims for universal validity or official status for a particular theology, say a western theology, which comes out of its own particular culture and context.

Latin American liberation theology was one of the first examples of a contextual theology. Even before Vatican II the Uruguayan Jesuit Juan Luis Segundo was calling for the Church to address the social situation and poverty of so much of Latin America, though he didn't yet use the term liberation theology. When the Latin America bishops returned from Vatican II, they sought to engage their churches in the renewal efforts mandated by the council, especially the engagement with social misery

---

[23] Thomas C. Fox, *Pentecost in Asia: A New Way of Being Church* (Marknoll, NY: Orbis, 2002) 8.

[24] See Robert J. Schreiter, *Constructing Local Theologies* (Maryknoll, NY: Orbis, 1985); also his *The New Catholicity: Theology Between the Global and the Local* (Maryknoll, NY: Orbis, 1997).

and support for economic justice and human rights called for by the Pastoral Constitution on the Church in the Modern World.

At their meeting at Medellín (1968) the Episcopal Conferences of Latin America (CELAM) produced sixteen documents that located the problems of their continent in what the bishops identified as "a situation of injustice that can be called institutional violence."[25] They embraced to a considerable extent the themes later given expression by Peru's Gustavo Gutiérrez in his 1971 book, *A Theology of Liberation*. As Gutiérrez defined it, liberation theology is "a critical reflection on praxis in the light of the Bible."[26] It sought to do theology from "the underside of history," that is, from the particular social context or situation of the poor in Latin America, stressing the importance of praxis, encouraging the formation of basic Christian communities, and challenging the Latin American churches to embrace a "preferential option for the poor," the title of one of the chapters adopted by the CELAM bishops at Puebla, Mexico (1979).

This new theology emerging from Latin America was the first of many contextual theologies of liberation—black, Asian, gay, and feminist, the last further divided into *"mujerista"* (Hispanic) and *"womanist"* (African American).[27] New contextual theologies have also emerged from Africa and Asia that are concerned with their unique cultural contexts. After long years of trying to move beyond the western theology brought by the missionaries, African churches are seeking to develop a genuine African theology that can integrate their pre-Christian spiritualities and cultural traditions.[28]

Similarly, theologian Peter Phan, a Vietnamese American, surveys various Asian attempts to construct a Christology "with an Asian face," among them Jesus as the poor monk (Aloysius Pieris), as marginal person *par excellence* (Jung Young Lee), or as eldest son and ancestor (Phan himself).[29] He notes that at Bangkok in 1982 and Bandung, Indonesia in 1990, the Federation of Asian Bishops' Conferences sought to construct an alterna-

---

[25] CELAM II, "Peace," no. 17; see Joseph Gremillion, *The Gospel of Peace and Justice: Catholic Social Teaching Since Pope John* (Maryknoll, NY: Orbis, 1976) 445–84 for the documents.

[26] Gustavo Gutiérrez, *A Theology of Liberation: History, Politics and Salvation*, trans. Caridad Inda and John Eagleson (Maryknoll, NY: Orbis, 1973) 9.

[27] See Alfred T. Hennelly, *Liberation Theologies: The Global Pursuit of Justice* (Mystic, CT: Twenty-Third Publications, 1995); also *Liberation Theology: An Introductory Reader*, ed. Curt Cadorette et al (Maryknoll, NY: Orbis, 1996).

[28] See Kwame Bediako, *Christianity in Africa: The Renewal of a Non-Western Religion* (Edinburgh: Edinburgh University Press/ Maryknoll, NY: Orbis Books, 1995).

[29] Peter C. Phan, *Christianity with an Asian Face: Asian American Theology in the Making* (Maryknoll, NY: Orbis, 2003) 104–32.

tive ecclesiology that makes not the Church but the reign of God the center of Christian life.[30] While the Asian bishops recognize the value of inculturation, they see it as a two way street. It means both "Christianizing" Asia but also "Asianizing" Christianity.[31] This sometimes brings them into conflict with Rome.

Tensions with Rome

One of the challenges for the Roman Catholic Church as a worldwide communion of churches is how to balance the local and the universal, collegiality and primacy, regional churches and Roman authority. The appearance of contextual local theologies was to exacerbate that tension.

Rome was not slow to respond to what it saw as the threat of Latin American liberation theology. In 1984 the Vatican's Congregation for the Doctrine of the Faith published an instruction on "certain aspects of liberation theology," warning against "risks of deviation" from the faith because of a borrowing from various currents of Marxist thought in "an insufficiently critical manner." Besides objecting to the concept of the class struggle, the instruction warned against identifying the kingdom of God with the movement for human liberation and challenging the sacramental and hierarchical structure of the Church.[32] A second instruction, still concerned with Marxist concepts but more positive in advocating the rights of the poor and the struggle against injustice, appeared two years later.[33] But Rome has remained uncomfortable with the new emphasis on liberation theology on the part of the Latin American churches, and has sought to counter it by the appointment of conservative bishops, many of them from Opus Dei.

The 1998 special assembly for Asia of the Synod of Bishops (held in Rome) was seen by many as a coming of age for the Asian churches. Clearly the Asian churches were finding their own voice. Representatives of the various Asian conferences criticized the *Lineamenta,* the Roman drafted outline document for the Synod, for being too western in its approach. Japanese and Indonesian bishops wondered why they should have to obtain Roman approval for their translations of liturgical and catechetical texts. Indian bishops argued for the right of local churches to develop

---

[30] Ibid, 176.

[31] Fox, *Pentecost in Asia*, 46.

[32] CDF, "Instruction on Certain Aspects of the 'Theology of Liberation'," *Origins* 14 (1984) 193–204.

[33] CDF, "Instruction on Christian Freedom and Liberation," *Origins* 15/44 (1986) 713–27.

their own methods and expressions for preaching the gospel. Some members were resentful of instructions from curial officials to avoid the word "subsidiarity" on the debatable grounds that it was not a theological term.[34]

Much of the controversy generated by the synod centered on how the Asian churches should proclaim Christ. The Roman drafted *Lineamenta* took as its theme "Jesus Christ as unique Savior of Asia."[35] Many of the bishops objected that the curial emphasis on proclaiming Christ as universal savior was not a good starting point in an Asian context. They objected that its approach to evangelization ignored the considerable experience of their conferences. Their concern was *how* Christ was proclaimed. They spoke of a "triple dialogue," with other religions, with local cultures, and with the poor.[36] Phan acknowledges that Pope John Paul II's post-synodal apostolic exhortation, *Ecclesia in Asia*, takes into account some of the bishops' concerns, among them the difficulties in proclaiming Jesus as the *only* savior, the fact that Christ is perceived as alien to Asia, and the need for a gradual pedagogy.[37] Finally, however, Phan says that in Asia the immediate goal of proclamation should be helping another to accept Jesus as his or her personal savior, with its implication of personal and total commitment, rather than as the only savior.[38] Tension between the Asian churches and Rome resulted in another Roman declaration when the CDF published *Dominus Iesus* (2000).[39] Among other things, the declaration stressed:

- Revelation in Christ is complete (no. 5) and is not complemented by other religions (no. 6).
- Christ is unique and has an absolute and universal significance (no. 15).
- Members of other religions, objectively speaking, are in a gravely deficient situation in comparison to those in the Church (no. 22).
- The Church must be committed to announcing the necessity of conversion to Christ (no. 22).

---

[34] See Fox, *Pentecost in Asia*, 170–84; also Peter C. Phan, (ed.), *The Asian Synod: Texts and Commentaries* (Maryknoll, NY: Orbis, 2002).

[35] Fox, *Pentecost in Asia*, 155.

[36] Fox, Pentecost in Asia, 158–59; on the triple dialogue, see *For All the Peoples of Asia: Federation of Asian Bishops' Conferences Documents from 1970 to 1991*, Vol. 1 (Maryknoll, NY: Orbis/Quezon City, Philippines: Claretian Publications, 1997) 1:15 ff.

[37] Phan, *Christianity with an Asian Face*, 180; for *Ecclesia in Asia*, see *Origins* 29/32 (1999) 358–84.

[38] Phan, *Christianity with an Asian Face*, 181.

[39] CDF, "*Dominus Iesus*," *Origins* 30/14 (2000) 209–19.

At the news conference announcing the release of the declaration, Cardinal Ratzinger said it had been prompted in part by the "worrisome influence" of the "negative theology" of Asia on the West.[40]

Inculturation in a multicultural, global church remains a difficult issue. In his study of evangelization and culture, Aylward Shorter cites Aidan Kavanagh of Yale and the Vatican's Cardinal Ratzinger as two theologians willing to contest inculturation. Kavanagh worries about local politicization of the liturgy and the "dispersal of the Church itself as a worshipping community."[41] Ratzinger has stressed "that there is no way back to the cultural situation which existed before the results of European thought spread to the whole world"[42] which seems to suggest the superiority of western culture for Christian theology. Recently he urged the Japanese bishops to replace the term "inculturation" with "interculturality," implying that Christian faith is communicated through western culture, which then becomes "fused" with the evangelized culture.[43] Shorter is not sympathetic with these objections, considering them expressions of an outmoded Eurocentric monoculturalism.

Yet the questions raised by inculturation cannot be simply dismissed, for they highlight the tensions between regional churches and Rome as those churches strive to develop theologies for their own particular contexts. This challenge has taken on particular ecclesiological expressions. Avery Dulles has described the tension between "particularist" and "universalist" tendencies in ecclesiology that in some ways reflect the tensions brought on by globalization and the diversity of the regional churches. The particularist tendency takes its departure from the local community, formed under the impulse of the Holy Spirit, while the universalist begins from the global community founded on Peter and the apostles.[44]

Perhaps the theoretical expression of this tension is best seen in a well-known debate that took place in 2001 between two cardinals, Ratzinger

[40] Cited by Fox, *Pentecost in Asia*, 192; see also *Sic et non: Encountering Dominus Iesus*, ed. Stephen J. Pope and Charles Hefling, (Maryknoll, NY: Orbis Books, 2002).

[41] Aylward Shorter, *Evangelization and Culture* (London: Geoffrey Chapman, 1994) 89; see Aidan Kavanagh, "Liturgical Inculturation: Looking to the Future," *Studia Liturgica*, 20 (1990) 98.

[42] *The Ratzinger Report: An Exclusive Interview on the State of the Church*, Joseph Cardinal Ratzinger with Vittorio Messori, trans. Salvator Attanasio and Graham Harrison (San Francisco: Ignatius Press, 1985) 193.

[43] Cited by Shorter, *Evangelization and Culture*, 90; see Joseph Ratzinger, UCAN (Union of Catholic Asian News), AS7025/705 (9 March 1993).

[44] Avery Dulles, "The Church as Communion," in *New Perspectives on Historical Theology: Essays in Memory of John Meyendorff*, ed. Bradley Nassif (Grand Rapids, MI: William B. Eerdmans, 1996) 133–34.

and Walter Kasper. In 1992, the CDF published a "Letter to the Bishops of the Catholic Church on Some Aspects of the Church Understood as Communion." The letter maintained that the universal Church "is a reality ontologically and temporally prior to every individual particular church."[45] Kasper, expressing his concern as a bishop that "The right balance between the universal church and the particular churches has been destroyed," argued that the one Church of Christ exists "in and from" the local churches.[46] He noted that Vatican II had sought to bring the beliefs and attitudes of the early Church into harmony with the First Vatican Council, and that after the council its teachings had been explicated through an "ecclesiology of communion."[47]

The 1992 letter had appropriately sought to address a one-sided emphasis on local churches, the effect of which was to reduce the universal Church to an assembly of all the particular churches. On the other hand, particular churches cannot be reduced to "parts" of the whole. Kasper stresses that the Church is present in each local church, especially in its celebration of the Eucharist, but at the same time he adds "there can be no local church in isolation, for its own sake, but only in communion with all other local churches. . . . The unity of the universal church is a unity in communion."[48] However he does not accept Ratzinger's argument for the historical and ontological primacy of the universal Church over the local churches. The debate between the two of them was not about any point of Catholic doctrine, but a "conflict between theological opinions and underlying philosophical assumptions." Ratzinger's argument, he maintained, is essentially Platonic, starting from the primacy of the idea, while his position is more Aristotelian, seeing the universal as existing in concrete reality.[49]

---

[45] CDF, "Some Aspects of the Church Understood as Communion" (no. 9); *Origins* 22 (June 25, 1992) 109.

[46] Walter Kasper, "On the Church: A Friendly Reply to Cardinal Ratzinger," *America* 184/14 (April 23, 2001) 12; in speaking of the particular churches, LG 23 says, "it is in and from these that the one and unique catholic church exists." See also Kasper, *Leadership in the Church: How Traditional Roles Can Serve the Christian Community Today*, trans. Brian McNeil (New York: Crossroad, 2003) chapter 6, "The Universal Church and the Local Church: A Friendly Rejoinder," 158–75.

[47] Ibid., 11.

[48] Ibid., 12.

[49] Ibid., 13.

A Renewed Catholicity

The very notion of catholicity means "both a fullness that unifies and a diversity that is reconciled."[50] This is what a world Church should be. It does not mean a single institution, but a communion of communions. In many ways the Roman Catholic Church is uniquely poised to provide the structures to link local and regional churches together into a truly catholic Church, an *ecclesia catholica* more inclusive than the current Catholic Church. It is already a world Church, "the oldest significant globe-oriented organization."[51] At the 1985 Extraordinary Synod of Bishops in Rome, 74 percent of the bishops came from countries other than those in Europe or North America, as do 70 percent of the world's Catholics today. The center of Catholicism has shifted to Asia and the Third World. It is estimated that by 2020 eighty percent of all Catholics will live in the eastern and southern hemispheres.[52] Catholicism's genius historically has been its ability to reconcile unity and diversity, holding them together in communion. As a world communion with international structures, networks, and a developed social teaching, it is uniquely positioned to carry out its social mission on a global scale.[53] But that does not mean that its present structure can simply be imposed on the other churches. As Francis Sullivan observes, "The unity which is the goal of the ecumenical movement may have to be different from the unity that exists in any present church."[54]

The challenge for the Catholic Church remains: how can it preserve the proper balance between global and local expressions of the Church? How can it support and encourage the emergence of authentic expressions of the Church in different cultures, which implies an acceptance of differences in law, liturgy, and theological expression, without sacrificing the communion of the Catholic Church as a world Church. In Avery Dulles' view, the Church's global character and the rapidity of modern communications media argues for a strong papacy, able to act decisively, while he suspects that not a few members of other churches "are looking toward Rome to provide effective leadership for the entire *oikoumene* (the whole

---

[50] Richard Marzheuser, "Globalization and Catholicity: Two Expressions of One Ecclesiology?" *Journal of Ecumenical Studies* 32/2 (1995) 186.

[51] See Roland Robertson, "Religion and the Global Field," *Social Compass* 41 (1994) 129.

[52] Fox, *Pentecost in Asia*, xiv.

[53] See T. Howland Sanks, "Globalization and the Church's Social Mission," *Theological Studies* 60/4 (1999) 651.

[54] Francis A. Sullivan, "Faith and Order: The Nature and Purpose of the Church: Comments on the 'material inside the boxes'," *Ecumenical Trends* 32/10 (November 2003) 5.

inhabited world)."[55] Others object that all the dialogues that have treated primacy call for serious reform, including a decentralized papacy and stronger intermediate structures of governance to support a more effective collegiality if this ministry is to be received by other churches.[56]

Robert Schreiter suggests that a renewed concept of catholicity could provide the key to meeting the challenges of a world Church.[57] Two traditional aspects of catholicity, extension throughout the world and fullness of faith, need to be understood more deeply. Global extension has important implications for the issues of inculturation and the tension between local churches and Rome that we have been considering. If diverse cultures can be at least imperfect vessels of faith, then a world Church should have much greater respect for local, non-western theologies and diverse cultural expressions.

Fullness is an ancient characteristic of catholicity, but the non-reception of the Gospel message by a culture should make us alert to the possible problems in the way the faith is presented. For Schreiter, the Christian message is more narrative than proposition or collection of doctrines; it is the story of the life, death, and resurrection of Jesus. "A new humanity, genuine peace, reconciliation as a new creation—these are the forms the Good News takes" in a pluralistic, globalized world.[58] While the western theological tradition is highly developed and has served the Church well, it is not inconceivable that the inculturation of the faith in Asian and African contexts will produce new theological languages, more dependent on Asian or African ways of thinking.

In addition, Schreiter suggests that a renewed understanding of catholicity should add the idea of communication and exchange, developing the structures and processes that facilitate "communicating interculturally between local, intermediate, and central levels of the Church." To fail to do this is to risk failing to grasp the fullness of the faith.[59] Schreiter's work is highly suggestive for he has taken seriously the challenge that globalization presents to the world Church, for its mission and for its theology. By both reclaiming and seeking to expand the concept of catholicity, he seeks to envision a truly universal, catholic Church and at the same time bring

[55] Avery Dulles, "The Papacy for a Global Church," *America* 183/2 (2000) 11.

[56] See Ladislas Orsy, "The Papacy for an Ecumenical Age," *America* 182/12 (2000) 9–15.

[57] Schreiter, "The World Church and Its Mission," 59; in his *The New Catholicity*, he explores a new understanding of catholicity, 127–33.

[58] Schreiter, *The New Catholicity*, 131.

[59] Schreiter, "The World Church and Its Mission," 60.

its message of the reconciliation of all peoples in Christ to bear in a critical way on the process of globalization itself. His work has consequences not just for Christian theology, but for its theology of the Church as well.

Conclusion

If the world today is shrinking because of the interconnectedness of its economies and its electronic nervous systems, the homogenization this brings is often perceived as a threat to the identities of peoples and their religious cultures. The resurgence of fundamentalisms and a new global terrorism both can be traced to a perception of this threat.

At the same time, Christianity in a global context gives evidence of the emergence of a world Church, a Church of churches on a planetary scale. While most of those churches are not yet in communion with each other, many are, and the existence of a number of world communions suggests perhaps for the first time the possibility of a truly catholic Church, global in its extension, embracing an incredible diversity of peoples and expressions of life in Christ.

The Roman Catholic Church offers an example of a world communion with the structures necessary to maintain and express the communion of a world Church as a communion of communions that would be truly catholic. The challenge is maintaining the proper relationship between the local and the global, the particular and the universal. In the final two chapters, we will examine the challenges that becoming a truly catholic Church presents to all the churches, to other Christian churches as well as to the Roman Catholic Church.

CHAPTER 10

Challenges for Other Christian Churches

I f the churches are to enter into visible communion in a world Church, if they are to be reunited in the *ecclesia catholica*, there are a number of issues that call for rethinking on the part of all the churches. If they are to move towards unity, they must have at least the desire to live in communion with each other. That is not yet a given. Some still have questions about the goal of visible unity or remain indifferent towards it, while others eagerly look forward to the day when Christians can celebrate together their unity in the Body of Christ.

In this chapter, we will consider some of the challenges facing the other Christian churches in the quest for a more inclusive communion. These include the goal of visible unity, the question of continuity with the Great Tradition, and finally, the difficult question of the future role of the bishop of Rome. In the following chapter we will consider some of the challenges facing the Roman Catholic Church.

Visible Unity

Many Christians today long for unity in the one Church of Christ, the *ecclesia catholica*, and there is a growing sense among many, particularly younger Christians, that the traditional differences between their churches are no longer that important. Their experience is not one of estrangement and hostility but rather of an acceptance of diverse expressions of Christian life unthinkable in another generation. Many have no problem with sharing worship and Eucharist, while most are unaware of traditional problems of doctrine, sacramental validity, or structures of authority that have kept the churches divided. From their perspective, it is often Church authorities themselves who insist on preserving boundaries, emphasizing differences rather than a common faith.

A Common Faith

At the same time, a pre-condition for the restoration of communion is the recognition of sharing a common faith, a faith which comes to expression in the ecumenical creeds, the great tradition of the Church, including its sacramental and liturgical life, and more recent agreements on the issues such as justification, Eucharist, ministry, and apostolicity that have divided the churches since the sixteenth century. The more than forty years of ecumenical dialogue involving Catholic, Orthodox, Reformation, and Evangelical churches have reached significant agreements on many of these issues,[1] and a number of churches have already entered into full communion, as we saw in the last chapter.

Some examples of significant agreed statements include the following. The Anglican-Roman Catholic International Commission claimed a significant doctrinal consensus on Eucharist and the ministry,[2] though only a convergence on the more difficult question of authority.[3] Since then there has been further progress, as we will see below. The WCC's widely known statement, *Baptism, Eucharist and Ministry*, while it remains a convergence statement, is acknowledged by the Holy See as "perhaps the most significant result of the (Faith and Order) movement so far."[4] Another WCC text, *Confessing the One Faith*, focuses on the Nicene Creed as a confessional statement common to a large number of churches.[5] Many in the Free Church and Pentecostal traditions accept Nicaea's Trinitarian faith, though they remain reluctant to take the creed itself as a standard. They have historically been wary of suggesting that creeds, whether ancient or post-Reformation, might be on a par with Scripture and they have warned against using creeds as exclusionary faith statements that are less than biblical.

One of the most interesting examples of an agreed statement is the 1998 Joint Declaration on the Doctrine of Justification between Lutherans and Catholics. In this international statement on the issue foundational to the Reformation, the two traditions found "a consensus in basic truths of the

---

[1] For an overview see Jeffrey Gros, "Toward Full Communion: Faith and Order and Catholic Ecumenism," *Theological Studies* 65 (2003) 23–43.

[2] Anglican-Roman Catholic International Commission, *The Final Report* (London: CTS/SPCK, 1982) 49.

[3] See Christopher Hill and Edward Yarnold, *Anglicans and Roman Catholics: The Search for Unity: The ARCIC Documents and Their Reception* (London: SPCK/CTS, 1994).

[4] WCC, *Baptism, Eucharist and Ministry: 1982–1990: Report on the Process and Responses* (Geneva: WCC, 1990) 18; see *Baptism, Eucharist and Ministry* (Geneva: WCC, 1982).

[5] *Confessing the One Faith* (Geneva: WCC, 1991).

doctrine of justification," in light of which "the remaining differences of language, theological elaboration and emphasis" in the understanding of justification were deemed acceptable.[6] Such an approach makes room for different theological languages and emphases, even if some important differences remain, as both Rome and some Evangelical commentators observed.[7]

Very different was the approach of the 1999 Evangelical statement, "The Gospel of Jesus Christ: An Evangelical Celebration," which in its "Affirmations and Denials" seems to rule out any understanding of justification not couched in the most traditional Evangelical categories (sinful rebellion, substitutionary satisfaction, imputed righteousness, forensic declaration, eternal punishment without personal faith in Christ).[8] As David Scott observes, there is no acknowledgment that there are other ways of reading Scripture and the Christian tradition, nor any effort to engage Catholic and Orthodox views.[9] Thus one statement seeks to make room for an acceptable theological diversity in expression, while the other is narrowly confessional and exclusive.

Basic consensus does not necessarily mean full agreement, nor does it mean identical languages, theologies, or practices. It "means that sufficient agreement has been reached so that a doctrinal issue, such as justification, is no longer church dividing."[10] Ecumenical theologians stress the importance of an "epistemological tolerance"[11] or "differentiated consensus"[12] or a "hierarchy" of truths (UR 11) to accommodate differences in religious consciousness and theological expression that are complementary rather than mutually exclusive and so can co-exist with an agreement on the fundamental substance of the faith. The Orthodox churches, which refuse any consideration of "intercommunion" because they consider other churches to be heterodox,[13] may need to reflect more deeply on this

---

[6] Lutheran-Catholic Dialogue, "Joint Declaration on the Doctrine of Justification," (no. 40); *Origins* 28/8 (1998) 124.

[7] See "Official Catholic Responses to Joint Declaration," *Origins* 28/8 (1998) 13–32; Douglas A. Sweeney, "Taming the Reformation," *Christianity Today* 44/1 (January 10, 2000) 63–65.

[8] Cf. *Christianity Today* 43/7 (June 14, 1999) 51–56.

[9] David Scott in "An Ecumenical Symposium on 'A Call to Evangelical Unity'," *Pro Ecclesia* 9/2 (2000) 142.

[10] Gros, "Toward Full Communion," 28.

[11] Heinrich Fries and Karl Rahner, *Unity of the Churches: An Actual Possibility,* trans. Ruth C. L. Gritsch and Eric W. Gritsch (Philadelphia/New York: Fortress/Paulist, 1985) 36–38.

[12] Ola Tjørhom, *Visible Church—Visible Unity: Ecumenical Ecclesiology and "the Great Tradition of the Church"* (Collegeville, MN: The Liturgical Press, 2004) 85.

[13] See John D. Zizioulas, *Eucharist, Bishop, Church: The Unity of the Church in the Divine Eucharist and the Bishop During the First Three Centuries,* trans. Elizabeth Theokritoff (Brookline, MA: Holy Cross Orthodox Press, 2001) 258.

difference between diverse theological languages and an underlying consensus in faith.

At the same time, the recognition of a certain theological pluralism makes room for doctrinal developments or confessional positions unique to a given tradition within a wider communion in the faith. Thus Orthodox and Protestant churches should not be obligated to accept modern doctrinal developments within Catholicism, for example the Marian dogmas of the Immaculate Conception (1854) and the Assumption (1950) as well as the definition of papal infallibility (1870), while Catholics would not be held bound to all the doctrines of the Protestant confessional statements. Not compatible with living in communion would be proclaiming such teachings or doctrines as contrary to the Gospel.

Avery Dulles finds such an approach "reductionistic," based on what he considers to be a "lowest common denominator" approach to ecumenism.[14] He points to issues such as papal primacy of jurisdiction, the Mass as a propitiatory sacrifice, purgatory, the Immaculate Conception of Mary, the invocation of saints, or the ordination of women as the "hard questions" on which the churches are yet to reach "convergence, let alone a consensus."[15] This, however, seems to require more than a basic consensus on the apostolic faith, as it might be expressed in the creeds, the great tradition of the united Church, and agreements such as we have been considering. It holds other churches to Roman Catholic doctrinal expressions and relatively recent doctrinal developments which—no matter how important for Catholics—were formulated without the participation of the entire Church. In the words of Yves Congar, "Numerous Catholic ecumenists think that one cannot impose dogmas defined without the participation of others and without any root in their tradition as a *sine qua non* for communion."[16]

Visible Unity and Ecumenism

Not all Christians accept the goal of visible unity. Some Roman Catholic and Orthodox Christians do not look on ecumenism positively. Many Evangelical and Pentecostal Christians have been reluctant to engage fully in the ecumenical movement. Some fear that the goal of ecumenism is a

[14] Avery Dulles, "Ecumenism Without Illusions: A Catholic Perspective," *First Things* 4 (June/July 1990) 23–24.

[15] Ibid., 22.

[16] Yves Congar, *Diversity and Communion*, trans. John Bowden (Mystic, CT: Twenty-Third Publications, 1984) 174.

"megachurch" which would threaten the very existence of their local churches. For example, Cecil M. Robeck voices the fears of many Pentecostals who "are frustrated by the Roman Catholic Church's exclusivist ecclesiology and believe that because of this ecclesiology the Roman Catholic Church is not genuinely committed to Christian unity or ecumenism except as a means of assimilating all others into its grasp."[17] And some Roman Catholics still hold this view of Christian unity.

Others have sought to redefine the goal of ecumenism. Konrad Raiser, former General Secretary of the World Council of Churches, has suggested that a new paradigm is emerging. Raiser maintains that from its beginning the ecumenical movement has been based on a christocentric universalism which presumed the lordship of Jesus and a concept of salvation history. He sees ecumenism today as shifting from the language of unity of doctrine and church order to an ecclesiology of *communio*.[18] Judging sacramental-hierarchical or organizational ecclesial self-understandings as bound to fail, he argues that in a world characterized by secularism and religious pluralism, the ecumenical task should be one of making visible the unity already given in the triune God, particularly by sharing in the Eucharist.[19] Thus he highlights a new vision of an ecumenism centered on issues of justice, peace and the integrity of creation through a conciliar process that offers a way of learning how to live together in the "household" of God.[20] Teresa Berger has suggested a similar reorientation of ecumenism from a feminist perspective.[21]

This tension between traditional ecumenism, focused on the unity of the Church, and a new one based on social concerns was already evident at the WCC Vancouver Assembly (1983).[22] Since then, this alternative vision has increasingly defined the WCC's understanding of the conciliar process. In Raiser's view, precisely because it has no institutional author-

[17] Cecil M. Robeck, Jr., "Roman Catholic-Pentecostal Dialogue: Some Pentecostal Assumptions," *Journal of the European Pentecostal Theological Association*, 21 (2001) 6.

[18] Konrad Raiser, *Ecumenism in Transition: A Paradigm Shift in the Ecumenical Movement*, trans. Tony Coates (Geneva: World Council of Churches, 1991) 72–73.

[19] Ibid., 109–11.

[20] Ibid., 117–20.

[21] Teresa Berger, "'Separated Brethren' and 'Separated Sisters': Feminist and/as Ecumenical Visions of the Church," in *Ecumenical Theology in Worship, Doctrine, and Life: Essays Presented to Geoffrey Wainwright on his Sixtieth Birthday*, ed. David S. Cunningham, Ralph Del Colle, and Lucas Lamadrid (New York/Oxford: Oxford University Press, 1999) 221–30.

[22] David Gill (ed.), *Gathered for Life: Official Report, VI Assembly World Council of Churches, Vancouver, Canada 24 July–10 August 1983* (Geneva: WCC, 1983) 49, footnote 192.

ity and must rely on its power to convince, the WCC is "the only appropriate expression for the fellowship of the church at world level."[23]

Roman Catholics and the Orthodox have generally not welcomed Raiser's "new paradigm," nor have all Protestants found it congenial. While sympathetic to Raiser's concern for a common mission expressed in terms of social-ethical responsibility, Harding Meyer argues that the ecumenical movement cannot be reduced to a "conciliar process" that gives up the goal of the visible unity of the churches in faith, sacraments, and ministry."[24]

Many of the more conservative churches are not comfortable with the word "ecumenical" and continue to object to what seems to them the liberal, activist agenda of the WCC; they have declined to participate as members. A concern to move towards better relationships and common witness with these often vital and rapidly growing churches has led to some new initiatives. In the late '90s the General Secretary of the WCC was instrumental in setting up a committee to bring together "Ecumenicals" and "Evangelicals," based on *participation* rather than *membership*. An initial meeting took place at the Chateau de Bossey near Geneva, August 26–29, 1998, with 28 participants. Another meeting with some twenty Evangelical and Pentecostal representatives gathered at Fuller Theological Seminary in Pasadena, September 9–11, 2000.

The first meeting of what would be known as the Global Christian Forum took place at Fuller Seminary, June 15–20, 2002. Bringing together 59 members from Orthodox, Protestant, Roman Catholic, Evangelical, Pentecostal, and African Instituted Churches, its purpose was not to create another organization, but rather an "open space" where Christians from diverse churches and interchurch organizations could gather to foster mutual respect, develop more inclusive relationships, and address common challenges. The Forum met again in Hong Kong April 28–May 4, 2004, and another meeting was planned for Lesotho in Zambia in February 2005. Hopefully the Forum will help those from more conservative churches see the possibilities of a more inclusive ecclesial communion.

A Visible Church?

What can be said about the goal of visible unity? Many argue that the metaphors of people of God and Body of Christ imply the visibility of the

---

[23] Raiser, *Ecumenism in Transition*, 116.

[24] Harding Meyer, *That All May Be One: Perceptions and Models of Ecumenicity*, trans. William G. Rusch (Grand Rapids, MI: William B. Eerdmans, 1999) 147–48.

Church. Ola Tjørhom maintains that many Protestants, misunderstanding the Reformers' view that the "real church" is "hidden" (*verborgen*), have misinterpreted the Church as essentially invisible. Such a Church becomes a *societas platonica*, a mere "idea' that has no "body."[25] For a Church that is fundamentally invisible, visible unity is not possible. According to Veli-Matti Kärkkäinen, "most Pentecostals emphasize the spiritual, thus invisible, nature of the church."[26] Geoffrey Wainwright agrees that institutional unity without the spiritual unity of heart and mind would be a mere facade; but he adds, "the alternative to visible unity is visible *dis*unity, and that is a witness against the gospel."[27]

Hans Küng has also stressed the necessarily visible nature of the Church. "A real Church made up of real people cannot possibly be invisible." The Church is not a Platonic idea; it is a real and therefore visible fellowship of people, rooted in history, comparable with other institutions. The Reformers, he argued, had no intention of founding an invisible Church; they sought to renew the visible Church.[28]

Küng certainly has not been one to overemphasize the visible, institutional dimension of the Church; few Catholic theologians have put as much emphasis on the Church's charismatic structure as he. He argues that the source of the Church's life is the Spirit, and stresses that "the Church will be heading for disaster if it abandons itself to its visible aspects and, forgetful of its true nature, put itself on the same level as other institutions."[29] Nevertheless, echoing *Lumen gentium*, he rejects any attempt to reduce the Church to two realities, one visible, the other invisible (cf. LG 8). The Church has an essentially public nature. It is the people of God; it has a real history that embraces sin as well as grace. Against the Free Church tendency to see the Church as a spiritual assembly of like-minded people, Küng argues "it is impossible to see the origins of the Church in individuals, in believing Christians. This misconception reduces the Church to something private, to an agglomeration of pious individuals."[30]

---

[25] Tjørhom, *Visible Church—Visible Unity*, 77.

[26] Veli-Matti Kärkkäinen, *An Introduction to Ecclesiology: Ecumenical, Historical and Global Perspectives* (Downers Grove, IL: InterVarsity, 2002) 73.

[27] Geoffrey Wainwright, *The Ecumenical Moment: Crisis and Opportunity for the Church* (Grand Rapids, MI: Eerdmans, 1983) 4.

[28] Hans Küng, *The Church*, trans. Ray and Rosaleen Ockenden (New York: Sheed and Ward, 1967) 35.

[29] Ibid., 37.

[30] Ibid., 127. Wolfhart Pannenberg takes a similar view; see his *Systematic Theology*, Vol. 3, trans Geoffrey W. Bromiley (Grand Rapids, MI: William B. Eerdmans, 1998) 100–01.

The people of God is a visible, historical community, embracing people of both covenants, prophets and patriarchs, saints and sinners.

Communion in the Apostolic Tradition

The principle, *ecclesia semper reformanda*, should apply to all the churches, not just to the Church of Rome. If this is so, then other churches also are called to reexamine their ecclesial lives and self-understandings. A Church is apostolic if it is in continuity in its life and faith with the apostolic faith, if it is faithful to the apostolic tradition of the Church. In the words of the WCC *Baptism, Eucharist and Ministry* statement:

> Apostolic tradition in the Church means continuity in the permanent characteristics of the Church of the apostles: witness to the apostolic faith, proclamation and fresh interpretation of the Gospel, celebration of baptism and the eucharist, the transmission of ministerial responsibilities, communion in prayer, love, joy and suffering, service to the sick and the needy, unity among the local churches and sharing the gifts which the Lord has given to each.[31]

Some have lost continuity with this "great tradition of the Church," which Tjørhom describes as grounded in the apostolic witness, shaped by the ecumenical creeds of the ancient Church, "catholic" in incorporating the faith of the Church in all its richness, with a foundation that is sacramental, ecclesiological, and liturgical.[32]

Some churches are challenged by ecumenical consensus statements like *Baptism, Ministry and Eucharist* to examine their practice of baptism or to renew their worship life, becoming eucharistic communities. Some need to renew their ministerial and authority structures, or to develop visible structures of communion. Some may need to formalize or establish a teaching office to safeguard their grasp of the apostolic tradition and occasionally to re-express their teaching in light of a deeper understanding of the Gospel. Communion in the great apostolic tradition provides the creedal and liturgical context for the interpretation of Scripture; without it, the Reformation Scripture principle has become for some churches a warrant for private interpretation, substituting the infallibility of a text for the Church's living tradition.

---

[31] WCC, *Baptism, Eucharist and Ministry* (M no. 34).

[32] See Tjørhom, *Visible Church—Visible Unity*, 27-28; Tjørhom argues that authentic Reformation ecclesiology, particularly Luther's, underwent a "Protestantization" in the 19th century, 1–2.

Eucharist

For almost two thousand years Christians have gathered on the Lord's Day under the presidency of the bishop or his delegate to break the bread and share the cup in memory of Jesus. The Eucharist is not just a ritual; it is a sacramental meal that unites people across differences personal, social, and geographic, enabling them to rediscover each other in Christ. Implied here is the notion of *koinōnia* or communion, so important in the life of the Church.

For both Roman Catholic and Orthodox ecclesiology the Eucharist is crucial; "where the Eucharist is, there is the Church."[33] But in many Protestant traditions, the Eucharist has been marginalized; it is celebrated rarely if at all or it is made a matter of private devotion rather than an ecclesial event. Luther and Calvin did not intend to replace the Church's eucharistic worship with a service of the Word, though Calvin did see it as subordinate to the Word. But Sunday celebration did not remain the norm. As David Carter says, at a time "when some Anglican churches only had a monthly eucharist and many more only three or four celebrations a year, Wesley's recovery of the centrality of the eucharist was remarkable: it is estimated that he celebrated on average twice a week, often to large congregations."[34] David Fergusson observes that weekly celebration of the Lord's Supper "is still largely foreign to the worship of most Reformed communities in the world today, and, if ecumenical progress is to be achieved, a commitment to the more frequent celebration of the Lord's Supper is probably required alongside a reassessment of its theological significance."[35] Tracing the process of the marginalization of the Eucharist within American Evangelicalism, Lutheran liturgist Gordon Lathrop asks, "Is the church centered on individuals and their processes of decision-making? Or is it centered on—indeed, created by—certain concrete and communal means that God has given, which bear witness to and give the grace of God, and in which God is present and active?"[36] In other words, the Church has a sacramental structure.

---

[33] Susan Wood, "Communion Ecclesiology: Source of Hope, Source of Controversy," *Pro Ecclesia* 2 (1993) 425.

[34] David Carter, "The Ecumenical Wesleys," *Ecumenical Trends* 33/2 (February 2004) 12; see John C. Bowmer, *The Sacrament of the Lord's Supper in Early Methodism* (Westminster [London]: Dacre Press, 1951).

[35] David Fergusson, "The Reformed Churches," in *The Christian Church: An Introduction of the Major Traditions*, ed. Paul Avis (London: SPCK, 2002) 41.

[36] In Gordon W. Lathrop and Timothy J. Wengert, *Christian Assembly: Marks of the Church in a Pluralistic Age* (Minneapolis: Fortress Press, 2004) 126.

Sacraments mediate the encounter with God by symbolizing; they need to be effective signs. Thus all traditions need to look to the renewal of their eucharistic practice. Michael Welker offers a catalogue of dismal eucharistic experiences: a Supper appended to the "worship" service, after most of the congregation has departed; people remaining in the pews like passengers on an airplane while plates of bread crumbs and plastic cups of wine are passed; the literal "feeding" of the faithful of a mushy mixture of bread and wine with long spoons; splendidly celebrated liturgies where no one responded to the invitation to the meal;[37] and we might add, the "private mass," solitary celebrations without any member of the faithful present.

The ecumenical dialogues of the last forty years have helped bridge many of the divides between Christians over the Eucharist. The WCC text, *Baptist, Eucharist and Ministry*, states that as "the eucharist celebrates the resurrection of Christ, it is appropriate that it should take place at least every Sunday."[38] Many churches have been moved to more frequent celebration through the modern liturgical movement. While theological languages and approaches differ with the traditions, Catholics, Orthodox, and many Protestants are much closer today to a common understanding of Christ's eucharistic presence.[39] Many Protestant Christians see the Lord's Supper as an act of communal worship and agree that communion with Jesus in his body and blood cannot be separated from the act of eating and drinking. Though their theological language is different from that of Roman Catholics and they do not use the language of transubstantiation, they agree that the risen Christ is really present in the Lord's Supper through his self-identification with the bread and wine, and that he is truly received in Holy Communion.

What is perhaps more of a problem is helping both Catholics and Protestants in the pews come to a better appreciation of how similar their understandings of the Eucharist are, rather than continuing to emphasize the distance between their respective positions. As Jeffrey VanderWilt observes, Catholics too often presume that belief in the real presence is unique to Catholics, in part because they have been told by non-Catholic friends that they are not supposed to believe in the real presence since "That's only for Catholics to believe. . . . Thus Protestant faith is wounded by these polemical dynamics no less than Catholic faith."[40]

[37] Michael Welker, *What Happens in Holy Communion?* (Grand Rapids, MI: William B. Eerdmans, 2000) 6–8.

[38] WCC, *Baptism, Eucharist and Ministry,* (E, no. 31).

[39] See Welker, *What Happens in Holy Communion?*

[40] Jeffrey VanderWilt, *Communion with Non-Catholic Christians: Risks, Challenges, and Opportunities* (Collegeville, MN: The Liturgical Press, 2003) 59.

Towards a Common Ministry

A mutually recognized ministry is another important step towards full communion. Some churches desirous of such communion are seeking to ordain their ministers in a way that invites recognition from all parts of the Church. For example, the 1985 Catholic-Lutheran statement *Facing Unity* suggests that with a fundamental consensus on faith and sacraments, there should be a mutual act of recognition of ministry. The Catholic side would affirm the presence of the ministry instituted by Christ in the Lutheran churches "while at the same time pointing to a lack of fullness of the ordained ministry as a *defectus* which, for the sake of church fellowship, has jointly to be overcome" (no. 124).[41] The two traditions could begin to exercise a single *episcope* in collegial form that would include joint ordinations (no. 127). Without judging Reformation ministries as invalid, something the Catholic Church has not yet done,[42] the Catholic Church could offer other churches the sign of continuity in the tradition as well as communion with the Roman Catholic Church.

Without necessarily acknowledging any defect, Lutherans and Anglicans have already taken steps towards joint ordinations with the *Porvoo Common Statement* involving Anglicans in the British and Irish churches and Lutherans in the Nordic and Baltic churches, though the Danish Church objected to the importance given to the bishop's role, particularly in ordination.[43] The document understands the episcopal succession, not as a juridical requirement, but as one of God's gifts that is to be shared in communion.[44] In the United States, Lutherans and Episcopalians entered into full communion with the Episcopal Church when the Evangelical Lutheran Church in America approved "Called to Common Mission," a re-

---

[41] Roman Catholic-Lutheran Joint Commission, *Facing Unity: Models, Forms and Phases of Catholic Lutheran Church Fellowship* (Geneva: Lutheran World Federation, 1985).

[42] Some might extrapolate to the Protestant churches from the judgment of *Apostolicae curae*, promulgated by Pope Leo XIII in 1896 that ordinations carried out according to the Anglican rite are "absolutely null and utterly void" (no. 36); in his "Commentary" on Pope John Paul II's Apostolic Letter, *Ad Tuendam Fidem*, Cardinal Joseph Ratzinger mentioned this judgment as among those truths "to be held definitively"; see "Commentary on Profession of Faith's Concluding Paragraphs," *Origins* 28/8 (July 16, 1998) 119. However, theologians like Avery Dulles continue to find this example debatable; see "Commentary," sidebar, 117.

[43] *Together in Mission and Ministry: The Porvoo Common Statement with Essays on Church and Ministry in Northern Europe* (London: Church Publishing House, 1993); see Peter Lodberg, in Ola Tjørhom (ed.), *Apostolicity and Unity: Essays on the Porvoo Common Statement* (Grand Rapids, MI: William B. Eerdmans, 2002) 76–86.

[44] Ola Tjørhom, in *Together in Mission and Ministry*, 179.

vision of the earlier Concordat of Agreement.[45] In the words of the U.S. Lutheran-Roman Catholic Dialogue, in 2001 the ELCA entered a new relation with the Episcopal Church, committing both to "share an episcopal succession that is both evangelical and historic."[46]

Shared Teaching Office

Ultimately, the churches should move towards the development of a common magisterium or teaching office. Without a primacy recognized by all, the Orthodox churches have been unable to convene a pan-Orthodox council, and some Orthodox scholars think it "unlikely that such a council could ever be convoked."[47] Some Evangelical scholars argue that Evangelical churches do have a magisterium, though they are usually reluctant to acknowledge it. Glenn Hinson says that Baptists have one, but he admits that it is indefinite and difficult to define: "It probably exists in individual interpretation, in congregational worship and Sunday school instruction; in denominational agencies, especially the seminaries; and in various 'leaders' within a democratic political body."[48] Cecil Robeck argues that Pentecostals have a developing magisterium, even though most Pentecostal leaders would deny its existence. "Unfortunately," he writes, "the teaching magisterium that is emerging is composed of ecclesiastical leaders who themselves are often little more than lay theologians, while their trained theologians are not trusted to play any ongoing role in such a magisterium."[49] He observes, the recent requirement of the Assemblies of God General Presbytery that all new candidates for ministry must answer a new question, "Do you believe that everyone who is baptized in the Holy Spirit speaks in tongues at the time they are baptized in the Spirit?" represents a change in the tradition without a vote of the General Council of the Assemblies of God.[50]

---

[45] See W. A. Norgren and William G. Rusch, (ed.), *"Toward Full Agreement" and "Concordat of Agreement"* (Augsburg: Fortress Press, 1991).

[46] U.S. Lutheran/Roman Catholic Dialogue, "The Church as Koinonia of Salvation: Its Structures and Ministries," no. 80; see http://www.usccb.org/seia/koinonia.

[47] Nicholas Afanassieff, "The Church Which Presides in Love," in *The Primacy of Peter: Essays in Ecclesiology and the Early Church*, ed. John Meyendorff (Crestwood, N.Y.: St. Vladimir's Seminary Press, 1992) 102.

[48] E. Glenn Hinson, "The Authority of Tradition: A Baptist View," in *The Free Church and the Early Church*, D. H. Williams (ed.), (Grand Rapids, MI: William B. Eerdmans, 2002) 146.

[49] Cecil M. Robeck, Jr., "The Challenge Pentecostalism Poses to the Quest for Ecclesial Unity," in *Kirche in ökumenischer Perspektive: Kardinal Walter Kasper zum 70. Geburtstag*, ed. Peter Walter, Klaus Krämer, and George Augustin (Freiburg: Herder, 2003) 314.

[50] Cecil M. Robeck, Jr., "An Emerging Magisterium? The Case of the Assemblies of God," *PNEUMA: The Journal for the Society of Pentecostal Studies* 25/2 (2003) 213.

The difficulty that Hinson and Robeck point to is that indefinite or un-acknowledged teaching offices are generally ineffective; the very lack of definition means that their "authorities" are not really accountable, personal influence is often more important than ordination or theological education, and without formal status they are not really able to make binding decisions on new questions. Robeck includes the subject of tradition and the role of a teaching magisterium as two questions on which the Pentecostal Movement needs to develop its own position, a challenge that could also be directed towards other Evangelical communities.[51] Perhaps Evangelicals might learn from Catholics in this area.

What if the Roman Catholic Church were to invite the Orthodox and Protestant churches into a shared exercise of the Church's teaching authority? There are many questions that divide our churches today, both internally and from others. Some of these might include the following: Can those "outside the Church" be saved? Are they excluded from God's grace if they have not made an explicit confession of faith in Jesus, a question extremely important today when dialogue with the great world religions is becoming increasingly urgent? Can grace be mediated by these other religious traditions? Can women be ordained to ministry in the Church? What about those who are homosexual, not by choice, but from an orientation, determined perhaps even before birth? What about human life questions such as abortion, the death penalty, and the possibilities raised by genetic engineering? And most important, how are these questions to be decided? Who speaks for the Church?

What if these questions were to be addressed by the whole Church, acting together, rather than separately? Would Christians from the different churches be willing to come together in a truly ecumenical council? Would they have the structures or authorized representatives to do so? When the different churches have built up a level of trust from working and praying together, will they move towards articulating the bonds of communion that would enable them to so assemble? Will they be willing to trust their deliberations together to the Holy Spirit?

Obviously I speak here with what may seem like naïve optimism. The churches remain divided over questions of biblical interpretation, the authority of tradition and how to recognize authentic tradition, how authority is exercised, whether it is personal or institutional, and the relationship between faith and reason. At the same time, there has been considerable convergence between many of them on these difficult questions. For example, the Fourth World Conference on Faith and Order of the WCC (Montreal 1963) ac-

---

[51] Robeck, "The Challenge Pentecostalism Poses," 314.

knowledged "we exist as Christians by the Tradition of the Gospel (the *para-dosis* of the *kerygma*) testified in Scripture, transmitted in and by the Church through the power of the Holy Spirit" (no. 45). Distinguishing between "the Christian Tradition" and "traditions," in the sense of a diversity of both forms of expression and separate communions (nos. 46-47), it noted that modern biblical scholarship had done much to bring the churches "towards the Tradition" and encouraged common study, including study of the Church fathers of all periods and reexamination of their particular traditions (no. 55).[52]

The 1982 WCC statement *Baptism, Eucharist and Ministry* balances the authority of Church leaders with the sense of the faithful: "Authority cannot be exercised without regard for the community. . . . Yet the authority of ordained ministers must not be so reduced as to make them dependent on the common opinion of the community. Their authority lies in the responsibility to express the will of God in the community."[53] While many in the Free Church tradition continue to be suspicious of any kind of institutionalized authority, there has been considerable convergence. What is needed is a vision of the future that will encourage the churches to begin addressing difficult problems together, rather than separately.

The Free Churches

As vital as the Free Church tradition is, it presents a greater challenge to the idea of union in a broader communion of the *ecclesia catholica*, and it is not at all clear that all of the churches in this tradition are really desirous of being included. Theologians from this tradition have complained that the Free Church and congregationalist ecclesiologies are generally ignored in the ecumenical discussions of the last decades.[54] Veli-Matti Kärkkäinen argues that the Faith and Order document *The Nature and Purpose [now "Mission"] of the Church* (NPC) in particular and mainstream ecumenism in general is almost exclusively based on the ecclesiologies of traditional churches in the West, ignoring the incredible growth of largely Pentecostal-Charismatic churches in the Southern Hemisphere.[55]

---

[52] See "Fourth World Conference on Faith and Order, Montreal, 1963," in *The Ecumenical Movement: An Anthology of Key Texts and Voices*, ed. Michael Kinnamon and Brian E. Cope (Geneva: WCC/Grand Rapids, MI: William B. Eerdmans, 1997) 139–44.

[53] WCC, *Baptism, Eucharist and Ministry,* Commentary no. 16.

[54] For example, Miroslav Volf, *After Our Likeness: The Church as the Image of the Trinity* (Grand Rapids, MI: William B. Eerdmans, 1998) 20.

[55] Veli-Matti Kärkkäinen, "'The Nature and Purpose of the Church': Theological and Ecumenical Reflections from Pentecostal/Free Church Perspectives," *Ecumenical Trends* 33/7 (July August 2004) 5–7.

While Kärkkäinen faults the western ecclesiologies for being one-sidedly christological,[56] one could argue that the restorationist ecclesiology of the Free Churches is one-sidedly pneumatological. At the same time one might ask if Kärkkäinen's emphasis on the charismatic gifts, "from prophecy to speaking in tongues to healing to visions to exorcism,"[57] is based on an overly idealized understanding of the apostolic Church. Pneumatology cannot be separated from Christology.

There are important ecclesiological questions implicit in Kärkkäinen's argument. He critiques the NPC draft for a "typically Protestant" idea that the church is the *creatura Verbi et creatura Spiritus*.[58] Though he wants to see greater emphasis on the Church as the Body of Christ, strangely he does not mention here the sacraments of baptism and particularly the Eucharist that for Paul constitute the Church as the Body of Christ (1 Cor 12:13; 10:16-17).

Thus we need to ask, what is the ecclesial reality of a Church whose members gather for Eucharist only infrequently or whose eucharistic faith differs substantially from that of the great tradition? Could it be considered a eucharistic community and thus a Church in the full sense? Ecclesial communities gathering for prayer, praise, and Bible study are important, but they are not "Church," at least in the Catholic and Orthodox sense. For both, the Eucharist is crucial; "where the Eucharist is, there is the Church."[59]

The Bishop of Rome

Clearly one of the most difficult problems remains the future role of the bishop of Rome. Without pursuing some kind of relationship to the bishop of Rome, restoration of communion between the Catholic Church and other churches is unimaginable.[60] Within an ecclesiology of communion, the pope has and will continue to have a crucial role to play. It is precisely through communion with the bishop of Rome that a particular Church and its ministry of oversight are shown to be visibly in communion with the Catholic Church. But if the bishop of Rome is to play again the role of universal pastor and servant of the Church's unity, the way this ministry is ex-

---

[56] Ibid., 6.
[57] Ibid.
[58] Ibid., 3.
[59] Wood, "Communion Ecclesiology," 425.
[60] Clint Le Bruyns, "*Ecclesia de Eucharistia*: On Its Ecumenical Import," *Ecumenical Trends* 32/8 (2003) 13.

ercised must be renewed and reformed, if other churches are to see in it a gift. Some have suggested that in a reconciled communion of churches the pope could continue to exercise his teaching ministry for the Catholic Church, while teaching directed at the whole Church would be by way of "authentic and non-defining declarations" that would not threaten the religious conscience of Christians from Reformation backgrounds.[61] This possibility should at least be considered.

Today an increasing number of Christians are coming to recognize the place of the bishop of Rome in the Church of tomorrow. Some Orthodox theologians are willing to recognize the historical priority or primacy of Rome, but not a primacy defined in terms of "supreme power" over other churches.[62] The Lutheran-Catholic Dialogue in the United States spoke of a "Petrine function," a ministry of unity on behalf of the Church as a whole. The Lutheran participants expressed an interest in a papal primacy renewed in the light of the gospel for tomorrow's Church.[63] The members of the Anglican-Roman Catholic International Commission (ARCIC I) have also stated that in any future union of the whole Christian community a universal primacy serving the communion of the churches should be exercised by the See of Rome, the only see that has exercised and still exercises such a ministry.[64]

Many years ago, while still a professor of theology, Joseph Ratzinger stated an important principle in regards to the primacy:

> One who stands on the ground of Catholic theology cannot consider the forms of the 19th and 20th century papacy as the only possible and necessary forms for all Christians. One cannot say that what was possible for a thousand years is not possible today. Rome should not demand from the East more on the doctrine of the primacy than was formulated and taught in the first thousand years. On this basis recognition is possible. The East should not describe the Western development as heretical.[65]

a deal

---

[61] Fries and Rahner, *Unity of the Churches*, 90.

[62] See Alexander Schmemann, "The Idea of Primacy in Orthodox Ecclesiology" in *The Primacy of Peter*, ed. John Meyendorff, 163.

[63] Paul C. Empie and T. Austin Murphy (ed), *Lutherans and Catholics in Dialogue V: Papal Primacy and the Universal Church* (Minneapolis: Augsburg, 1974) (no. 32).

[64] "Authority in the Church I" (no. 23); text in the Anglican-Roman Catholic International Commission, *The Final Report* (Washington: USCC, 1982) 64.

[65] Joseph Ratzinger, cited by Heinrich Fries, "Katholische Anerkennung des Augsburger Bekenntnisses?" *Stimmen der Zeit* 7 (1978) 476; Ratzinger's statement appears in his "Prognosen für die Zukunft des Ökumenismus" in *Bausteine für die Einheit der Christen* 17 (1977) 10.

Pope John Paul II himself has suggested the need for a rethinking of the primacy in his 1995 encyclical on ecumenism, *Ut unum sint*.[66] Without minimizing the difficult questions that remain, he invited representatives of the other Christian churches to join him in the search for "a way of exercising the primacy which, while in no way renouncing what is essential to its mission, is nonetheless open to a new situation" (no. 95). While the response was not overwhelming, some theologians and dialogue groups have been quite positive.

Lutheran theologian Wolfhart Pannenberg has stated that since the Church of Rome has been the historical center of Christianity since the end of the primitive Jerusalem Church, "We ought freely to admit the fact of the primacy of the Roman Church and its bishop in Christianity."[67] The Anglican-Roman Catholic International Commission in its 1999 statement, "The Gift of Authority," stated that as sufficient agreement on universal primacy as a "gift of God" had been reached in the Commission's work, its members proposed that the ministry of the bishop of Rome "could be offered and received" by the Anglicans even before the two communions were in full communion. "We envisage a primacy that will even now help to uphold the legitimate diversity of traditions, strengthening and safeguarding them in fidelity to the Gospel."[68]

The Princeton Proposal, formulated by a group of scholars chosen by the independent Center for Catholic and Evangelical Theology, states that the bishop of Rome is "the only historically plausible candidate to exercise an effective worldwide ministry of unity," but notes that the "bishop of Rome and the magisterium of the Roman Catholic Church must teach in a fashion capable of shaping the minds of the faithful beyond those currently in communion with Rome."[69]

Responding from an Orthodox perspective, Olivier Clément challenges both Roman Catholics and the Orthodox. He calls on the Orthodox to move beyond the temptation to autocephalism and religious nationalism to recognize a primacy such as it was in the first millennium, balanced by collegiality. The challenge for Catholicism is "to return to the authentic conception of primacy as the servant of communion, within a framework of genuine interdependence between her bishops and all other bishops,

---

[66] John Paul II, *Ut unum sint*, *Origins* 25 (1995) 49–72.

[67] Pannenberg, *Systematic Theology*, Vol. 3, 421.

[68] ARCIC, "The Gift of Authority" (no. 60); *Origins* 29/2 (1999) 29.

[69] *In One Body Through the Cross: The Princeton Proposal for Christian Unity*, ed. Carl E. Braaten and Robert W. Jenson, (Grand Rapids, MI: William B. Eerdmans, 2003) 54–55.

and also of real dialogue with the entire people of God."[70] The WCC draft statement, *The Nature and Mission of the Church*, points to a new climate in which a universal primacy can be seen as a gift rather than a threat to other churches (no. 103, Crete text).

The emerging consensus on the Petrine ministry is a hopeful sign, though it does not yet represent a general consensus in the Reformation churches. Walter Kasper speaks of two fundamentally different interpretations of the sixteenth century Reformation. He calls one an "ecumenism of consensus," a unity in diversity that would recognize the episcopal ministry in apostolic succession and—with some reservations—the Petrine ministry. The other, an "ecumenism of difference" insists on eucharistic hospitality on the basis of a consensus in principle regarding the gospel, while the churches remain separated from a confessional and institutional point of view. Until the Protestant churches are able to resolve this divergence, he judges that "no substantial progress can be made with the Ecclesial Communities of the Reformation traditions."[71]

Conclusion

The potential of a world Church, organized and focused, to bring about change should not be underestimated. José Casanova shows how the Catholic Church, having accommodated itself to modernity at the Second Vatican Council, officially recognizing the principle of religious liberty and committed to the defense of human rights, "has become such an important transnational organization in the emerging world system that no state can afford to ignore it."[72] Of course, this matters little if salvation is understood in a personal and individualistic way. This does not require global organization. But if the Church understands the kingdom of God as including the transformation of the world, witnessing to it in its life and enacting it through its ministry, it needs effective structures and organization for common action.

Perhaps the greatest obstacle to the churches living in communion in a truly catholic Church is the lack of will on all sides. Most understand that living in visible unity will demand some changes on the part of all. But a unity that is not visible is not real.

[70] Olivier Clément, *You Are Peter: An Orthodox Theologian's Reflection on the Exercise of Papal Primacy* (New York: New City Press, 2003) 75–76.

[71] Walter Kasper, "Prolusio," *PCPCU Information Service* 115 (2004/I-II) 29.

[72] José Casanova, "Globalizing Catholicism and the Return to a 'Universal Church'," in *Transnational Religion and Fading States*, ed. Susanne Hoeber Rudolph and James Piscatori (Boulder, CO: Westview Press, 1997) 130–32 at 132.

Yet so much progress has already been made. After long years of dialogue, many of the churches are joined in a consensus on the basic truths of the faith, and recognize that such consensus can co-exist with a diversity of theological expressions and understandings. Many have moved closer to communion in the great tradition of the Church. Some have reached consensus on the Eucharist and Christ's eucharistic presence and are moving towards weekly celebration. Some have already begun taking steps towards ordaining new ministers together in a way that can be recognized by all the churches. Recovering this tradition would signify recognition that the Church is more than a Church of the Word; it has a visible, sacramental structure.

More difficult questions include moving towards an ability to teach together, to face new problems jointly rather than separately, integrating those in the Free Church tradition into a visible communion of the *ecclesia catholica,* and the question of embracing the ministry of the bishop of Rome. For some, these questions appear as irresolvable or the suggested steps forward too idealistic.

On the other hand, the long years of dialogue have led to widespread agreement that each local church needs a ministry of *episkopē*, to watch over its life and safeguard its unity with the wider communion of the Church. So, too, the universal Church needs a ministry of unity. Not a few theologians speak openly of a new communion with the bishop of Rome, the only See to have historically exercised this ministry. We will return to this subject in the following chapter in the context of the challenges facing the Roman Catholic Church.

CHAPTER 11

Challenges for the Roman Catholic Church

T he genius of the Roman Catholic Church over the centuries has been its ability to preserve <u>unity within diversity</u>. This ability gives the Catholic Church a singular advantage in a fragmented world. With its structures of communion in place, it is uniquely positioned as a world Church. Already representing almost fifty percent of world Christianity, it offers the framework for a larger communion of communions, a more encompassing *ecclesia catholica* embracing all Christians. Yet this vision will not be realized without a renewal of its own structures so that it might function more effectively as a communion. As Hermann Pottmeyer observes, Vatican II provides the theological foundations for an ecclesiology of communion, but the idea of papal primacy as sovereignty is still operative in its documents.[1] Similarly, Joseph Komonchak characterizes the council doctrine on the Church as "transitional." While the council began from the perspective of the universalist ecclesiology long dominant in the west, "its recovery of an ecclesiology of communion that underlies a theology of the local church was hesitant and unsystematic."[2]

What steps might the Roman Catholic Church take towards a more inclusive communion with Orthodox and Protestant Christians that would represent a truly catholic Church? In this chapter, we will consider some of those steps. They include a reform of its structures, some positive initiatives towards other churches, and reclaiming its identity precisely as catholic.

---

[1] Herman J. Pottmeyer, *Towards a Papacy in Communion: Perspectives from Vatican Councils I & II*, trans. Matthew J. O'Connell (New York: Crossroad, 1998) 129.

[2] Joseph Komonchak, "The Local Church and the Church Catholic: The Contemporary Theological Problematic," *The Jurist* 52 (1952) 427.

Reform of Structures

The *ecclesia catholica* means both the fullness of the church and the communion of all the churches. The Roman Catholic Church could embrace other churches within a more encompassing communion, for it already embraces the theologically and liturgically diverse Eastern Catholic churches. But without a profound renewal of its own structures of government and decision-making, its promise will remain unfulfilled. If other churches see Rome as monarchical in its exercise of authority, imposing a crushing uniformity on its own local churches, or as not being open to local concerns, they will not recognize the universal Catholic Church as able to function as a true communion of churches.

"Catholicity" necessarily entails inclusivity. As a worldwide communion of churches, the Roman Catholic Church needs to model a diversity in communion that could accommodate the identity and traditions of the Orthodox and Protestant churches and grant its own episcopal conferences greater freedom to address issues specific to their regions. Since Vatican II, the Church has developed a multiplicity of consultative bodies—pastoral councils on parish and diocesan levels, national and regional episcopal conferences, and international synods of bishops, but most have little real authority. Thus the Church needs to acknowledge the value of the principle of subsidiarity for its own life, to maintain the proper tension between primacy and collegiality, the global and the local, the universal and the particular Church. It needs a system of checks and balances and greater accountability, to ensure that the Church functions as a true communion and not simply as a monarchical institution, and it needs to make it possible for lay men and women to express more adequately their share in the mission of the Church. As Roger Haight observes, if even the Roman Catholic Church has become a voluntary organization to which people freely commit to belong, "will not church authority have to involve dialogue and consent as in a congregational or free church polity"?[3]

Many theologians and bishops have sought to address issues of renewal and reform in the Catholic Church. In an important address given at Oxford University in 1996, retired San Francisco Archbishop John Quinn called for a reform of the Roman Curia. In addition, he asked for wider and more serious consultation with bishops and episcopal conferences on a number of "grave questions" that have been closed to discussion, for a "true, active collegiality and not merely a passive collegiality," for a greater involvement

---

[3] Roger Haight, *Christian Community in History*: Vol. I: *Historical Ecclesiology* (New York: Continuum, 2004) 34.

of local churches in the selection of bishops, and for the implementation within the church of the principle of subsidiarity, allowing local decisions to be made at local levels rather than by higher authorities.[4] He has also called for reexamining the role played by the College of Cardinals over the bishops and international synods of bishops, including their exclusive role in the election of the bishop of Rome. In addition to the royal embellishments of this office, he objects to "the creation of a distinct body superior to and set apart from the rest of the College of Bishops, making the rest of the episcopate a body of secondary importance."[5]

Other theologians have made similar suggestions. Richard Gaillardetz points out that the distinction between the pope and bishops as legislators for the Church and the curial dicasteries as executors has been ignored, "with the result that the congregations of the Roman curia have virtually replaced the college of bishops as the principal legislators of the Church."[6] Michael Buckley has recommended returning to the ancient practice that bound a bishop to his see as a way of short-circuiting clerical ambition and careerism, and he cites Vatican Cardinals Gantin and Ratzinger as having condemned the current practice of translating bishops from one see to another.[7] Others have proposed strengthening the power of national episcopal conferences and promoting local, regional, and supranational synods as ways of providing for more effective decision-making at local and regional levels.[8] With power over liturgy, discipline, and the ability to name local bishops, such regional structures would make possible both subsidiarity and decentralization within the universal Church.[9]

Such reform is badly needed. Indeed, Cardinal Walter Kasper speaks of "a mental or practical schism" between the universal church—by which he means Rome—and local practice. "Many laypersons and priests can no

---

[4] John R. Quinn, "Considering the Papacy," *Origins* 26/8 (July 18, 1996) 121–25 at 123.

[5] John R. Quinn, *The Reform of the Papacy: The Costly Call to Christian Unity* (New York: Crossroad, 1999) 145.

[6] Richard R. Gaillardetz, *Teaching With Authority: A Theology of the Magisterium in the Church* (Collegeville, MN: The Liturgical Press, 1997) 287.

[7] Michael J. Buckley, "What Can We Learn from the Church in the First Millennium," in *The Catholic Church in the 21st Century: Finding Hope for its Future in the Wisdom of the Past*, ed. Michael J. Himes (Ligouri, MO: Liguori, 2004) 19–21.

[8] See Brian Daley, "Structures of Charity: Bishops' Gathering and the See of Rome in the Early Church," in *Episcopal Conferences: Historical, Canonical and Theological Studies*, ed. Thomas J. Reese (Washington: Georgetown University Press, 1989) 28–29.

[9] Andrew Greeley, "Information Deficit: Why the Church's Hierarchy Isn't Working," *Commonweal* 131/5 (March 12, 2004) 14–15; Rembert G. Weakland, "Looking Forward: An Archbishop Examines Himself and Church Structures," *Commonweal* 18 (August 15, 2003) 21; Weakland suggests reviving the ancient structure of patriarchates.

longer understand universal church regulations, and simply ignore them."[10] As for the other churches with which the Catholic Church is in dialogue, they will find its vision of "communion-unity of the church" credible "only if the relationship between universal and local church—as unity in plurality and plurality in unity—is realized in an exemplary manner in our own church." A model of unity in communion should not crush or absorb local churches and their traditions, whether Catholic, Orthodox, or Protestant. At the same time, each local Church or communion of churches "can be the church of Jesus Christ in the full sense only in fellowship with the universal church."[11]

Thus, without serious reform emanating from Rome, Christian unity will remain only a dream. While the challenges for Rome are considerable, the Church has much more freedom to move in new directions than is generally acknowledged. The Church's structures developed, were reshaped, and sometimes changed in the course of its history. For example, the election of the pope by the cardinals was introduced in 1059 as a reform; from the end of the ninth to well into the eleventh century, popes had generally been appointed by the German emperor or the powerful Roman families.[12] The present system of papal elections could be expanded or changed to make it once again more representative. Similarly, there are precedents in history of the medieval Church for the modern practice of representative government that according to Brian Tierney begins in ecclesiastical institutions, for example, the Dominican order.[13]

If Vatican II taught that lay Christians share in the mission of the Church through their baptism and confirmation (LG 33), with the implication of a co-responsibility for its life, the Roman Catholic Church has yet to find ways to express this effectively in its governance. Three issues seem of particular importance; they include greater local involvement in the selection of bishops, respect for the principle of subsidiarity, and revising the rules for the synod of bishops.

Selection of Bishops

How bishops are selected remains a critical issue today, both for Roman Catholics, but also for other Christians who are considering the possibil-

---

[10] Walter Kasper, *Leadership in the Church: How Traditional Roles Can Serve the Christian Community Today*, trans. Brian McNeil (New York: Crossroad, 2003) 159.

[11] Kasper, *Leadership in the Church*, 174.

[12] See Haight, *Historical Ecclesiology*, 272, 277–78.

[13] Brian Tierney, "Church Law and Alternative Structures: A Medieval Perspective," in *Governance, Accountability, and the Future of the Catholic Church*, ed. Francis Oakley and Bruce Russett (New York: Continuum, 2004) 58–59.

ity of living in communion with a broader *ecclesia catholica*, with but not under the bishop of Rome. A review of Church history shows a number of ways for choosing a bishop, most of them involving some input from both clergy and laity in the local church.[14]

In the first four centuries local churches generally chose their own bishops, with the involvement of all their people. In the fourth to sixth centuries, it was common for the bishops of the province to select and consecrate a bishop chosen by the people and clergy of the local church, though influential community leaders increasingly supplanted direct involvement of the people. From the sixth to the eleventh centuries cathedral chapters or other representatives of the clergy elected their bishops, though kings and other secular powers increasingly imposed their own candidates, particularly under the influence of feudalism.

The Gregorian reform in the eleventh century sought to restrict the influence of secular rulers. Gratian's *Decretum*, a collection of some 4000 canonical rulings which served as the standard text of canon law until the promulgation of the 1917 Code, had a number of canons stating that a bishop was not to be imposed on a church against the wishes of the people and that the clergy and people were to be involved in choosing or at least consenting to a candidate's election. But Gregory's reforms frequently were ineffective because of local rivalries, the inability of local electors to reach a decision, and powerful metropolitans—all of which led to appeals to Rome or to Roman confirmation of local elections.

While Pope Urban V claimed the right to appoint all bishops, abbots, and abbesses, in some churches his claim was ignored, while in others the Holy See either appointed bishops directly or confirmed those chosen locally. In spite of considerable debate, the Council of Trent failed to reach a consensus on the appointment of bishops, though it stressed the role of provincial synods in investigating and judging the suitability of candidates. After Trent, papal appointment prevailed in most places; in others the popes confirmed those chosen by provincial synods or cathedral chapters, chose from a *terna* (Ireland), or confirmed those chosen by secular rulers (kings in France, Spain, Portugal, Bavaria, and Sicily, presidents in South America).

Thus, it is only in relatively recent times that all bishops in the Catholic Church have been appointed by Rome. The 1917 Code of Canon Law stated that the Roman Pontiff freely appoints bishops (c. 329, #2), though

---

[14] See John M. Huels and Richard R. Gaillardetz, "The Selection of Bishops: Recovering the Traditions," *The Jurist* 59 (1999) 348–76; I am dependent on their survey here.

it still acknowledged exceptions. Some argue that Roman appointment helps to safeguard unity in a world Church. But clearly the great tradition of the Church gives far more weight to provincial and local church structures in the selection of bishops. A return to local selection, confirmed by the bishop of Rome, would respect the integrity of the local church to provide for its own needs, and thus, honor the principle of subsidiarity. It would better maintain the necessary tension between conciliarity and primacy, local Church and universal Church in the communion of the Church. Finally, as Huels and Gaillardetz argue, returning to the tradition "would go a long way to reassuring other Christians that the Roman Catholic Church is not a papal monarchy intolerant of diversity."[15]

Principle of Subsidiarity

Another important step towards the reform of the way the Catholic Church exercises authority would be to find effective ways to give expression to the principle of subsidiarity in the Church's life. The principle of subsidiarity means that larger social bodies should not take over decisions that are responsibilities of smaller groups or associations. It has its roots in 19th century social thinkers in France and Germany and first appears in Roman Catholic social teaching in Pope Pius XI's encyclical *Quadragesimo anno* (1931).

While subsidiarity is presumed as a principle in Catholic social teaching, there is some debate as to whether or not it applies also to the government of the Church.[16] Pope Pius XII twice said that it did. He stated that the principle was valid "also for the life of the Church without prejudice to its hierarchical structure."[17] Vatican II, however, did not follow his lead in this respect. The Preface to the 1983 revised Code of Canon Law referred to it, but as Ad Leys contends, the Code's failure to develop the consequences of subsidiarity and its accentuating the power of the pope at the expense of the bishops "opens all the doors to a centralist exercise of primacy."[18]

---

[15] Huels and Gaillardetz, "The Selection of Bishops," 374; in an appendix they suggest some canons for a future edition of the Latin Code of Canon Law, based on the values of the tradition, 369–76.

[16] See Joseph A. Komonchak, "Subsidiarity in the Church: The State of the Question," *The Jurist* 48 (1988) 298.

[17] *La elevatezza, AAS* 38 (1946) 144–45; see also his address to the Second World Congress of the Lay Apostolate, *AAS* 49 (1957) 926–28.

[18] Ad Leys, *Ecclesiological Impacts of the Principle of Subsidiarity*, trans. A. van Santvoord (Kampen: Kok, 1995) 100.

Leys argues that the key issue involved in the principle of subsidiarity is the "balance between freedom and restraint."[19] If the Church is a communion of churches, it is characterized by a tensile relationship that needs to be maintained between the universal and the particular, the papacy and the bishops, the Church of Rome and the local churches. The principle of subsidiarity helps maintain this tensile relationship.[20]

For example, at the 1998 Synod of Bishops for Asia, one Indonesian bishop stated: "The Catholic church is not a monolithic pyramid. Bishops are not branch secretaries waiting for instructions from Headquarters! We are a communion of local churches." He pointed out that the Indonesian Bishops' Conference had been asking the Vatican for permission to ordain married men for over thirty years, noting that the shortage of celibate priests to celebrate the Eucharist meant that Indonesian Catholics were becoming Protestant "by default."[21]

Respecting the ability of local churches to make pastoral decisions affecting their own ecclesial lives is particularly important to other churches considering reestablishing full communion with the Catholic Church. As Archbishop John Quinn said in his Oxford Address, "Large segments of the Catholic Church as well as many Orthodox and other Christians do not believe that collegiality and subsidiarity are being practiced in the Catholic Church in a sufficiently meaningful way."[22] For the Orthodox, considering living in communion with the bishop of Rome, this is particularly important. Without a reform in these areas, reconciliation and the restoration of communion will be unlikely.

Synod of Bishops

One way to provide for a more effective exercise of collegiality would be to revise the rules for the international synod of bishops, a suggestion made by Archbishop Quinn, among others. Quinn argued that the synod had not lived up to its expectations, that its procedures were outdated, and that giving it a deliberative vote, not merely a consultative one, would make the synod a more truly collegial undertaking.[23]

---

[19] Ad Leys, "Structuring Communion: The Importance of the Principle of Subsidiarity," *The Jurist* 58 (1998) 117.

[20] Leys, "Structuring Communion," 108–10.

[21] Thomas C. Fox, *Pentecost in Asia: A New Way of Being Church* (Maryknoll, NY: Orbis, 2002) 178.

[22] Quinn, "Considering the Papacy," 123.

[23] Ibid., 123–24.

Formally established by Pope Paul VI in September 1965, the synod was to provide a structure for bringing together with the pope representatives of the bishops throughout the Church.[24] While its role is consultative, canon law allows for the possibility of the pope giving synods deliberative power in certain cases (can. 343). Once the pope has chosen a topic, preparation for the synod takes place under the guidance of a synod secretariat. The general secretary of the synod calls together various specialists who draw up a document, called the "outline" (*lineamenta*) which will be discussed, revised, and approved by the pope, after which it is sent to the episcopal conferences for study and discussion. From their reports, the secretariat draws up a "working paper" (*instrumentum laboris*) for the synod itself.

For the synod assembly at Rome, each episcopal conference elects several bishops to represent it. The pope can name other representatives, up to 15 percent of the total. At the synod itself bishops can address the synod topics, usually in brief interventions limited to about eight minutes. The real discussion takes place in smaller groups, organized by language, and often with clerical or lay auditors present. One of the flaws in the synod process is that the suggestions and recommendations from the bishops and the small groups are gathered and presented to the pope by a Vatican-appointed synod editorial committee which often filters out unwanted views. The final synod report is prepared, not by the synod participants, but by the pope and a post-synod committee, usually issued as an apostolic exhortation. Thus real power remains in the hands of the Vatican bureaucracy.

There has been general dissatisfaction with the synod process. Michael Fahey writes: "Unfortunately, despite high hopes for their success, results of synods have been negligible. Each new synod attracts less and less attention; the structure of their sessions has become unwieldy, they have become rituals with little practical impact on the life of the Church. In the last 30 years the institution has not been notable as a wellspring of new ideas or strategies."[25] Much of the frustration is due to the gap that so often exists between the issues presented at the synod and the official response that follows it.

The synod process might be improved considerably by giving the bishops more voice in preparing its agenda, by relaxing the rule of secrecy,

[24] Paul VI, apostolic constitution *Apostolica sollicitudo*, September 15, 1965; *AAS* 57 (1965) 775–80.

[25] Michael A. Fahey, "The Synod of America: Reflections of a Nonparticipant," *Theological Studies* 59 (1998) 489; see also Peter C. Phan (ed.), *The Asian Synod: Text and Commentary* (Maryknoll, NY: Orbis, 2002).

revising the reporting process, expanding the membership, providing for more effective participation by the laity, and giving the bishops a greater voice in preparing the final report.[26] Still the synod has considerable potential; it provides the bishops with an international forum to raise problems facing the Church, should they choose to so use it. Even if the synod's recommendations are not deliberative, they carry a moral authority that the pope cannot afford to ignore.

Ecumenical Initiatives

In addition to reforming its structures of authority, there are a number of ecumenical initiatives the Catholic Church might consider.

Sacramental Validity and Ecclesial Status

What is the position of the Catholic Church concerning other Christian churches, those it calls "Churches and ecclesial communities"? The Catholic Church has always recognized the ecclesial status of the Orthodox Churches which are seen as having preserved the apostolic succession and true sacraments (UR 15). The only times "ecclesial communities" appears by itself is in UR 22, in reference to ecclesial communities in the West, in other words, the Reformation churches. It asserts "we believe they have not preserved the proper reality of the eucharistic mystery in its fullness, especially because of the absence [Latin, *defectum*] of the sacrament of Orders."[27] Thus for official Roman Catholicism, sacramental validity and full ecclesiality are linked.

But one cannot immediately conclude that the council decided that the Reformation churches were not churches or that their sacraments were invalid. The issue is complicated. While the method of the council was to move from the recognition of valid orders to the title "church," Jerome Hamer who had served as the secretary of what was then known as the Secretariat for Promoting Christian Unity says that the council did not restrict the name Church to those communities that had valid orders and Eucharist; nor did it say that they could legitimately be called Church. It did not want to limit the debate of theologians on this point or to prejudge it.[28]

---

[26] See Thomas P. Rausch, "The Synod of Bishops: Improving the Synod Process," *The Jurist*, 49 (1989) 248–57.

[27] The conciliar texts do not use the word "absence" or "lack of" in this context.

[28] Jerome Hamer, "la terminologie ecclésiologique de Vatican II et les ministères protestants," *Documentation catholique* 68 (1971) 628.

The Congregation for the Doctrine of the Faith may have sought to close these questions in its controversial 2000 declaration, *Dominus Iesus*. The declaration stated, "the ecclesial communities which have not preserved the valid episcopate and the genuine and integral substance of the eucharistic mystery, are not churches in the proper sense."[29] While this may indeed have been implied by the logic of Vatican II's Decree on Ecumenism, *Dominus Iesus* seems to go beyond what the council actually said.[30] Francis Sullivan agrees that "the council never flatly declared that the ecclesial communities are 'not churches in the proper sense.'"[31] He notes that the Decree on Ecumenism spoke without hesitation of the separated Eastern churches as "particular churches," and that "it was the mind of the commission responsible for this text that the Western communities that lack the full reality of the Eucharist—without attempting to decide which ones these were—still have an ecclesial character, and are at least analogous to particular churches of the Catholic Church."[32]

Nor did the council decide the question of the validity of ministry in the Protestant communities. Hamer has stated that the theological language of the council does not permit a conclusion concerning the validity of ministry in the Protestant communities.[33] More recently, Bishop Richard Sklba of Milwaukee observed that Trent left open many questions regarding ministry, not wishing "to resolve issues prematurely or contrary to more ancient opinions in the church."[34] Thus the Roman Catholic Church does not deny ecclesial reality to the Reformation churches.[35] It sees them as ecclesial communities of Christians united with Christ, consecrated by baptism, living in his Spirit, nourished by the Word, and celebrating other sacraments (cf. LG 15; UR 22).

[29] Congregation for the Doctrine of the Faith, "*Dominus Iesus,*" (no. 17); *Origins* 30/14 (Sept 14, 2000) 216; cf. UR (no. 22).

[30] See Thomas P. Rausch, "Has the Congregation for the Doctrine of the Faith Exceeded Its Authority?" *Theological Studies* 62 (2001) 802–10.

[31] Francis A. Sullivan, "The Impact of *Dominus Iesus* on Ecumenism," *America* 183 (October 28, 2000) 10.

[32] Francis A. Sullivan, *The Church We Believe In: One, Holy, Catholic and Apostolic* (New York: Paulist, 1988) 32; see his discussion on "The One Church of Christ," 23–33.

[33] Hamer, "La terminiologie ecclésiologique," 628.

[34] Richard Sklba, "Four Important Truths Learned in Lutheran-Catholic Dialogue," *Origins* 30 (December 21, 2000) 452; see however Chapter 10, note 42 below.

[35] See Francis A. Sullivan's commentary on NPC, "Faith and Order: The Nature and Purpose of the Church; Comments on the 'material inside the boxes'," *Ecumenical Trends* 32/10 (November 2003) 5; also *The Church We Believe In,* 34–65.

Apostolic Succession

What about the related question of apostolic succession? Few today would want to limit genuine ecclesiality and sacramentality validity to the question of apostolic succession, narrowly understood as a succession of episcopal ordinations considered by itself. John Burkhard includes Yves Congar, Joseph Ratzinger, and Francis Sullivan among those who have serious reservations about this mechanical theory of apostolic succession.[36] Nevertheless Pope John Paul II's 2003 encyclical *Ecclesia de Eucharistia* seems to have taken this position; it says that "the uninterrupted sequence of valid episcopal ordinations . . . is essential for the church to exist in a proper and full sense"[37] and a genuine eucharistic assembly requires a priest ordained "through episcopal succession going back to the apostles."[38] This seems to make both full ecclesial status and ministerial validity depend on apostolic succession, narrowly understood. This was the position of *Dominus Iesus* a few years earlier.

Yet Walter Kasper, in a 2001 report to the Pontifical Council for Promoting Christian Unity, has stated that *Dominus Iesus* went beyond the council in stating that the Church of Jesus Christ is "fully" realized only in the Catholic Church. This language, for Kasper, does not mean that there is an "ecclesial vacuum" outside the Catholic Church. *Dominus Iesus* "does not state that the ecclesial communities which issued from the Reformation are not churches; it only maintains that they are not churches in the proper sense, which means that in an improper sense, analogous to the Catholic Church, they are church. Indeed . . . they do not want to be church in the Catholic sense." The lack (*defectus*) is on the level of the signs and instruments of grace, not on the level of the *res*, the grace of salvation itself.[39]

Susan Wood suggests that John Paul's judgment regarding both the nature of the Lord's Supper in Protestant communities and the nature of their ordinations "seems to be of an all-or-nothing nature."[40] She cites a 1993 letter of Cardinal Ratzinger to Bavarian Lutheran bishop Johannes Hanselmann acknowledging the Lord's presence in the Lutheran Lord's Supper:

---

[36] John J. Burkhard, *Apostolicity Then and Now: An Ecumenical Church in a Postmodern World* (Collegeville, MN: The Liturgical Press, 2004) 39.

[37] John Paul II, *Ecclesia de Eucharistia*, (no. 28); *Origins* 32/46 (2003) 760.

[38] Ibid., no. 29.

[39] Walter Kasper, *"Prolusio,"* in PCPCU *Information Service* 109 (2002/I-II) 18.

[40] Susan K. Wood, *"Ecclesia de Eucharistia*: A Roman Catholic Response," in *Pro Ecclesia* 12 (2003) 397.

I count among the most important results of the ecumenical dialogues the insight that the issue of the eucharist cannot be narrowed to the problem of 'validity.' Even a theology oriented to the concept of succession, such as that which holds in the Catholic and in the Orthodox church, need not in any way deny the salvation-granting presence of the Lord [Heilschaffende Gegenwart des Herrn] in a Lutheran [evangelische] Lord's Supper.[41]

Like Kasper and others, Wood argues that a more developed understanding of ministry, sacramental life, and ecclesiology would translate the "*defectus*" of *Lumen gentium* 22 as "deficiency" or "defect," rather than simply as "lack."[42] The issue is not validity, the "*res sacramenti*," but a defect in regards to the sign.[43]

Kasper has argued that the Second Vatican Council left open the possibility "that the *una sancta* could recognize more than one exclusive form and conception of apostolic succession."[44] And he appeals to the Orthodox churches' more pneumatological understanding of the Church's episcopal structure to suggest that "the continuity of the apostolic ministry can no longer be understood in terms of a purely historical linear succession; rather this continuity is realized ever anew in the Holy Spirit."[45] If this is so, it should not be impossible for the Roman Catholic Church to move forward to recognize the validity of the sacraments in the Reformation confessional churches, and thus their substantial ecclesiality, even if from a Catholic perspective they "are invalid according to purely institutional criteria."[46] Even more specifically, Kasper states that "it is certainly possible for the *successio*, understood as sign, to part company with the *res* that it designates and attests, namely, the tradition. . . . But one should not turn exceptional situations into the normal case; rather, one should adopt the patristic view that *traditio*, *successio*, and *communio* are essentially interrelated."[47]

---

[41] Wood, "*Ecclesia de Eucharistia*." 398; see "Briefwechsel von Landesbischof Johannes Hanselmann und Joseph Kardinal Ratzinger über das communion-Schreiben der Römanischen Glaubenskongregation," *Una Sancta* 48 (1993) 348.

[42] Ibid. See Burkhard's extended discussion of the concept of sacramental validity, *Apostolicity Then and Now*, 218-23.

[43] This is the position of the U.S. Lutheran-Roman Catholic Dialogue Common Statement, *The Church as Koinonia of Salvation: Its Structures and Ministries*, (no. 108); see www.usccb.org/seia/ koinonia.htm.

[44] Kasper, *Leadership in the Church,* 135; see also Wood, "*Ecclesia de Eucharistia*," 395-96.

[45] Kasper, *Leadership in the Church*, 141.

[46] Ibid.

[47] Ibid., 126.

Thus it seems clear that the Roman Catholic Church could do considerably more to move towards greater communion with these churches and ecclesial communities. A deeper understanding of apostolicity has placed the thorny problem of the recognition of ministries in a new context. If apostolicity is seen, not as a pipeline of episcopal ordinations, but as fidelity to the life and mission of the apostolic Church, then authentic ministry, ecclesiologically grounded, can coexist with what from a Catholic perspective is a *defectus* in the ritual, sacramental sign.[48] Some churches have begun to address this, as we saw in the last chapter.

At the same time, a church is not apostolic merely by claiming to be so. To be apostolic a church needs to express in its life a fidelity to the life and mission of the apostolic church; it must be faithful to the apostolic tradition (cf. Acts 2:42). A church that was not evangelical, not a eucharistic community, did not encourage discipleship and holiness of life, did not witness to the kingdom of God through compassionate service of the poor, that was not willing to live in visible, sacramental communion with other churches—would be seriously deficient.

If the Roman Catholic Church could move beyond its often too narrow concept of sacramental validity, and thus understand "Church" in a more inclusive way, Evangelical Christians might also need to acknowledge the ecclesial status of the Catholic Church more explicitly. For example, in a report of a conversation between representatives of the Catholic Church and the World Evangelical Alliance (2003), the Evangelical participants acknowledge the "presence of true believers indwelt by Christ's Spirit among Catholics," but the report is less clear on the ecclesial status of the Catholic Church.[49] Certainly the ecumenical dialogues of the last forty years have moved this question forward considerably.

Eucharistic Hospitality

Could the Roman Catholic Church relax its discipline and welcome non-Catholic Christians to share in its Eucharist? Pope John Paul II again reiterated the impossibility of eucharistic sharing in his encyclical on the Eucharist.[50] But Vatican II's position on eucharistic sharing is more ambiguous:

[48] See for example, Kilian McDonnell, "Ways of Validating Ministry," *Journal of Ecumenical Studies* 7 (1970) 209–65.

[49] Roman Catholic Church/World Evangelical Alliance, "Church, Evangelization, and 'Koinonia'," (no. 11); see *Origins* 33/19 (2003) 313.

[50] John Paul II, *Ecclesia de Eucharistia*, (nos. 40-44); *Origins* 763.

Worship in common (*communicatio in sacris*) is not to be considered as a means to be used indiscriminately for the restoration of unity among Christians. There are two main principles upon which the practice of such common worship depends: first, that of the unity of the church which ought to be expressed; and second, that of the sharing in the means of grace. The expression of unity generally forbids common worship. Grace to be obtained sometimes commends it (UR 8).

Note that the council did not forbid *communicatio in sacris* (which includes the possibility of receiving the Eucharist), though it said that it should not be used "without discretion (*indiscretim*)."[51] While the council left concrete cases up to local episcopal authority, subsequent instructions from Rome have forbidden eucharistic sharing in almost all cases involving Protestant churches. However, the council did allow for the possibility of eucharistic sharing between Catholic and Orthodox Christians, on the basis of the Orthodox having "true sacraments, above all—by apostolic succession—the priesthood and the Eucharist" (UR 15; cf. OE 26-29). According to the 1993 Ecumenical Directory, "Catholic ministers may lawfully administer the sacraments of penance, Eucharist and the anointing of the sick to members of the Eastern churches who ask for these sacraments of their own free will and are properly disposed."[52] However, the Orthodox have been reluctant to welcome eucharistic sharing with Roman Catholics. They believe the term "intercommunion" itself is inept, as eucharistic communion makes sense only in a fully united Church.[53] As far as Protestant Christians are concerned, the Catholic Church has questions about the validity of their sacraments and the full ecclesial reality of their churches, though, as we have seen, progress since the council should make movement forward on these questions possible.

Eucharistic sharing continues to remain a barrier for the Catholic Church. Perhaps in part this reflects a fear that if the Protestant churches reached their long-sought goal of intercommunion, they would settle for the present divided state of the Church. There may indeed be a danger of this. In the last chapter, we saw Kasper contrasting an "ecumenism of consensus," open to a qualified recognition of the Petrine ministry, with an

[51] See Jeffrey VanderWilt, *Communion with Non-Catholic Christians: Risks, Challenges, and Opportunities* (Collegeville, MN: The Liturgical Press, 2003) 39.

[52] PCPCU, *Directory for the Application of Principles and Norms on Ecumenism* (no. 125); see *Origins* 23/9 (1993) 148.

[53] John D. Zizioulas, *Eucharist, Bishop, Church: The Unity of the Church in the Divine Eucharist and the Bishop During the First Three Centuries*, trans. Elizabeth Theokritoff (Brookline, MA: Holy Cross Orthodox Press, 2001) 258.

"ecumenism of difference" that insists on eucharistic hospitality while the churches remain confessionally and institutionally separated.[54]

Being Truly Catholic

Perhaps at this point the Roman Catholic Church needs to reflect more profoundly on its own claim to catholicity. Catholicity cannot be limited to geographical extension; it means to embrace the whole (*kat' holos*). Nor can it be reduced to the fullness of present day Roman Catholicism. As confessed in the ancient creeds, catholicity means not full or perfect, but universal, in contrast to what is local or particular.[55] For Roman Catholics, Catholicism is not the product of a single reformer or historical movement in post-New Testament Christian history. It does not find its identity in a single doctrine, like Lutheranism, with its emphasis on justification by faith alone. Unlike Reformed or Calvinist Christianity, it is not based on a single theological tradition. It is not defined by a single liturgical tradition, as is Anglicanism, which finds its principle of unity in the Book of Common Prayer. Nor is it committed to a single method of biblical interpretation, like fundamentalist and much of Evangelical Protestantism, bound to a confessional notion of biblical inerrancy. Catholicism includes within itself a wide variety of theologies, spiritualities, liturgies, and expressions of the Christian life.

If catholic means universal, to embrace the whole, the Roman Catholic Church should take its catholicity more seriously. If it is to be truly catholic, there should be an inclusiveness or fullness in its catholicity. It should be willing to embrace and include within its communion all legitimate expressions of life in Christ, even if from its own perspective one or another is less than perfect or full.

On the one hand, the Catholic Church does not want to reduce ecclesiality to submission to the bishop of Rome. It already recognizes the Orthodox churches as true churches with valid sacraments. Given that it has not authoritatively declared ministry in the Reformation churches as invalid, it is difficult to see why it could not recognize the ecclesial status of the Reformation churches when they are eucharistic communities, joined in a communion with other churches, and with the Catholic Church through the historic creeds and more recent consensus statements on justification, Eucharist, and ministry.

[54] Walter Kasper, "Prolusio," *PCPCU Information Service* 115 (2004/I-II) 29.
[55] See Johannes Brosseder, (ed.), *Von der Verwerfung zur Versöhnung* (Hamburg: Neukirchener Verlag, 1996), "Steht uns unsere Geschichte im Wege?" 27.

On the other hand, communion should be visibly, sacramentally expressed. What if the Catholic Church were to extend an offer of eucharistic hospitality to those churches? If the Catholic Church could acknowledge them as churches with valid sacraments, why not invite them to share in the Eucharist? And what if it were to invite the Reformation and Orthodox churches into a shared exercise of the Church's magisterium? Would the Catholic Church and the other churches be willing to trust in the Spirit's guidance in some future synodal or conciliar assembly?

The Roman Catholic Church and other churches are already in imperfect communion with each other. They share baptism and life in the Spirit; they are nourished by the Word, and celebrate other sacraments (cf. LG 15; UR 22). While their communion is not yet full, it admits of different degrees. Some "interchurch" families are united in faith but divided at the altar. Bilateral and multilateral consensus statements, new attitudes on the part of the faithful of different churches, ecumenical communities, covenants on local levels, the desire to live in communion and worship together——all these are signs of a growing communion. What is to prevent the Catholic Church from recognizing this growing communion sacramentally? Communion cannot be reduced to doctrine and authority; it must also include shared life.

The Free Churches

The Free Churches present a more difficult problem. Rooted in the radical reformation, they appeal in matters of doctrine, ministry, and structure, not to the great liturgical and sacramental tradition of the Church, but directly to the New Testament.[56] While some gather for the Lord's Supper weekly, others celebrate it monthly, quarterly, or not at all.[57] Some understand the Church as a eucharistic community, others do not. Congregational in inspiration, they lack visible bonds of communion with each other and with the wider Church. Some do not recognize Catholics as Christians or honor their baptism. Thus they often vary widely among themselves and in their attitude towards the Catholic Church.

There is at least the potential of an ecclesial individualism or sectarianism in the Free Church position, for example, in that of Miroslav Volf, who does not require sacramental relations between churches as a condition of

---

[56] See Veli-Matti Kärkkäinen, *An Introduction to Ecclesiology: Ecumenical, Historical and Global Perspectives* (Downers Grove, IL: InterVarsity Press, 2002) 64–66.

[57] According to *BEM* (Geneva: WCC, 1982), the Eucharist "should take place at least every Sunday." See Eucharist, no. 31.

ecclesiality, but only that each church retains an *openness* towards all other churches.[58] But openness is not communion, a network of relationships uniting the Church of Christ, enabling it to function as "one" in its witness, ministry, and ecclesial life. In the pre-Constantinian period a particular church was seen as authentically Church only if it lived in fellowship with other churches.[59] Can an ecclesial community today truly be Church without such relations of *communio*? Or do we simply embrace the multiplicity of forms emergent in modern times, no matter how different from the historic Christian community, and call each "Church"?

Roman Catholic, Orthodox, and many Protestant Christians understand the word Church differently from the way it is understood by many in the Pentecostal and Free Church traditions. It is difficult to recognize "Church" in the full sense in a community that does not understand the Eucharist as it was understood in the great tradition, to live in visible, sacramental communion with other Christians, or to seek communion with the worldwide communion of the *ecclesia catholica*. Theologically, the Church is more than an ecclesial community; it is a eucharistic community, made one body through its participation in the body and blood of Christ (cf. 1 Cor 10:26-17).

Thus, from a Roman Catholic perspective, many churches in the Free Church tradition correspond more closely to ecclesial communities than to churches in the full sense. Though some of their members are reluctant to recognize Roman Catholics even as Christians, the Catholic Church does not deny the ecclesial status of these communities. They are communities of Christians, disciples of Jesus, consecrated by baptism, nourished by the Word, deeply committed to his mission, living in his Spirit, and rich in spiritual gifts and graces (cf. LG 15; UR 3).

Communion in the Ecclesia Catholica

The Church has included a rich diversity of communities within its communion throughout its history.[60] In the early centuries it embraced monastic communities that occasionally lived in some tension with the official Church. Roger Haight speaks of the monastic movement as sharing many of the characteristics of Troeltsch's sect type of Church. If they represented a critique of the institutional Church, it remained implicit and

---

[58] Miroslav Volf, *After Our Likeness: The Church as the Image of the Trinity* (Grand Rapids, MI: William B. Eerdmans, 1998) 156–57.

[59] Ulrich Kühn, "Reception—An Imperative and an Opportunity," in *Ecumenical Perspectives on Baptism, Eucharist and Ministry*, ed. Max Thurian (Geneva: WCC, 1983) 166.

[60] See Thomas P. Rausch, *Radical Christian Communities* (Collegeville, MN: The Liturgical Press, 1990).

they remained completely contained within it, unlike the Cathars who defined themselves over and against it.[61] Other religious movements and ecclesial communities were able to find a home in the Church. The evangelical movement in medieval Europe, known as the *vita apostolica*, led to new religious congregations, some of which were lay in origin. While the Reformation generally was hostile to monasticism and religious congregations, the radical Reformation produced its own ecclesial communities, among them the Moravians, the Hutterites, the Mennonites, and the Quakers. Today they are considered churches in their own right, though it could be argued that they might more appropriately be considered communities within the universal Church. The contemporary Catholic Church is enriched by a rich diversity of communities, both lay and religious and there has been a rediscovery of monasticism in the Protestant tradition today.

If catholicity means embracing all legitimate expressions of life in Christ and if the Roman Catholic Church acknowledges a "certain communion with other churches and ecclesial communities,"[62] why could it not embrace the Free Churches as ecclesial communities with rich apostolic lives, their own traditions, a unique mission, and their own structures of governance within its communion? Could it not welcome baptized members of the Free Churches to share in its ecclesial life in different ways, even to participate in its eucharistic celebrations, provided that they desired to live in communion with the Roman Catholic Church? What would be required of the Evangelical and Free Church communities? They should, as a minimum, respect the validity (thus the non-repetition) of Roman Catholic baptism, refrain from aggressive proselytizing of Catholics,[63] and be able to recognize the presence of the risen Jesus in the breaking of the eucharistic bread and the sharing of the cup. Their desire to live in communion would be exemplified by their willingness to enter into dialogue on those questions that continue to remain divisive.

With so much held in common, the inclusion of the Free churches within the communion of the Catholic Church could enrich the mission of the whole Church. If the principle *lex orandi lex credendi* (the law of praying

---

[61] Haight, *Historical Ecclesiology*, 344.

[62] *Ecumenical Directory*, (no. 18); *Origins* 23 (1993).

[63] On the difficult subject of ethics and evangelization see *Evangelization, Proselytism and Common Witness*, The Report from the Fourth Phase of the International Dialogue 1990-1997 Between the Roman Catholic Church and Some Classical Pentecostal Churches and Leaders, *PCPCU Information Service* 97 (1998/I-II) no. 93; see also John C. Haughey, "The Ethics of Evangelization," in *Evangelizing America*, ed. Thomas P. Rausch (New York: Paulist Press, 2004) 152–71.

is the law of believing) is valid, might not living again in communion draw the different churches and communities closer together, enriching them with each other's gifts, manifesting the unity of the disciples of Jesus with God and with one another, "so that the world may believe" (John 17:21)?

The Bishop of Rome

What might a universal ministry of unity, exercised by the bishop of Rome, look like in a wider communion of the *ecclesia catholica*? In suggesting the need for a rethinking of the primacy in his 1995 encyclical on ecumenism, Pope John Paul II pointed to the structures of the Church of the first millennium as the model for unity with the East: "Her unity during the first millennium was maintained within those same structures through the bishops, successors of the apostles, in communion with the bishop of Rome. If today at the end of the second millennium we are seeking to restore full communion, it is to that unity, *thus structured*, which we must look."[64]

Pottmeyer observes that when the Latin patriarchate of the bishop of Rome came to be understood as the structure for the universal Church, the Church of the West lost its character as a communion of churches. At the same time, without a center of unity and ministry of communion, the Eastern churches disintegrated into a multiplicity of autocephalous or autonomous churches.[65] Some commentators suggest the possibility of regional structures of decision-making and communion—metropolitans, patriarchates, and synods, as we saw earlier.[66]

The bishop of Rome could be recognized as a spokesman for world Christianity and servant of the unity of the churches, occasionally calling representatives of the churches together to discuss common problems. Churches embracing such a ministry of unity should see their new unity, not "as a unity *under* Rome, but as a unity *with* Rome, in which 'the Western patriarch' has a special responsibility for the Church's universal unity within the framework of a comprehensive collegial and synodal structure."[67] Collegiality would be a key requirement. As Heinrich Fries and Karl Rahner have suggested, papal teaching procedures should include the bishops (or presiding ministers), including those of future partner churches,

---

[64] *Ut unum sint*, (no. 55); *Origins*, 62.

[65] Pottmeyer, *Towards a Papacy in Communion*, 133–34.

[66] Weakland, "Looking Forward," 21; also Olivier Clément, *You Are Peter: An Orthodox Theologian's Reflection on the Exercise of the Primacy* (New York: New City Press, 2003) 92.

[67] Ola Tjørhom, *Visible Church—Visible Unity: Ecumenical Ecclesiology and "The Great Tradition of the Church"* (Collegeville, MN: The Liturgical Press, 2004) 31.

and infallible definitions would be limited to those clarifying the substance of the faith. Future encyclicals would be addressed to all Christian churches, taking into account their different theologies and ways of thinking.[68] How the pope exercises authority over the communion of the Roman Catholic Church would remain the concern of that communion.

What is clear however is that the ministry of the bishop of Rome cannot and will not be seen as a gift for all the churches without the reform of the way that ministry is exercised. Those churches joining the wider communion of the *ecclesia catholica* would have to continue to govern themselves and choose their own bishops or presiding ministers. In this way, the principle of subsidiarity would find full expression in the life of the Church. But if Rome must change in the way it presides over the communion of the churches, without some recognition by the other churches of the Petrine ministry, exercised by the bishop of Rome, substantial progress will remain unlikely.

Conclusion

As we come to the end of our study we need to draw together in summary fashion some of the threads of our argument. The phenomenon of globalization shows a joining of peoples through economic and communication systems that has far outdistanced the ability of the churches to symbolize their reconciliation and unity with God and with each other. Thus globalization illustrates the importance of a truly catholic world Church.

Furthermore, the more than forty years of dialogue and encounter since the end of the Second Vatican Council have narrowed traditional doctrinal differences and helped Christians from different traditions to discover how much they genuinely have in common. In the process new relationships of friendship and mutual respect have developed and many Christians have begun to discover a common identity in Christ that often transcends ecclesial differences, without diminishing the richness they find in their own traditions. Those who have begun this journey towards reconciliation often encounter other Christians living lives of great generosity, sacrifice, and holiness, and they have been changed by the experience. There are Evangelicals today who read and quote with appreciation the writings of recent popes and seek in their ministry, not to lure Catholics into their own communities, but to renew Catholic parishes. There are Catholics doing graduate degrees with Evangelical faculties, eager to learn from their ex-

---

[68] Heinrich Fries and Karl Rahner, *Unity of the Churches: An Actual Possibility*, trans. Ruth C. L. Gritsch and Eric W. Gritsch (Philadelphia/New York: Fortress Press/Paulist Press, 1983) 83–89.

perience in intercultural ministry and missiology. There are Protestants and Catholics who live, work, and pray together in ecumenical communities, some lay, others monastic.

Thus turning back the clock to the divided Church of the second millennium is neither possible nor desirable. In a secular world, often hostile to the Christian message and yet sensing the emptiness and anomie that lies beneath the surface of modern life, the good news of the Gospel is more important than ever. Those who claim to be disciples of Jesus need to rediscover the unity that is already theirs. They need to put aside their stereotypes, their fear of the ecclesial "Other." Their focus should be the reign of God, not just their own ecclesial identity. We need bridges today, not the strengthening of barriers.

While there are some remaining differences, many today are coming to a greater appreciation of the diversity of God's gifts and the limitations of our theological languages. But in spite of the progress made, many churches have been reluctant to take the necessary steps towards visible unity in a communion of communions. In concluding I would like to suggest in outline fashion some of those steps.

1. Most important is the desire to live in communion with each other within the *ecclesia catholica*. Communion admits of different degrees; full communion may take considerable time. At the same time, each tradition has unique gifts to bring to this communion of communions. But without a desire to live in communion, a truly catholic Church remains only a dream.

2. Unity if it is to be real must be visible. The Church is not a Platonic idea. It is a real, historical community, the people of God, showing God's historical relationship with humankind. As the Body of Christ, the Church makes visible in human history the presence of the risen Jesus among his own for the sake of the world.

3. A basic consensus in faith is a precondition for the restoration of communion. The work of the Faith and Order Commission since its founding in 1927 and the dialogues carried on since the end of the Second Vatican Council in 1965 have addressed many of the questions that have divided the churches historically, finding both significant convergences and often consensus. Walter Kasper points to two milestones on the road to full unity, the agreements between Rome and the Oriental churches on the union of the divine and human in the one person of Christ, and the Common Declaration on the Doctrine of Justification, signed in Augsburg in 1999 between the Roman Catholic Church and the Lutheran World Federation.[69]

---

[69] Kasper, *Leadership in the Church*, 187.

4. Basic consensus is different from full agreement. It makes room for differences in theological expression, doctrinal developments, and confessional positions that can co-exist within a wider communion in faith and Christian life. It means that study and dialogue have found that these remaining differences do not contradict the Gospel and so are no longer to be considered Church dividing. Furthermore, dogmas defined by one tradition without the participation of others should not be considered as a *sine qua non* for communion.[70]

5. A shared faith means living in continuity with the great tradition of the Church. Agreed statements such as the WCC *Baptism, Eucharist and Ministry* text represent a challenge to all the churches to renew their sacramental practice as well as their ministerial and authority structures, including their ability to reach decisions and teach in communion. Baptism, the centrality of the Eucharist, and performing ordinations in a way that can be recognized by all the churches show forth the sacramental nature of the Church itself.

6. The Roman Catholic Church has the structures to foster and express communion in a world Church, but without the reform of those structures, to make them more collegial, transparent, and accountable, other churches will not be able to see them as gifts. Providing for more involvement of local churches in the selection of their bishops, honoring the principle of subsidiarity in the Church as well as in society, particularly in regard to national and regional conferences of bishops, and reforming the way the international synod of bishops works would be important steps in this direction.

7. The history of the development of structures of authority and governance in the Catholic Church gives evidence of considerable flexibility. The Church has always learned and borrowed from its historical and cultural surroundings, so that what is presumed in one moment may have been quite differently understood and exercised in another.

8. The Church's teaching office or magisterium has been exercised historically in various forms. In the late Middle Ages it included the university faculties of theology. University theologians reviewed the doctrinal decrees of the general councils of Lyons I, 1245; Lyons II, 1274; and Vienne, 1312 and voted at the Councils of Constance (1415) and Basel (1439); Aquinas juxtaposed the teaching magisterium of the university theologians to the pastoral magisterium of the bishops. Certainly their expertise could prove helpful in the future.

---

[70] See Yves Congar, *Diversity and Communion*, trans. John Bowden (Mystic, CT: Twenty-Third Publications, 1985) 174.

9. If eucharistic hospitality is possible in principle with the Orthodox churches (UR 15), it should also be possible with the Reformation churches, since the Catholic Church has not definitively denied their ecclesial status or the validity of their ministries and sacraments, though from its perspective there is a defect on the level of sign of apostolic succession. There is a broad consensus today that apostolic succession cannot be reduced to a succession of episcopal ordinations, considered by itself. Offering mutual eucharistic hospitality to the churches of the Reformation could acknowledge their status as churches of the Word and the sacraments, even if they are not Church in the same way as the Roman Catholic Church understands itself. They are analogous to particular churches.

10. The ecclesial status of the churches in the Free Church tradition is more problematic. They are generally not eucharistic communities, living in visible, sacramental communion with other Christians. Some have little concern for continuity with the great tradition of the Church. Thus, from a Roman Catholic perspective, it is difficult to see them as churches in the proper sense. Nevertheless, many are vital ecclesial communities of Christians, centered on the Word and life in the Spirit, rich in spiritual gifts. While not all Free churches desire to live in communion with the Catholic Church, those that do could be welcomed as ecclesial communities within its communion, sharing its sacramental life and contributing their unique gifts.

11. Communion with the bishop of Rome symbolizes that a particular church is in communion with the Catholic Church. There are degrees of communion, but it must be real, even visible. For many Orthodox and Protestant churches, the real obstacle to communion with Rome is not the preeminent position of the bishop of Rome, his role as servant of unity, or even his ability to speak for the Church, but supreme power claimed over the universal Church and the personal way the pope and his curial assistants exercise the Church's magisterium, without the effective involvement of all the bishops. This obviously calls for change on the part of Rome.

12. But not just Rome. If Rome must change, so must the other churches. As globalization knits the secular world together, the churches remain divided. A truly catholic Church is possible. What its realization requires is becoming increasingly clear. Only the will is missing.

Index of Names

Index of Subjects

Canon within the canon, 125
Cardinals, college of, 203
Catholicity, 12–13, 138–42, 215
    and other churches, 12, 202
    renewed, 179–81
    truly catholic, 13, 170, 199, 215–16
CELAM, 174
Celibacy, 83, 104, 207
Chalcedon, Council of, 97
Charisms, 28, 59, 82–84; *see also*
    spiritual gifts
    and office, 106
China, Church in, 11, 171–72
Christianity, demographics, 11–12,
    133, 179
Christology, 7, 149
Church,
    and ecclesial communities, 30–31,
        135, 209–13
    and historical precedent, 7, 222, 204
    and Jesus movement, 50–52
    and state, 42, 155
    and Trinity, 23, 33, 46, 67
    as apostolic, 142–47, 189, 213
    as Body of Christ, 57–60, 81, 85–86
    as catholic, 12, 138-142
    as communion, 68, 130, 133
    as community of disciples, 66–67
    as *ekklēsia*, 46–49, 67
    as eucharistic community, 190, 196,
        217, 223
    as herald, 65
    as holy, 136–38
    as institution, 15–16, 63–64, 66
    as mystical communion, 64
    as one, 132–36, 138, 162
    as sacrament, sacramental, 24–25,
        64–65, 134, 162, 200, 222
    as servant, 65–66
    as universal, 136, 139–40
    as world church, 169–70, 179–80
    christological foundation of, 5,
        51–52, 87, 149, 196

diverse views of, 1, 68, 132, 178
house church, 47–48, 92
images of, 23–25, 45–47
local and universal, 48–49, 166,
    178, 204, 207
marks of, 131–51
    as analogical, 151
    Free church and Pentecostal
        view of, 148–49
    in Luther, 131
membership in, 20, 23, 29–30
mission of, 44, 53–54, 166
models of, 63–68
one or many, 1–4, 48, 70, 133–36,
    160
particular, 48, 153, 178
pneumatological foundation of, 4,
    5, 28, 82–83, 99, 196
sins of members, 138
undivided, 134
visible or invisible, 4, 132, 134–36,
    187–89
Clement, First letter, 92, 98, 117, 144
Clergy, 99, 102
Clericalism, 18, 27–28, 95, 102–06
Collegiality, 4, 20–22, 26–27
    and primacy, 202–04, 207, 223
Common good, 38, 42
Communicatio in sacris, 161, 214
Communio sanctorum, 71, 137, 160
    Protestant view of, 160
Communion (*koinōnia*), 1, 20, 59,
    64, 69–86, 122, 152, 159–65,
    216–18, 223
    and Eucharist, 59, 69–71, 81,
        160–61
    as participation in divine life, 71,
        84, 159
    CDF letter on, 178
    full, 163–66, 221
    in *Lumen gentium*, 27, 31, 33
    loss of, 7, 84, 133, 162
    of churches, 13, 27, 163, 166,

on biblical interpretation, 125–26, 130
on intercommunion, 214

Reception, 9, 152–59
Reform of structures, 197, 201–09, 222
Reformation, 7, 123–26, 162
and tradition, 124
and unity, 135, 199
and visibility of Church, 135, 188
hermeneutics, 124
on apostolic succession, 143
on catholicity, 141
Radical, 1, 135–36, 216, 218
Religious liberty, 8, 199
Religious life, 28, 217–18
Respect for Life, 37, 194
Ressourcement, 9
Restorationist Movement, 148
Revelation, 97
Roman Catholic Church, 12–13, 23
and apostolicity, 146
and catholicity, 140–42
and Free churches, 217, 223
and holiness, 138
and modernity, 8–9, 44, 199
and mystical Body of Christ, 29–30
and other churches, 29–31, 135, 209–13
Eastern rite Catholics, 12–13, 202
Roman Curia, 8, 19, 202, 203, 223
Roman church, primacy of, 117–18

Sacraments, 65, 79, 85, 190
validity of, 117, 146, 182, 209–13, 223
Salvation, 50, 53–54, 65, 71, 73, 78
outside the Church, 31–32, 126, 129, 155
Scripture principle, 110, 123–26, 189
crisis of, 125–26, 128–29,
Sectarianism, 5, 110, 169, 216
Sensus fidelium, 26, 126, 127
Slavery, 155

Social justice, 34, 38, 44, 53, 66
Societas perfecta, 25, 63, 147
Spirit, holy, 5, 7, 36, 61–62, 171
Spiritual gifts, 6, 28, 61, 62, 82–85, 196
Subsidiarity, principle of, 3, 176, 206–07
Syllabus of Errors, 42
Synod of bishops, 25, 27, 118, 120, 207–09
Asian Synod, 173, 175–77, 207
Extraordinary Synod, 70, 163, 179

Table-fellowship tradition, 74
Teaching Office, 110–15, 126–28, 222
of doctors, 113–14
ordinary universal magisterium, 121
shared, 193–95, 216
unacknowledged, 129, 193–94
The Twelve, 5, 51, 89–92
role of, 90–92, 105
Theological Commission, 18, 22
Theology, 40–41, 53–54
and models, 63
and pluralism, 4, 185, 200, 222
and university theologians, 113–14, 222
as "second order" language, 80–81
contextual, 170, 173–75
feminist, 44, 54, 174, 186
liberal, 51, 126
liberation, 44, 53–54, 66, 173–75
non-western, 180
Protestant, 87, 126
scholastic, 8, 112
Tongues, gift of, 82–84, 94, 193
Torture, 155
Tradition, 69, 108–30, 195, 212
Transubstantiation, 76, 79–81, 191
Trent, Council of, 27, 119, 205
Triumphalism, 18
Tübingen school, 64

Unam sanctam, 154
United Nations, 35, 36